OBAMA'S ENFORCER

ALSO BY JOHN FUND AND HANS VON SPAKOVSKY

Who's Counting? How Fraudsters and Bureaucrats Put Your Vote at Risk

ALSO BY JOHN FUND

Stealing Elections: How Voter Fraud Threatens Our Democracy

OBAMA'S ENFORCER

ERIC HOLDER'S JUSTICE DEPARTMENT

JOHN FUND AND HANS VON SPAKOVSKY

BROADSIDE BOOKS
An Imprint of HarperCollins*Publishers*
www.broadsidebooks.net

HarperCollins books may be purchased for educational, business, or sales promotional use. For information, please e-mail the Special Markets Department at SPsales@harpercollins.com.

FIRST EDITION

Designed by William Ruoto

Library of Congress Cataloging-in-Publication Data has been applied for.

ISBN: 978-0-06-232092-6

14 15 16 17 18 OV/RRD 10 9 8 7 6 5 4 3 2 1

To my parents, Anatol and Traudel von Spakovsky, who passed from this world too soon, and to my wife, Susan, who has stood with me during the best and worst of times.

—Hans von Spakovsky

ACKNOWLEDGMENTS

Working at the Justice Department was a real honor, and I met many dedicated professionals there who were interested in representing the American people to the best of their abilities and making sure that justice was served. But I also met too many biased partisans whose lack of professionalism and ideological extremism was an embarrassment to the legal profession and a danger to the liberty of Americans. With very few exceptions, such as J. Christian Adams and Andrew McCarthy, almost no one has been willing to expose this because of the fear of being targeted by the Justice Department, the most powerful law enforcement agency in America. When the Justice Department abuses its power, it threatens the freedom and well-being of Americans.

This book would not have been possible without the help of sources who are still inside Justice, and who provided much of the information in this book. Many of them have been subject to harassment and intimidation under the tenure of Eric Holder because of their dedication to the rule of law and their belief that the Justice Department should act in the best interests of the public. They know who they are and I extend to them my sincere thanks not just for their help, but for staying at Justice in a very hostile atmosphere and trying to do the right thing.

No one could ask for a better coauthor than John Fund, a journalist dedicated to ferreting out the truth. Our many years of collaborating on stories and sharing information have been very fruitful, to the obvious chagrin of our critics and those who have opposed our efforts to improve the integrity of the election process and expose the wrongdoing of government agencies like the Justice Department.

Thanks to my wife, Susan, with whom I celebrated our twenty-fifth wedding anniversary during the writing of this book. She has always been my first-line editor, and none of this would have been possible without her. To my children—Elisabeth, Christopher, and Anna—thanks for putting up with my many weekends of writing when I couldn't spend time with you.

I have to acknowledge the many brilliant lawyers and analysts at The Heritage Foundation, where I have had a home for the past six years. Some like Cully Stimson helped to improve the chapters. Other people have helped me over some difficult years, including Cleta Mitchell, one of the fiercest advocates for conservatives in Washington, former attorney general Ed Meese, who was without question the best person I've ever worked for, and Todd Gaziano and Robert Alt, my former colleagues at Heritage.

Thanks to PJ Media and *National Review*, who took a chance on me and started publishing my commentaries after I left the Federal Election Commission in 2008 after a vitriolic nomination fight that illustrated everything that is wrong with Washington today.

Finally, I can't say enough about my family. My parents, Anatol and Traudel von Spakovsky, met in a refugee camp in occupied Germany after the end of World War II, having barely survived being killed on numerous occasions, including when my mother was arrested by the Gestapo. They immigrated to the United States in 1951 and had five children in this great democracy that gave the von Spakovsky family refuge. We all love America and we want to see our country prosper. To my brothers, Alexis and Michael, and my sisters, Christine and Ingrid, don't you think Anatol and Traudel are smiling down at all of us and saying, "They've done well!"?

—Hans von Spakovsky

CONTENTS

OBAMA'S ENFORCER

CHAPTER 1

JUSTICE IN CHARGE

How Holder Came to Justice

The ornate, spacious committee room used by the House Judiciary Committee has seen a lot of Washington legal drama—from the impeachment proceedings against Presidents Richard Nixon and Bill Clinton to vigorous and spirited debates on issues ranging from gay rights to immigration policy.

In May 2013, the room was the scene of an oversight hearing on the activities of the Obama Justice Department that provided a fascinating look into its methods of misleading the American people about the truth of its actions.

In sworn testimony on May 15, Attorney General Eric Holder told the House Judiciary Committee that he had never been involved in or even thought about prosecuting the press over the publication of classified material. Yet, as the Judiciary Committee learned after the hearing, Holder had specifically approved a search warrant for Fox News reporter James Rosen's emails by "swearing to a federal court that Mr. Rosen was a co-conspirator in a national security leak investigation." When questioned by the committee about the obvious clash between his testimony and the truth, Mr. Holder refused to answer.[1]

An investigation by the Judiciary Committee concluded that Holder's testimony about the Rosen investigation was "deceptive and misleading" and damaged the "credibility and professionalism" of the Justice Department.[2] But as Charles Krauthammer accurately predicted, the attorney general was not punished for lying about the Justice Department's investigation of Rosen because Holder is one of Obama's "cronies" and is "too much of a friend of the president."[3]

Some (including the Justice Department) have contended that Holder's statement was not a lie because even though he approved the search warrant application, Holder never intended to actually prosecute Rosen. But Bill Otis, a twenty-year veteran of the Justice Department and the U.S. attorney's office, points out:

> When an officer of the Department of Justice tells a court that a search warrant target probably either committed, or aided the commission of, a very serious federal felony, and that extraordinary means are required forthwith to investigate the target's activities in that he is a risk to flee, the idea that the officer is *not* asserting the basis of a "potential prosecution" is—how shall I say this?—bordering on silly. This can only be defended by re-defining, or more precisely by defining out of existence, the word "potential . . . .
>
> Whether there is a *potential* prosecution does not depend on Holder's state of mind, or the state of mind of anyone currently in power at DOJ; the notion that psychology is everything is, while unfortunately widespread, complete baloney. When the Department goes on record with a court as being of the view Mr. X is at the minimum an aider or abettor or co-conspirator in a federal felony, and must immediately be investigated through extraordinary means because of, among other possible reasons, the risk that he'll flee, then it is nothing

more than blinking reality to say that there is no potential persecution of Mr. X.[4]

The James Rosen incident wasn't the first time that Holder was caught in an outright misrepresentation of the facts. On May 3, 2011, Holder testified before the House Judiciary Committee and was asked by Chairman Darrell Issa when Holder learned of the Fast and Furious scandal, a gun-running operation in which federal agents allowed illegal guns to be smuggled into Mexico, one of which was used to murder U.S. Border Patrol agent Brian Terry in 2010. Holder replied that he was "not sure of the exact date, but I probably heard about Fast and Furious over the last few weeks."[5]

The congressional investigation continued for several months afterward, and in early October 2011, documents surfaced that showed the attorney general himself was sent several briefing documents that specifically mentioned Fast and Furious. The DOJ initially responded to these documents by saying that Holder does not always read his briefings. When that explanation wasn't accepted, Holder wrote a long letter to Issa, which stated in part: "Much has been made in the past few days about my congressional testimony earlier this year regarding Fast and Furious. My testimony was truthful and accurate and I have been consistent on this point throughout. I have no recollection of knowing about Fast and Furious or of hearing its name prior to the public controversy about it."[6]

But when that didn't dampen congressional suspicion, Holder finally retracted his May 3, 2011, testimony before the Senate Judiciary Committee in November 2011, revising his statement of a "few weeks" to a "couple months."

"I did say a 'few weeks,'" Holder testified at the Senate hearing when asked questions by Senator Patrick Leahy (D-VT), the chairman of the committee. "I probably could've said 'a couple of months.' I didn't think the term I said, 'few weeks,' was inaccurate based on what happened."[7] Shortly thereafter, Justice withdrew the February 2011 letter it had sent to Senator Chuck Grassley in which it had denied that Justice had ever encouraged the shipment of illicit guns into Mexico. The administration admitted that statement was false when it retracted the letter.[8]

The evidence is overwhelming that Holder has lied under oath to Congress on numerous occasions. At other times, his testimony has been astonishingly vague or uninformed. At a Senate Judiciary Committee hearing in January 2014, Holder had no relevant information for senators who wanted to know why "many if not all" of the targeted groups or individuals in the IRS scandal had not been interviewed 280 days after the targeting of political opponents of the administration had been revealed by an inspector general report in May 2013. Holder said he was constrained in discussing any "steps that have been taken in connection with that investigation."

Senator Ted Cruz of Texas was having none of it. "In the 280 days since that inspector general report, it's been publicly reported that no indictments are planned. Today in this hearing, you were unwilling to answer a question whether even a single victim of targeting has been interviewed," he told Holder. "In my view, the integrity of the Department of Justice has been severely compromised. Predecessors of yours in both parties, Democrat and Republican, when faced with serious charges of abuse of power for partisan gain have made the right decision and appointed special prosecutors."

"I would call upon you to carry out the tradition of independence that attorneys general have honored that office with for centuries and protect the integrity of the Department of Justice," he later added. "Given the political sensitivities, given the fact that individual citizens believe they are being persecuted by the federal government for partisan reasons."

Holder replied that there isn't a basis for the DOJ to appoint an independent counsel. He said he has "faith in the career people who are handling this matter." He bristled when Cruz pointed out that a lead lawyer in the investigation, Justice Department attorney Barbara Kay Bosserman, was a large donor to President Obama, having given $5,600 to his presidential campaigns, $500 to the 2012 Obama Victory Fund, and $650 to the Democratic National Committee. "I don't know anything about the political activities of any of the people who are involved in this investigation." He told the committee that he doesn't "have any basis to believe that the people who are engaged in this investigation are doing so in a way other than investigations are normally done."

Holder conveniently ignored applicable Justice Department regulations that DOJ lawyers like Bosserman must avoid even "an appearance of a conflict of interest likely to affect the public perception of the integrity" of an investigation or prosecution. The Justice Department removes attorneys from cases all the time for such perceived conflicts of interest and there is no question that Bosserman fit squarely within this prohibition.

Cruz was clearly frustrated, noting that he "heard from dozens of financial supporters of Governor Romney that told me they had never been audited in their life, and within a week, a month of it becoming public they were raising money for Mitt Romney, they discovered they were being audited." Cruz said he found it troubling that so few people had been interviewed in the Justice probe and that "280 days have passed and apparently the anger and outrage that both the president and you expressed has utterly disappeared." He concluded by calling on "the tradition of independence" that previous attorneys general had exercised in appointing special prosecutors, ranging from Janet Reno, Holder's old boss at the Justice Department in the 1990s, to John Ashcroft, who appointed a special counsel to investigate the Valerie Plame CIA leak case.[9]

Holder has consistently refused to appoint special counsels to investigate serious problems within the Obama administration, including the IRS targeting of conservative organizations. Of course, he was apparently willing to appoint such a counsel to prosecute CIA interrogators, going to the extent of asking his staff for a list of possible candidates.[10] But this was squashed by the White House, including then–chief of staff Rahm Emanuel, who did not want the political fallout from such a move.

Senator Mike Lee of Utah had his own set of questions for Holder about the flurry of executive orders President Obama has issued on everything from delaying the small business mandate in ObamaCare to raising the minimum wage federal contractors must pay. Holder couldn't explain the constitutional basis for executive orders because "I have not seen—I don't remember looking at or having seen the analysis in some time, so I'm not sure where along the spectrum that would come," Holder replied when Senator Lee, a Republican, asked him to explain the basis of Obama's constitutional power to delay the employer mandate.

Lee had based his question on a three-part legal test, first described by Supreme Court justice Robert Jackson in the *Youngstown Sheet & Tube* case of 1952. Jackson said the president's authority to issue executive orders is strongest when he does so with the backing of Congress (category one), more dubious when he issues an order pertaining to a topic on which Congress has not passed a law (category two), and weakest when the executive order is "incompatible with a congressional command" (category three).

Holder told Lee that Jackson's analysis is factored into any decision on presidential power, but said he couldn't use that test to explain in any detail what kind of authority the president employed when he delayed the employer mandate.

"I've not had a chance to look at, you know, for some time, exactly what the analysis was there, so I'm not sure that I would be able to put it in what category," Holder told Lee. He believes that Obama "is probably at the height of his constitutional power" in issuing an executive order to raise the minimum wage paid by vendors who work for the federal government, though, and concluded that the same is true for the employer mandate delay despite the fact that Obama's actions actually conflicted with applicable federal laws.

"I would think that given that we're talking about a statute passed by Congress that delegates or devolves to the executive branch certain authorities, I would think that you're probably in category one there as well," Holder said of the delayed employer mandate, which the ObamaCare law stated was to have taken effect on January 1, 2014. "But, again, I have not looked at the analysis in some time."[11]

Senator Ted Cruz found Holder's answers exasperating, calling them "Orwellian doublespeak" that "clearly clashes with the text of the law President Obama signed and swore to faithfully execute."[12]

He also noted that in the past, previous attorneys general have been fully briefed by their staff on the questions senators have indicated in advance that they will pose. Eric Holder is apparently an exception. Senator Lee then called on Holder "to release legal analysis produced by [Justice's] Office of Legal Counsel, or whoever is advising the president on these issues." Holder deflected that request without a direct answer.

Holder was better briefed when it came to President Obama's potential future use of executive orders. Senator Richard Blumenthal, a Connecticut Democrat and top supporter of gun control, lamented that President Obama had made only a "very brief" reference to gun violence in his 2014 State of the Union address.

"The bill that was before us [after the 2012 Sandy Hook massacre] unfortunately failed to pass, but I'd like your commitment on behalf of the administration that he remains resolutely and steadfastly in support of these initiatives," Blumenthal told Holder.

"Our commitment is real and we will revisit these issues," the attorney general replied. "The president—it is his intention to again try to work with Congress, but in the absence of meaningful action to explore all the possibilities and use all the powers that he has to, frankly, just protect the American people." In other words, President Obama is contemplating a new executive order to push through gun control measures that have already failed in a Senate controlled by his own party.[13]

The January oversight hearing in the Senate was emblematic of the Obama administration's approach to questioning—slippery and nonresponsive.

Under Eric Holder, the Justice Department has stood the old Ronald Reagan maxim "trust but verify" on its head and adopted a "trust and we won't let you verify" approach to its activities. Even Jill Abramson, the executive editor of the staunchly liberal *New York Times*, in the wake of the revelations about the Justice Department's monitoring of Fox News reporter James Rosen, whom the DOJ labeled a "co-conspirator" in a leak case, said that "the Obama administration has moved beyond protecting government secrets to threatening fundamental freedoms of the press to gather news."[14]

How much is the Justice Department's uncooperative and secretive approach the product of Eric Holder's management style and how much is in response to President Obama's wishes? We would argue that the most likely explanation is that presidents almost always appoint the attorney general they're most comfortable with, someone who will watch their back on institutional issues and vigorously pursue their enforcement priorities. In Eric Holder, Barack Obama has found both a kindred spirit and a heat shield against criticism that would often be directed at the White House. And Holder has made it clear that he is "part of the president's team. I want the president to succeed; I campaigned for him. I share his world view and values."[15]

Eric Holder and Barack Obama first met in November 2004, at a small Washington, D.C., dinner party celebrating Obama's election to the Senate that month. It was hosted by Ann Walker Marchant, a niece of Vernon Jordan and a former Clinton administration White House aide.[16] "Obama sat next to Eric Holder, a former Justice Department official in the Clinton administration. The two found they had much in common—they were lawyers, they had gone to Columbia University and they were basketball enthusiasts. The party was the start of a continuing Holder-Obama relationship," reported *Newsday*.[17] "We just clicked," said Holder.[18]

Holder was expected to support Hillary Clinton for president in 2008, but his meeting with Obama changed everything. "Loyalty is something I value an awful lot. And so my decision to support Barack was not necessarily a difficult one, but I had to be really moved by him. My inclination would be to support Senator Clinton, but I was overwhelmed by Barack," he told *American Lawyer* magazine in 2008. He added that when it came to race, he and Obama "share a worldview."[19] Holder also became close to Valerie Jarrett, a highly influential, highly political Obama adviser. In fact, Jarrett said in 2008 about Holder that "there isn't a day that we don't talk."[20]

By the summer of 2008, Holder was "the utility infielder for Team Obama, playing a variety of positions: surrogate, fundraiser, strategist and source of wisdom in the ways of Washington."[21] He was a key player in the search committee that settled on Delaware senator Joe Biden to be Obama's vice presidential running mate.

Eric Holder was born in the Bronx in 1951, but grew up in Queens, another borough of New York City, with his brother, Billy.

His father was an immigrant from Barbados who became a real estate agent and his mother was a secretary from New Jersey. The family's neighbors included Louis Armstrong, Dizzy Gillespie, Willie Mays, Malcom X, and Louis Farrakhan.[22] Holder's early school years "remained mostly free of racial tension. His classmates were more concerned with who was free to play softball after school than the color of anyone's skin."[23] A 1997 NPR profile said Holder found "his childhood was free of racial strife and full of opportunities." He became racially and politically conscious in 1963, when the civil rights struggle and the assassination of President Kennedy led him to read books on the lives of great leaders. He was inspired by *The Autobiography of Malcolm X* and its story of redemption.

An overachiever, Holder was removed from his local school in fifth grade "and sent to a gifted program in Manhattan, making the hour-long commute each day at age 10."[24] He then won a prized place at New York's prestigious Stuyvesant High School, an even longer hour-and-a-half commute. He joined the Afro-American Society and was co-captain of the basketball team. He had felt overwhelmed at first by the school's academic demands but he later credited his mother for giving him the confidence he needed to succeed there, because she reassured him that he was "capable" and that he could "compete."[25]

He was accepted at Columbia University and entered its freshman class in 1969, a time of great political turmoil. As a freshman and a leader of the Student Afro-American Society (SAAS), he joined student protesters who occupied the campus ROTC office and christened it as a student center named for Malcolm X. A deleted Web page of the Black Students' Organization, a successor organization to the SAAS, claimed the students were "armed," but the Justice Department refused to answer whether Holder was armed, when contacted by reporters from the *Daily Caller* after a report of this surfaced in 2012.[26]

Holder went on to attend law school at Columbia, where he did an internship with the NAACP Legal Defense and Educational Fund. Upon graduation in 1976, he immediately joined the newly formed Public Integrity Section of the Justice Department. It was not his first choice, but his application to the Civil Rights Division had been rejected.[27] The Justice Department normally only hires lawyers laterally, that is, lawyers who have been out and working for a number of years. But there is an exception for the Attorney General's Honors Program, which selects a small number of recent law graduates for employment at the department.

Craig Donsanto, head of the Election Crimes Unit within the Public Integrity Section, spoke with us about his time working with Eric Holder during the 1970s and 1980s.[28]

Donsanto was a career prosecutor who worked for the Justice Department for forty years before retiring in 2010. He is well-known to election officials across the country, as well as campaign finance lawyers, because Donsanto was responsible for managing the Justice Department's investigation and prosecution of voter fraud, campaign finance violations, and other forms of public corruption related to elections and political fund-raising. In fact, he wrote the department's manual on "Federal Prosecution of Election Offenses."

Starting in 1976, he began working very closely with Holder investigating and prosecuting cases for a number of years. The two men frequently traveled together on Justice Department business. They and their colleagues helped secure convictions for everyone from a judge to a diplomat to an organized crime figure.

Donsanto liked Holder and thought he was "a damn good lawyer . . . young, but very bright." Donsanto was "proud to be his colleague" and was close enough to Holder that he was invited to attend Holder's swearing in as a Superior Court judge in the District of Columbia in 1988.

But Donsanto expressed his chagrin over the change that came over Holder as the years went by, particularly how Holder's approach to the law seemed to change from an objective, professional one to a much more political one, and he shakes his head at Holder's conduct over the past five years. Donsanto believes Holder became "politicized" as he apparently let his political ambitions seize hold of his professional judgment.

Donsanto also thinks that the bitter contempt that Holder has displayed for the political right and his apparent view that racism is rampant everywhere in America because we are a "nation of cowards" may have been at least in part influenced by his marriage to Sharon Malone. Holder "changed" after his marriage, says Donsanto. Holder himself has admitted that his wife has an "edge" that he doesn't have because he "never saw the reality of racism or felt the insecurity that comes with it."[29]

Malone was the sister of a civil rights icon, Vivian Malone Jones, one of the two black students who helped break the color barrier at the University of Alabama when they enrolled in 1963. Jones was made famous by Alabama governor George Wallace's attempt to block her admission when she arrived at the university with Justice Department deputy attorney general Nicholas Katzenbach and a phalanx of federal marshals. In talking about her husband, Malone has said that "he experienced a kinder, gentler version of the black experience" than her family.[30]

Sharon Malone is a doctor in Washington who is very involved with organizations like the Coalition of 100 Black Women and makes no secret of her anger at the wrongs her family and other black Americans suffered, to which the "American government was, I wouldn't say complicit, but at least indifferent."[31] She told her family's story in a PBS documentary, *Slavery by Another Name*. Malone said she was "forever colored by my experiences growing up in the segregated South."[32]

According to a reporter for *Newsweek* who attended a dinner party with Holder and Malone in 2009, she drew "a direct line from the sins of America's racial past to the abuses of the Guantanamo Bay detention center." In fact, she not only equates the two but sees both as examples of "what we have not done in the face of injustice" as her "voice rose with indignation," according to the *Newsweek* reporter.[33]

After his stint at Justice, Holder served four years as a judge in Washington, D.C., where he became deeply affected by having to sentence upwards of thirty black males to jail every week. "The thing that I think most moves me in this is the notion that no matter how successful you become, there is still something that ties you to a person who is dealing with a drug problem, who is an unwed mother, that as long as there are people who are discriminated against because of their race, there is still something that must bind us as black people."[34]

Holder's passionate belief in racial preferences stems from this period of his life, and he has very passionate views on the subject. In 2012, he returned to his alma mater Columbia for a World Leaders Forum. He was asked by Lee Bollinger, Columbia's president, about Supreme Court cases on affirmative action that had involved Bollinger in his former role as president of the University of Michigan. In 2003, then-justice Sandra Day O'Connor was the deciding vote in *Grutter v. Bollinger*, which allowed racial preferences at universities to continue. But she made it clear that their days should be numbered: "We expect that 25 years from now, the use of racial preferences will no longer be necessary to further the interest approved today."[35]

But Holder's response to the *Grutter* case made it clear that for him that day will never come. Holder "can't actually imagine a time in which the need for more diversity would ever cease." "Affirmative action has been an issue since segregation practices," he declared. "The question is not when does it end, but when does it begin. . . . When do people of color truly get the benefits to which they are entitled?"[36]

While he was serving as a Superior Court judge in Washington, Bill Clinton was elected president in 1992. The next year, Holder became the first African-American U.S. attorney in the District of Columbia.

As the U.S. attorney, Holder took a lead role in prosecuting Dan Rostenkowski, the chairman of the powerful House Ways and Means Committee, for corruption in office. His critics charged he was less aggressive in pursuing the pervasive political corruption among the many associates of Washington, D.C., mayor Marion Barry, who returned to a fourth term in the mayor's office in 1995 after serving six months in jail for drug possession.

While he was U.S. attorney, Holder's commitment to the First Amendment was also questioned. Many legal scholars believed he overreacted and abused his authority when he became the subject of harsh verbal attacks by a Romanian immigrant.

Ion Cornel Popa fled communist Romania in 1986 as a political refugee and was granted legal residence in the United States. In 1992, he claimed to be a victim of police brutality committed by African-American police officers who were not brought to justice. His claim was believable. In the 1990s, the District of Columbia police department was a cesspool of corruption and incompetence, according to Carl Rowan Jr., the son of the late African-American columnist Carl Rowan, as well as a former FBI agent and police chief. Rowan says that after the election of Marion Barry as D.C. mayor in 1978, "They took the police department and changed it from a career service of people dedicated to law enforcement [to] just another patronage opportunity. They'd say, 'We don't have any jobs open in the department of recreation, but hey, wanna be a cop?' People who were looking for a paycheck found one at the police department."[37]

But rather than take out his grievances on local law enforcement, Popa decided to blame U.S. attorney Holder for not doing his job prosecuting the city's corruption. During April and May of 1997, Popa made seven anonymous phone calls to Holder's office. He claimed that Holder "violated . . . our rights" and then in one passage ranted: "Eric Holder is a negro. Is a negro. Which is a criminal. He make a violent crime against me, violating the rights in court of the white people. [Inaudible] negro. He's negro. Eric Holder. Criminal."[38]

Nasty stuff, but not nearly as bad as many insults in our coarse culture of today. Nonetheless, Popa was charged by Holder's office with violating 47 U.S.C. §223(a)(1)(c), which makes it a crime punishable by up to two years in prison to make anonymous phone calls "with intent to annoy, abuse, threaten, or harass any person at the called number or who receives the communications." Popa claimed in his defense that he had given his name during some of the calls and that they were made to placate an acquaintance with whom he was staying, who plied him with liquor, made him read racist literature, and threatened to turn him out into the street if he didn't make the calls. A Washington, D.C., jury didn't buy Popa's account, convicted him after deliberating only an hour, and sentenced him to the nine months in jail he had already served.

Popa appealed his conviction, claiming that "this type of speech directed at a public official . . . is entitled to First Amendment protection." He argued that his derogatory references to Holder were not punishable as "fighting words." The government claimed that Popa's speech was not political in nature and therefore not protected.[39]

But in late 1999, a three-judge panel of the U.S. Court of Appeals for the District of Columbia Circuit unanimously accepted Popa's political speech argument. The D.C. Circuit vacated his conviction, concluding that the statute "could have been drawn more narrowly, without any loss of utility to the Government, by excluding from its scope those who intend to engage in public or political discourse." The appellate court remarked that people who make anonymous and abusive phone calls with the intent to communicate a political message should be given "a pass."[40]

Eugene Volokh, a law professor at the University of California, Los Angeles, says Holder's efforts to prosecute Popa were a troubling early harbinger of an increasing tendency to criminalize offensive speech. He notes one case involving Philip Speulda, a Democratic candidate for city council in Hawthorne, New Jersey, in 2011. Speulda sent out a flyer that included a photo of his Republican opponent in a hot tub with two other men. The Republican charged that the photo was intended to indicate he was gay and he convinced the police to issue a criminal summons for "harassment." The charges were later dismissed, but certainly created a "chilling effect" on Speulda's campaign.[41]

"Unwanted speech to some recipients—for instance, government officials, candidates for office, and possibly businesses that serve the public—might have constitutional value even when the listener doesn't want to hear it. People may have the right to remonstrate with government agencies and petition for redress of grievances even when the target doesn't want to hear the petitions or the petitions are offensively worded," Volokh wrote.[42]

Eric Holder clearly didn't want to hear Ion Cornel Popa's message and went to great lengths to prosecute him criminally for his harsh criticism, which, as coarse and nasty as it was, was fully protected by the First Amendment.

In 1997, Holder left the U.S. attorney job when he was elevated by Bill Clinton to the number-two slot at Justice. There he not only had major administrative duties but became increasingly important as Attorney General Janet Reno struggled with Parkinson's disease. Insiders at Justice say Holder was influential in convincing Reno to stop appointing independent counsels to investigate Clinton scandals such as Chinagate, the flow of illegal campaign contributions from foreign sources to the 1996 Clinton reelection effort.

At the end of Clinton's second term, Holder's image was tarnished by his role in the pardon of Marc Rich, a fugitive financier who had been indicted in 1983 on charges of tax evasion and selling oil to Iran during the hostage crisis involving U.S. diplomats. Rich fled to Switzerland to escape a trial, but employed top-shelf lawyers and lobbyists to plead his case for a presidential pardon. According to the *Wall Street Journal*, his former wife, Denise Rich, donated more than $1 million to the president's party and Hillary Clinton's 2000 Senate race, and raised millions more from others. One event at her Fifth Avenue penthouse brought in $3 million during the dark days of the Lewinsky-Clinton scandal. "It means more now than ever, and we'll never forget it," President Clinton said at that event. The *Journal* reported, "By the time the Clintons left the White House, Ms. Rich had become a close enough friend that she was able to lobby the president on three occasions—once in person, once on the phone and once in a letter."[43]

All this apparently moved Rich's pardon application to the top of various Clinton administration in-boxes. Holder was asked his opinion of the pardon and responded he was "neutral leaning toward favorable." Clinton issued the pardon the next day, just hours before leaving office. *Time* magazine has placed it on its list of the ten most notorious presidential pardons, along with those of Richard Nixon and Patty Hearst.[44]

Holder has since said he "regretted" his role in the Rich pardon. He concluded his testimony to the House Government Reform Committee in February 2001 by saying that "knowing everything that I know now, I would not have recommended to the president that he grant the pardon." But sometime before the 2000 election, Holder had told Rich's lawyer, Jack Quinn, someone Holder knew very well was "a close confidant of Vice President Al Gore, that [Holder] wanted to be attorney general in a Gore administration."[45]

Holder may have regretted the political fallout he received from the deal, but as Representative Dan Burton (R-IN) said to Holder at the February hearing, "You wanted something from Mr. Quinn. You wanted his support for attorney general of the United States, and he wanted a pardon for Mr. Rich and his partner."[46] In fact, for Eric Holder, "the position of attorney general had always loomed in the distance like a grail—the pinnacle of influence for a public-service lawyer."[47]

During the eight years of the Bush administration, Holder was a lawyer with the Washington, D.C., firm of Covington & Burling, where he represented major clients such as the National Football League and Chiquita Brands International and earned a great deal more money than he had in government.[48] An example of his work there was his securing a "slap-on-the-wrist plea deal" with federal prosecutors for Chiquita to charges that the company had paid off terrorists in Colombia.[49] He briefly served on the board of MCI and even joined an investor group that made an unsuccessful bid for a major-league baseball team, losing the contest for the Washington Nationals.[50]

But Holder also found time to remain politically active, becoming, as *ABA Journal* noted, "the consummate Washington insider." Then came that fateful dinner party with Barack Obama. The mind-meld the two men had culminated in Holder's nomination to become attorney general and his Senate confirmation by a vote of 75 to 21. At Justice, he has become the "vanguard for the administration's progressive wing."[51]

Why does it matter who runs the U.S. Justice Department? Because that person heads one of the most powerful executive branch agencies in the federal government—one that has enormous discretionary power to pursue people accused of breaking the law and to exert major influence over social, economic, and national security policies by the choices its leader makes in enforcement. It requires someone who understands that while the attorney general is a political appointee, he (or she) has a sworn duty to uphold the Constitution and enforce the law in an objective, nonpolitical manner. One of Holder's own friends, a former DOJ official, said Holder's weakness is his "instinct to please." Holder "doesn't have to be told what to do—he's willing to do whatever it takes. It's his survival mechanism in Washington."[52]

In 2013, the Justice Department had a budget of almost $27 billion, 114,000 employees, and was America's largest law firm.[53] It has more employees today than it has ever had in its history, with a sharp increase in the number of staff occurring during the Obama administration (it only had a little over 105,000 employees in 2008).[54] There are more than forty different offices, including the Civil Rights, Criminal, Anti-Trust, Environment and Natural Resources, and Tax divisions. But the attorney general does far more than merely oversee the federal government's prosecution of cases in these areas of the law.

The department's Civil Division defends the government when it is sued and the Office of the Solicitor General represents the government before the Supreme Court. The Office of Justice Programs dispenses hundreds of millions of dollars in federal grants of all kinds, giving it extraordinary power over state and local law enforcement agencies as well as many other organizations, including nonprofit groups.

Eric Holder also oversees the Bureau of Prisons, which runs all of the federal prisons in the country; the Federal Bureau of Investigation (the FBI); the Bureau of Alcohol, Tobacco, Firearms and Explosives (the ATF); the U.S. Marshals Service; and the Drug Enforcement Administration, all of which are part of the Department of Justice. In essence, the Justice Department is the largest law enforcement agency in the world with investigators and agents, lawyers, and prison officials all combined in one government department.

Although the Office of the Attorney General was created by the Judiciary Act of 1789, making it the fourth cabinet-level post, the Justice Department has only been in existence since an act of Congress signed by President Ulysses S. Grant in 1870. Holder is the eighty-second American to hold that position; he has been preceded by some very distinguished jurists.

The very first attorney general was Edmund Jennings Randolph, a delegate to the Constitutional Convention of 1787 and a former aide-de-camp to George Washington, and who served from 1789 to 1794. Other well-known attorneys general include Robert H. Jackson, the fifty-seventh attorney general, who went on to become a member of the U.S. Supreme Court and, most famously, one of the chief prosecutors in the Nuremberg trials of Nazi leaders after the end of World War II; Edwin Meese III, the seventy-fifth attorney general, who started a legal revolution with his remarks about originalism and the Constitution in a speech to the ABA in 1985 during the Reagan administration; and of course, Robert F. Kennedy, the brother of President John F. Kennedy, who served as the sixty-fourth attorney general from 1961 to 1964 during the crucial period of the civil rights movement.[55]

Holder's spacious and well-furnished offices are located on the fifth floor of the main Justice Department building, located at 950 Pennsylvania Avenue in Washington, about halfway between the

White House and Congress, and they include a small private apartment where the attorney general can sleep when he needs to stay at the office during crises. Named the Robert F. Kennedy Building since 2001, it was completed in 1935 and occupies the entire block between Pennsylvania and Constitution Avenues, and Ninth and Tenth Streets. It was built in the Classical Revival style of that time period, combined with Art Deco and Greek features, and surrounds a central courtyard. It is filled with beautiful murals and statutes depicting scenes of daily life at home and in the workplace throughout American history, as well as symbolic themes about the role of justice in our society.

The Justice Department's motto, contained on the seal of the Department, is "Qui Pro Domina Justitia Sequitur." It has been roughly translated to refer to the attorney general as he who "prosecutes on behalf of justice."[56] But as we will see, Eric Holder seems to have changed that motto so that it sometimes can be read to mean "the attorney general prosecutes on behalf of his political and ideological allies." Eric Holder is almost certainly the most liberal attorney general of the modern era, but he has also liberally bent the rule of law and established internal practices that harm the cause of justice. His tenure at the Justice Department has been marked by one scandal after another and abusive behavior by Justice Department lawyers in unwarranted, ideologically driven prosecutions.

Holder is the first attorney general in history to be held in contempt by the House of Representatives for his unjustified refusal to turn over documents related to what may be the most reckless law enforcement operation of the Justice Department: Operation Fast and Furious. He has launched more investigations and prosecutions of leaks than any prior attorney general, yet he has studiously ignored high-level "friendly leaks" by White House officials in the Obama administration.

Holder has racialized the prosecution of federal discrimination laws and led an unprecedented attack on election integrity laws, thus making it easier for people to commit voter fraud and facilitating the election of members of his political party. His handling of national security issues has been dismal and he has filled the career ranks of the Justice Department with political allies, cronies, and Democratic Party donors, in clear violation of civil service rules. Holder has treated Congress with contempt and has done everything he can to evade its oversight responsibilities by misleading, misinforming, and ignoring members of Congress and its committees. Holder has attacked pro-life protesters, trying to use federal power to restrict their First Amendment right to speak, has prosecuted American companies for engaging in behavior that is routinely done by government officials, and has on numerous occasions ignored his duty to defend the law and to enforce statutes passed by Congress.

For these reasons and many others, former career lawyer Christopher Coates, who served in the Clinton, Bush, and Obama administrations, says that in his opinion, "Holder is the worst person to hold the position of Attorney General since the disgraced John Mitchell, who went to jail as a result of the Watergate scandal."[57]

CHAPTER 2

GIBSON GUITAR'S GREEN RAID

Gibson Guitar is a 112-year-old company with a peerless reputation. It makes the renowned Les Paul electric guitar and is famous for being the source of John Lennon's J-160E acoustic guitar. But to the Obama Justice Department it was a target of opportunity, worthy of being treated as if it were run by dangerous drug dealers or the mob.

In August 2009, Justice sent federal agents armed with automatic weapons on raids of Gibson's offices and factories in Nashville and Memphis, Tennessee, seizing computers, files, guitars, pallets of wood, and ebony fingerboard blanks. In April 2011, DOJ executed another similar raid of Gibson, even though no criminal charges had been filed.

Initially, the big mystery for Gibson was why the first raid had even been conducted. "Everything is sealed" said Gibson CEO Henry Juszkiewicz: "They won't tell us anything."[1] Apparently, Justice's Environmental and Resources Division was investigating possible violations of the Lacey Act, which makes it a crime to import flora or fauna in violation of a foreign nation's laws. In other words, if a country like India makes it illegal to export a certain type of wood, then it is a criminal violation for an American company to import the Indian wood into the United States. Gibson tried to point out to the Justice Department, apparently to no avail, that the wood seized in both raids, ebony and rosewood from India and ebony from Madagascar, was legally exported under both countries' laws. The wood from India had been certified by the Forest Stewardship Council, an independent nonprofit that monitors the sale and export of wood to make sure it is legal. Gibson had sworn statements and documents from the Madagascar government that the wood was legally exported under Madagascar law.

As Juszkiewicz said after the 2011 raid, "armed people came in our factory . . . evacuated our employees, then seized half a million dollars of our goods without any charges having been filed. . . . I think it's a clear overreach."[2] Juszkiewicz added that "the federal bureaucracy is just out of hand. . . . We feel totally abused. We believe the arrogance of federal power is impacting me personally, our company personally and the employees here in Tennessee, and it's just plain wrong."[3]

The actual amount of rosewood, ebony, and finished guitars seized by the feds was worth more than a million dollars. The raids crippled Gibson's production because the "raids took most of the company's raw materials." The company filed a civil lawsuit in federal court to recover the seized material.[4]

The Justice Department received a blaze of bad publicity and congressional inquiries because of its SWAT-style armed raids on a guitar maker, particularly since Gibson had cooperated with Justice after the first raid by providing documentation and information. As Gibson pointed out, the second raid was conducted "without warning or communication of any kind." If Justice had simply contacted Gibson, the company "would have cooperated without having to stop its production and send workers home."[5] But the administration's environmental allies were happy about the administration's enforcement of the Lacey Act and had no sympathy for Gibson or its employees: "Gibson clearly understood the risks involved," said Andrea Johnson, director of the Environmental Investigation Agency, which, despite its name, is a private liberal organization.[6]

But it turned out in the end that the Justice Department really had overreached—conducting armed raids and threatening criminal charges without the evidence to back up its claims. Because of the threat to the continued operations of his business, Juszkiewicz finally agreed to a settlement with the Justice Department despite the frivolous nature of the department's case. As he said, he really didn't have any choice because the criminal proceedings had cut off Gibson's access to sources of hardwood needed to manufacture guitars:

"The alternative was pretty onerous. We would have had to have gone to trial and we would have been precluded from buying wood from our major source country. For the ability to carry on with the business and remove this onerous Sword of Damocles, if you will, we feel this is about as good a settlement as we can get."[7]

But the "deferred prosecution" settlement agreement signed by the Justice Department with Gibson in 2012 reveals the weakness of the threatened prosecution—in fact, DOJ had no case at all.[8] For example, Justice acknowledged that "certain questions and inconsistencies now exist regarding the tariff classification of ebony and rosewood fingerboard blanks pursuant to the Indian government's Foreign Trade Policy. Accordingly, the Government will not undertake enforcement actions related to Gibson's future orders, purchases, or imports of ebony and rosewood fingerboard blanks from India."

In other words, the Justice Department essentially admitted that it had improperly seized Gibson's stock of fingerboards from India because it was "unclear" if they had been illegally exported under the relevant law, not U.S. law, but India's law. And Justice not only agreed to return all of the Indian wood it had seized but also not to object to future importation from India.[9]

Justice's case for the Madagascar wood was no stronger. Appendix A to the settlement agreement goes into a lengthy explanation of "Madagascar Interministerial Order 16.030/2006," as well as a whole series of other "interministerial orders," all of which concerned the export of certain woods. According to a translation of these orders, wood products considered "finished" could be exported, and listed under the examples of "finished" wood products were "guitar fingerboards."

In the same appendix, however, Justice then recites that a Gibson representative flew to Madagascar on a trip organized by "Greenpeace and other non-profit environmental groups." The trip's organizers received a "translation" of Order 16.030/2006 and gave Gibson their opinion that fingerboard blanks were not "finished" products and therefore could not be exported. So to make its case, the Justice Department was relying on the opinion of the trip organizers about the interpretation of a translation of a foreign government order. No mention is made of who made the translation.

As Paul Larkin, a veteran Justice Department lawyer who worked in both the Criminal Division and the solicitor general's office says, putting "aside the obvious problems with government reliance on the opinion by the trip's 'organizers' of a *foreign order* written in a *foreign tongue*—Gibson was given conflicting views of the law. That should have ended the matter entirely."[10] Because Gibson had received conflicting advice, the government could not prove that it had the required criminal intent or that the exportation of the fingerboards even violated Madagascar law. When combined with the "questions and inconsistencies" over India's law, the government should have dropped all the charges.

Instead, in conduct bordering on unethical, it forced Gibson into a settlement that Gibson agreed to in order to be able to remain in business. Gibson was required to pay a $300,000 fine, to make a $50,000 payment to the National Fish and Wildlife Foundation, and improve its internal compliance program to make sure it did not violate the Lacey Act in the future—even though the government was essentially agreeing it had not violated the Lacey Act in the first place.

After the prosecution was settled, some very interesting facts came to light. It turned out that Henry Juszkiewicz, Gibson's CEO, had contributed to Republican politicians, including Senator Lamar Alexander (R-TN) and Representative Marsha Blackburn (R-TN). Chris Martin, the head of Gibson's biggest competitor, C. F. Martin & Company, was a "longtime Democratic supporter, with $35,400 in contributions to Democratic candidates and the Democratic National Committee over the past couple of election cycles."[11] C. F. Martin's catalog showed several guitars containing "East Indian Rosewood," which is the exact same wood that was at issue in the Gibson case and seized during the militia-style SWAT raid.

Moreover, at the same time that Gibson Guitar was raided in 2011, federal agents also seized "$200,000 worth of Indian ebony and rosewood" from Gibson's supplier, Luthiers Mercantile International, which was destined to be shipped to Gibson.[12] The sixty thousand fingerboards were the "same cut and kind of wood that the company routinely sells to other guitar manufacturers," according to Natalie Swango, Luther Mercantile's general manager.[13] "Other guitar manufacturers"—like C. F. Martin perhaps? But C. F. Martin was never raided by federal agents or threatened with criminal prosecution by the Justice Department.

The Justice Department's press release about the settlement is full of praise for itself and says that it "goes a long way in demonstrating the government's commitment to protecting the world's natural resources." It does not acknowledge the lack of evidence that Gibson violated the law or the baselessness of the government's prosecution. As former DOJ prosecutor Paul Larkin pointedly says: "The government has made a federal case out of 'fretboards' or 'fingerboards.' . . . Is that how we want federal tax dollars spent—punishing domestic companies that purchase a valuable, harmless product from foreign companies that, in turn, purchase it from an exporter in a foreign land, where the alleged illegality is the violation of an ambiguous order written in a foreign language? All that not to prevent the import of toxic waste but guitar fretboards?"[14]

According to *Investor's Business Daily*, the Justice Department claimed it "acted to save the environment from greedy plunderers." But 95 percent of the rosewood from Madagascar and India goes to China: "America is a trivial importer . . . so putting Gibson out of business wasn't going to do a whole lot to save their forests."[15]

The effect of the Gibson prosecution on musicians was to inspire fear and uncertainty. John Thomas, a blues and ragtime guitarist, says, "there's a lot of anxiety, and it's well justified."[16] He will never go out of the country anymore "with a wooden guitar" for fear it will be seized and criminal charges filed against him. Musicians "who play vintage guitars and other instruments made of environmentally protected materials are worried the authorities may be coming for them next."[17] "People are very confused," said George Gruhn, a Nashville-based vintage guitar dealer, because "there is uncertainty about what the federal government expects."[18] Apparently, what the government expects is for Americans to have detailed knowledge about the laws of foreign countries like India and Madagascar or else risk imprisonment. As Larkin says, "*that* is the biggest crime of all."

Despite the expensive and unnecessary ordeal that Gibson and its employees went through, they obviously have not lost their sense of humor. Gibson is now advertising the "Government Series II Les Paul," which celebrates "an infamous moment in Gibson history." Gibson electric guitars "have long been a means of fighting the establishment," so musicians can now "fight the powers that be with this powerful Les Paul!" that features some of the rosewood seized by the Justice Department in its raids.[19]

The Gibson Guitar fiasco put a spotlight on a little-known division of Justice, the Environment & Natural Resources Division (ENRD). If you ask most Department of Justice veterans (the ones who will give you a straight answer) which division is full of the craziest, most ideologically driven lawyers, they will immediately say the Civil Rights Division. But if you ask them which division comes in second, they will tell you it is ENRD, which boasts on its website that it is "the nation's environmental lawyer, and the largest environmental law firm in the country."[20] When one of the authors worked in the Civil Rights Division at the Justice Department, he was told by a lawyer who worked in ENRD that all of the lawyers there thought of the ENRD as simply an extension of Greenpeace, the Natural Resources Defense Council, or the Sierra Club. They did not think of themselves as government attorneys who are supposed to act in the best interests of the public, both individual citizens and businesses, by enforcing our nation's environmental laws in a fair and judicious manner.

That their extremism has simply accelerated under the Obama administration is no surprise—the ENRD in June 2013 was headed by Acting Assistant Attorney General Robert Dreher, the former general counsel for the Defenders of Wildlife and a former attorney at the Sierra Club Legal Defense Fund (now Earthjustice). By an odd coincidence, Earthjustice, Dreher's former employer, has been the biggest beneficiary of attorneys' fees paid out by American taxpayers in litigation against the Environmental Protection Agency

(EPA) and lawsuits handled by the ENRD when it represents the EPA (more on that later).

All Americans want to protect wildlife and foster a cleaner and healthier environment. And it is ENRD's job to enforce the laws that Congress has passed to do exactly that. But it is not ENRD's job to do so in a way that goes beyond the law, abuses its authority, criminalizes ordinary conduct, and benefits the political allies of the president who holds the White House.

As Kim Strassel of the *Wall Street Journal* has pointed out, the EPA—and thus the ENRD lawyers representing the agency—has suffered an "embarrassing string of defeats" in the courts.[21] Those "judicial slapdowns are making a mockery of former Obama EPA Administrator Lisa Jackson's promise in 2009 to restore the [EPA]'s 'stature' with rulemaking that 'stands up in court.'"[22] Part of the job of a lawyer, including a government lawyer, is telling clients that the positions they are taking are outside of or not in accord with the applicable law. This is particularly important for Justice Department lawyers who have an obligation to ensure that the agencies they represent are not acting beyond the authority granted to them by Congress. But because most ENRD lawyers agree ideologically with the extreme and often radical positions taken by the EPA and other federal agencies like the Department of the Interior, they are not willing to objectively assess the legality of the government's misbehavior and regulatory overreach.

This caused the U.S. Court of Appeals for the Federal Circuit, which has jurisdiction over many claims made against the federal government, to recently accuse the Justice Department, and specifically lawyers in the ENRD, of making legal arguments in court that were "so thin as to border on the frivolous."[23] They made such "frivolous" arguments in a rails-to-trails suit in which the federal government was making vigorous efforts to avoid paying landowners any compensation for the portions of their land taken through a program under the National Trails System Act. As the Federal Circuit Court of Appeals said, it could not understand the "sturm und drang" (storm and stress) pushing the Justice Department to fight lower-court judgments against the government. The rails-to-trails program is one that takes railroad corridors established by easements through private land that have been abandoned by the railroads and converts them to biking and hiking trails.

No one doubts the power of the government to take private land for a *public* purpose, but the Fifth Amendment requires the government to pay "just compensation" for such a taking. However, the Justice Department under Eric Holder has refused to accept that situation and has instead taken what many have called a "scorched earth" approach, arguing in court that private landowners don't actually own their property that is taken for the environmentally popular rails-to-trails programs. This position is contrary to a 1990 Supreme Court and a subsequent Federal Circuit Court of Appeals decision that the government is taking private property when it converts a railroad line to a trail, as opposed to the government's claim that the property reverted to the government, not the original property owner, when the railroads stopped using the property.[24]

After these decisions and several others, according to one analyst, Cecilia Fex, the Justice Department "started stipulating liability" for taking private property, making the only issue in such seizure cases what "just compensation" would be for the homeowner.[25] But in recent years, the Justice Department has "resurrected its challenges to the government's liability . . . [and] in an apparent coordinated litigation strategy, the DOJ routinely raises arguments that the Federal Circuit has previously rejected. Worse for the attorneys and the courts who do not deal with these [types of] cases, the DOJ advances these arguments without acknowledging the contrary law that was established during its earlier attempts to escape the government's liability."[26] In other words, in addition to trying to prevent private homeowners from being compensated for their property being taken, the ENRD lawyers violate basic ethics requirements by failing to inform courts of controlling authority that is contrary to the position the government is taking. Such outrageous behavior is per se unethical under professional codes of conduct.

Some of ENRD's arguments aren't just frivolous, they defy common sense. In one recent case, the Federal Circuit rejected a claim by Justice lawyers that the statute of limitations barred homeowners from making a claim for compensation even though the government had not informed the homeowners of the government's intent to use their land for a trail, the very action that normally triggers the right of the homeowner to make a claim against the government.[27] In fact, Thor Hearne, a lawyer who has represented numerous landowners in these cases, says the government often fails to notify homeowners and many "owners only learn that their property has been taken when a bulldozer shows up and begins grading a public recreational trail across their land."[28]

And the Justice Department's strategy to fight these just claims is costing taxpayers big money. Under the Uniform Relocation Assistance Act, the federal government has to reimburse the litigation expenses of homeowners when they win a case, including attorneys' fees, as well as pay them compensation for the government's delay between the date the property is taken and the date the owner is finally paid. In one case in Idaho where the homeowners finally beat the government, a federal court awarded them $2.24 million in attorneys' fees and costs in addition to $883,312 in "just compensation" for their confiscated property. So the Justice Department's senseless litigation strategy increased the cost to the American taxpayer of this exercise of eminent domain by more than 250 percent.[29]

Thor Hearne had a case in which his client, a small village, agreed to forfeit any compensation for the strip of land the government took. All the village wanted was for the feds to agree to mark the boundaries of the land it had taken. But the Justice Department lawyers refused unless the village first sued the government and won on the issue of liability—which was unquestioned under federal law. So the village sued, won, and taxpayers had to pay the village $19,000 for the strip of land and almost $300,000 in attorneys' fees.

As Hearne says, "the Justice Department's history of repeatedly taking frivolous and losing arguments—and recycling these same losing arguments—can only be explained by an intentional strategy of trying to make this litigation so lengthy and so expensive that landowners will let the government simply take their land without being" compensated. Hearne adds that the Justice Department should be interested in not just seeing that citizens are justly compensated, but that the government does it "cost-efficiently using taxpayer resources to promptly resolve the claims." That has not been his experience with ENRD lawyers. He says he is aware of at least twenty cases that Justice lawyers have lost in which they made "essentially the exact same losing argument" each time.[30] The cost to taxpayers of the obstreperous behavior of ENRD lawyers has been enormous. A former Justice Department lawyer who also worked at the EPA told one of the authors that based on his experience, the ENRD lawyers are "zealots" who have a "religious fervor" for environmentalism—they see no reason why the government should have to pay private landowners for anything that helps further their green agenda, and they act accordingly.

Often Justice uses its power over private landowners, business owners, and other parties to indulge in its habit of sending money to a favored organization of its own choosing. Part of the Gibson Guitar settlement required Gibson to "make a community service payment of $50,000 to the National Fish and Wildlife Foundation." In other words, instead of making a payment to the U.S. Treasury Department for the American taxpayer, Justice in essence extorted money from Gibson Guitar to help fund the NFWF, a congressionally created private charity that hands out funds "to some of the nation's largest environmental organizations, as well as some of the smallest," according to its own website.

So basically, the Justice Department used its authority to engineer a settlement of government claims requiring the defendant to provide benefits to a private group that was not involved in the lawsuit and was not injured by the defendants' actions. These kinds of settlements create a conflict of interest for government lawyers, since their client is the federal government and they are supposed to be acting in the best interest of the public at large, as expressed through the statutes passed by Congress. It is an abuse of their authority to provide a windfall to an outside group instead of the American taxpayer and the government. This is a conflict of interest that Eric Holder simply ignores.

But then, Justice has done a lot of funding of private advocacy groups in its environmental litigation. In 2011, the Government Accountability Office issued a report on the costs of lawsuits filed against the EPA, which were defended by the Justice Department.[31] Under various federal statutes, the EPA and the Treasury Department are required to award attorneys' fees to plaintiffs that successfully challenge the EPA. The intent of such statutes is a good one—reimbursing the costs of those who have to sue the government when bureaucrats do something wrong—but that is not what is happening in the environmental area. Instead, the Justice Department and the EPA have engaged in collusive litigation with political allies and friends of the Obama administration in order to implement regulations and new requirements without the regular process, including public notice, and at the same time using taxpayer money to fund the budgets of liberal environmental organizations.

According to the GAO report, Earthjustice, the former employer of Robert Dreher, who was the acting head of ENRD at Justice in 2013, received 32 percent of the attorneys' fees paid to EPA litigants. When combined with the attorneys' fees received by the Sierra Club and the Natural Resources Defense Council, these three groups received 41 percent of the millions of dollars paid out by the American taxpayer to environmental groups who were successful in their lawsuits against the federal government. As Senator David Vitter (R-LA), a member of the Senate Committee on Environment and Public Works, said, "The GAO report shows that taxpayers have been on the hook for years while 'Big Green' trial lawyers have raked in millions of dollars suing the government. Even worse, because of sloppy record keeping by the EPA and other agencies and a lack of cooperation by the Justice Department, we're not even sure how bad the problem really is."[32]

Another serious problem with ENRD is its handling of lawsuits over agency regulations. Rule-making by federal agencies is regulated by the Administrative Procedure Act[33] and other statutes, such as the Clean Air Act, which outlines its own procedures for creating new regulations. The purpose of these rules is to provide public notice of an agency's intent to promulgate a new regulation and give an opportunity for comment by affected parties. Federal law also very importantly requires the federal agency to "reference the legal authority under which the rule" is being proposed, in order to ensure that agencies stay within the legal authority that gives them the power to act.[34] All of this is intended to prevent arbitrary and capricious actions by unaccountable federal bureaucrats.

Usually, the Justice Department vigorously defends the federal government and agencies when they are sued. But in at least sixty cases between 2009 and 2012, the EPA through its Justice Department lawyers "chose not to defend itself in lawsuits brought by special interest advocacy groups" and in each case "agreed to settlements on terms favorable to those groups."[35] Those cases resulted in "more than 100 new federal rules, many of which are major rules with estimated compliance costs of more than $100 million annually."[36] That is more than double the number of lawsuits settled during the second term of President George W. Bush (only twenty-eight settlements). But almost all of the most costly of EPA's rule-makings have been settled by Justice Department lawyers through consent decrees without defending the suit. With such "losses," the lawyers of the ENRD are either professionally incompetent or willing participants in betraying their professional obligations to represent the public rather than the interests of advocacy groups and the particular policy choices of the administration.

The advantage to the Obama administration is that these lawsuits and resulting settlements, known as "sue and settle," provided an end run around the normal agency rule-making process, cutting out the public and affected parties, like the business community, that might protest or try to stop a bad regulation. Neither the EPA nor the Justice Department discloses the filing of such a lawsuit by a group like the Sierra Club until the case is over, when a settlement agreement has been negotiated and filed with the court. Often this allows the administration to issue regulations or requirements that go beyond their statutory authority.

Thus they can use a legally binding, court-approved settlement agreement "negotiated behind close doors" as their authority to issue, for example, a new regulation on a specific timetable and with specific requirements. As one critic says, "there shouldn't be secret deals in the determination of how someone regulates a sector, an industry, a pollutant."[37] But by colluding with their political and ideological allies in the radical environmental movement, the administration can essentially short-circuit the regulatory process and implement whatever rules the administration wants by throwing the case, failing to defend, waving the white flag of surrender, and agreeing to a settlement that has what both sides (who are really on the same side) want. There is no participation by the public, the business world, or anyone else in the national economy who would be affected by the new regulation.

Unfortunately, the vast majority of courts will simply rubber-stamp a settlement agreement without looking at its substance or questioning the circumstances under which a group such as Earthjustice and the Justice Department negotiated the deal. At that point the federal statutes awarding attorneys' fees to winning parties allow taxpayer funds to be transferred to the organizations that initiated the friendly lawsuits the administration wanted filed. The administration gets the burdensome new rules it wants without having to go through the normal transparency and review process, while at the same time helping its political allies. And the American taxpayer pays for it all.

As has been the practice of the Obama administration in many different areas, "sue and settle" actions expand the power of the executive branch and executive agencies at the expense of congressional oversight and authority, including over budget appropriations. The court-approved settlements help drive an agency's budget, taking it out of the hands of elected representatives in Congress. Such court decrees result in congressionally directed policies being "reprioritized by court orders that the agency asks the court to issue." This allows an agency like the EPA to "tell Congress 'we are acting under court order and we must publish a new regulation.' "[38]

According to the U.S. Chamber of Commerce, which is the largest trade association in the country, this collusive "sue and settle" process allows an agency like the EPA to intentionally transform itself

> from an independent actor that has discretion to perform its duties in a manner best serving the public interest into an actor subservient to the binding terms of settlement agreements, which includes using congressionally appropriated funds to achieve the demands of specific outside groups. This process also allows agencies to avoid the normal protections built into the rulemaking process—review by the Office of Management and Budget and the public, and compliance with executive orders—at the critical moment when the agency's new obligation is created.[39]

A graphic example of the conspiracy between the administration, Justice Department lawyers, and environmental groups is the litigation filed in December 2008 against the EPA by a coalition of environmental organizations, *American Nurses Association v. Jackson*. The suit claimed that the EPA had failed to issue "maximum achievable control technology (MACT)" emissions standards for "hazardous air pollutants" from coal- and oil-fired electric utility plants. This was a very questionable claim, and in fact the Bush administration had taken the position that there was no such requirement under the applicable law.

But without notice to the public or the industry members who had been allowed to intervene in the case by the court, the EPA and the environmental groups negotiated a settlement behind closed doors and filed a proposed consent decree to approve the settlement with the court in October 2009. In the settlement agreement, the EPA admitted that it had "failed" to comply with the Clean Air Act by not issuing a MACT rule and specified that the EPA would put out a proposed rule by March 16, 2011, and a final rule by November 16, 2011. The EPA essentially abandoned its ability to argue that no such regulation was needed or that a less burdensome regulation would meet the requirements of the law. It gained the ability through the litigation and court approval to issue a new regulation far more expensive and burdensome than what it could have issued through the normal rule-making process. And it got a very short regulatory approval process, one much shorter than needed for such a complex problem, making it much more difficult for those affected by the proposed regulation to analyze its effects and provide criticisms and comments to the EPA.

Any professional, objective lawyer representing the government would look at this settlement as a severe setback and a loss. But that is not how the White House saw it. In a "Presidential Memorandum" issued on December 21, 2011, President Obama called the new regulation issued as a result of this settlement "a major step forward in my Administration's efforts to protect public-health and the environment."[40] President Obama clearly welcomed the lawsuit and was glad that his lawyers had lost. But the regulatory process set up by the settlement engineered by Eric Holder's lawyers in the ENRD was so rushed that the EPA's proposed rule contained numerous errors. For example, a crucial conversion factor used by the EPA to determine the emissions history of power plants was "incorrect by a factor of 1,000."[41]

The new regulatory process was called one of the "most far-reaching and expensive rules" in the history of the EPA, by the non-profit trade association Utility Air Regulatory Group.[42] In fact, the new rule issued through this collusive lawsuit is so onerous and so burdensome that an assessment by the North American Electric Reliability Corporation said that it could force enough shutdowns of major power plants in the future to threaten reliable electric service in some areas of the country.[43]

If and when that happens, it will be the fault of not only the Obama White House and its political appointees at the EPA, but the lawyers within the Justice Department who engineered a politically convenient settlement rather than carry out their professional duty to represent the American people in the highest traditions of the legal profession and the prior history of the Justice Department.

CHAPTER 3

A CONTEMPT FOR THE CONSTITUTION AND THE RULE OF LAW

One of the most unfortunate and dangerous hallmarks of the Obama administration has been its contempt for the rule of law and its sweeping view of executive power that is well outside the bounds of the Constitution and the legal mainstream. Eric Holder has been the president's chief "aider and abettor and/or coconspirator" (to use the same language he approved in the search warrant application against Fox News reporter James Rosen) in this effort to bend, break, or ignore laws passed by Congress, since it is the Justice Department that not only makes decisions about the enforcement of federal laws, but also defends their constitutionality in court.

Jonathan Turley, a law professor at George Washington University who voted for Obama and agrees with many of his policy positions, nevertheless has expressed his grave concern over the unilateral actions of Obama and Holder, saying that the "actions of the Obama Administration challenge core principles of the separation of powers and lack meaningful limiting principles." According to Turley, "when a president claims the inherent power of both legislation and enforcement, he becomes a virtual government unto himself." Obama "is not simply posing a danger to the constitutional system; he becomes the very danger that the Constitution was designed to avoid." Holder's willingness to politicize his decision making on the enforcement (or in some cases nonenforcement) of federal law instead of carrying out his duties as the chief law enforcement officer of the United States guided by objective, nonpartisan standards of justice has directly aided Obama's expansion of executive power. As Turley says, these actions "fit an undeniable pattern of circumventing Congress."[1]

Holder revealed the politicized nature of his decision making almost as soon as he was confirmed as the new attorney general in February 2009. At that time, another push was being made in Congress to pass a bill that would provide the District of Columbia, the nation's capital, with a voting member of the House of Representatives. Both President Obama and Eric Holder had made it clear in the past that they supported D.C. voting rights. In fact, Holder had cosigned a letter in 2007 urging the passage of a D.C. voting bill.[2]

Regardless of the merits of whether the residents of Washington, D.C., should have a voting representative, the legal issue is how to achieve that goal. This is where Holder demonstrated that his professional judgment was subordinate to his political views. The only way for the District of Columbia to gain representation is through a constitutional amendment, not a congressional statute. This is because Article I of the Constitution specifies that "Representatives . . . shall be apportioned among the several *States*," which is confirmed by Section 2 of the Fourteenth Amendment. One of the qualifications to be a congressmen is to "be an Inhabitant of that *State* in which he shall be chosen." Under the Constitution, the District is not a state, and therefore cannot have a representative.

In the past Congress itself recognized that the only way the District could get representation was through a constitutional amendment—it passed one in 1977 that failed to be ratified by the states The Twenty-third Amendment (ratified in 1961) gave District residents the right to vote for president. If that right could have been granted through legislation, there would have been no need to get thirty-eight states to sign off on a constitutional amendment. The courts have recognized this; in 2000, a federal court ruled that D.C. residents were not entitled to representation in Congress since the "Constitution does not contemplate that the District may serve as a state." The Congressional Research Service concluded in 2007 that Congress doesn't have the authority to grant voting representation to the District.[3]

As far back as the Kennedy administration, the Justice Department had agreed that any effort to give the District a vote in Congress had to be done by a constitutional amendment. That had been the consistent opinion of the Office of Legal Counsel (OLC), which is the high-powered office within the Justice Department that "provides authoritative legal advice to the President and all the Executive Branch agencies," as described on its Web page.

OLC has some of the best lawyers in the entire federal government and is considered one of the most prestigious offices to work for within the Justice Department. It is tasked with acting as counsel to the president and the attorney general, including giving them legal opinions on the constitutionality of proposed legislation in Congress. Just two years before Holder became attorney general, the deputy assistant attorney general for OLC, John Elwood, reiterated OLC's long-held legal opinion in congressional testimony that "[in the absence of a constitutional amendment, therefore, the explicit provisions of the Constitution do not permit Congress to grant congressional representation to the District through legislation."[4]

Because of criticism over the legal memos it had issued on enhanced interrogation techniques during the Bush administration, Holder was specifically asked about the legal opinions of OLC during his confirmation hearing in January 2009. Holder guaranteed the sanctity of the formulation of those opinions and promised not to politicize them when he said that "[w]e don't change OLC opinions simply because a new administration takes over. The review that we would conduct would be a substantive one and reflect the best opinions of probably the best lawyers in the department as to where the law would be, what their opinions should be. It will not be a political process, it will be one based solely on our interpretation of the law."[5] Yet Holder proceeded almost immediately to break that guarantee of professionalism to run "roughshod over OLC," as it was characterized by OLC veteran Ed Whelan.[6]

Because supporters of the D.C. effort know that there is insufficient support nationwide to amend the Constitution to give the District a voting member of Congress, they had resorted to trying to get a bill passed in Congress in 2009. This was also a clear power grab since the supporters know, given the political makeup of the District, that this would be a permanent Democratic seat.

David Barron, a liberal Harvard law professor and Democrat, was appointed by Holder to be the acting head of OLC. In reviewing that pending legislation, he signed an opinion concluding that the D.C. voting bill was unconstitutional, in complete accord with five decades of OLC opinions by both Republican and Democratic administrations.[7] Because of his (and the president's) support for the D.C. legislation, however, Holder acted to override OLC's opinion so that the Justice Department's official position would instead be that the legislation was constitutional.

There is no question that an attorney general can disagree with an OLC opinion, since OLC is "exercising the advisory function the attorney general has delegated to it."[8] Although this is rare, it has happened on occasion. But in those circumstances, previous attorneys general have conducted extensive reviews of the legal issue in question and then signed a written opinion explaining their position. Instead, Holder contacted another one of his political appointees, Neal K. Katyal, the deputy solicitor general, who is responsible for representing the Justice Department and the government before the Supreme Court. Holder asked whether the solicitor general's office could defend the D.C. legislation in court.

As Ed Whelan says:

> Holder instead adopted a sham review that abused OLC's institutional role. In particular, the answer he solicited and received from Katyal was virtually meaningless. Holder didn't ask for Katyal's best judgment as to whether the D.C. bill was constitutional. He instead asked merely whether his own position that the bill is constitutional was so beyond the pale, so beneath the low level of plausible lawyers' arguments, so legally frivolous, that the Solicitor General's office, under its traditional commitment to defend any federal laws for which any reasonable defense can be offered wouldn't be able to defend it in court.[9]

The question for the president that OLC and the attorney general are supposed to answer is not whether a law can be defended in court; it is whether the legislation is constitutional, because the president has his own separate and unique duty to uphold the Constitution. Holder deliberately and intentionally bypassed and disregarded the established internal procedures at the Justice Department that were carefully designed to give the attorney general and the president the best objective, nonpartisan advice on the constitutionality of proposed congressional action. And Holder did so almost immediately after promising in his confirmation hearing that he would not engage in such misbehavior. But he took such action because OLC's opinion did not match his (and the president's) political goals.

This was almost an exact mirror of Holder's prior misconduct during the Clinton administration, when he disregarded established Justice procedures and recommended pardons for more than a dozen terrorists and fugitive financier Marc Rich, against the recommendations of the Pardons Office and Justice Department prosecutors. Ultimately, the D.C. voting bill passed the Senate, but it never passed the House of Representatives.

For all of the criticism from some about John Ashcroft's tenure as attorney general, it is especially revealing that, unlike Eric Holder, when he was faced with a similar dilemma Ashcroft supported the OLC lawyers rather than give in to politics or the White House. In 2004, White House counsel Alberto Gonzales and chief of staff Andrew Card tried to persuade Ashcroft (who was in the intensive care unit of a hospital) to overrule OLC's opinion that President Bush's warrantless surveillance program was unlawful. This program allowed the NSA to monitor emails and phone calls between individuals in the U.S. and overseas if at least one of them was linked to a terrorist group. Ashcroft refused and threatened to resign, as did several other top Justice Department officials.[10]

Given that OLC had issued an opinion that Holder did not like shortly after he arrived, it should come as no surprise that David Barron, the acting head of OLC, was not the man put forward to become the confirmed head of the office. Holder and his boss, President Obama, clearly wanted someone who would produce opinions that allowed the attorney general and the administration to do what they wanted to do politically without regard to the law. They found the lawyer they needed in Virginia Seitz, a very liberal Democratic lawyer and longtime member of the leftist American Constitution

Society, who was confirmed as the new assistant attorney general of OLC by the Senate in June 2011. Additionally, Seitz had the same distorted views on race that Holder would want in the head of OLC, having filed an amicus brief with the Supreme Court when she was in private practice arguing that the military academies should be allowed to take race into account in their admissions policies (effectively a form of racial discrimination) because it helped "military cohesiveness."[11]

OLC's transformation under Holder from a nonpartisan, professional office providing high-quality legal opinions to one that gives the attorney general political cover for the administration's actions is illustrated in an opinion Seitz issued on January 6, 2012.[12] It concerned one of the most controversial actions of Obama's tenure: his "recess" appointment of three individuals to seats on the National Labor Relations Board and Richard Cordray to head the new Consumer Financial Protection Bureau on January 4, 2012. The Constitution allows the president to make appointments without the normal Senate vote during a Senate recess. As the Senate has done for the past several years during the December and January holidays, the Senate does not recess, but instead holds a pro forma session, where every few days a senator would open the Senate and immediately adjourn, usually conducting no business. Without a recess, the president does not have the constitutional authority to make recess appointments,

While the OLC has always had an expansive view of presidential authority, including recess appointments, Seitz's opinion, issued two days *after* the president's action, was unprecedented: she said that the president has the ability to ignore the Senate's own recognition that it was in session (albeit a pro forma session) and decide on his own that the Senate was in a recess. *Three* different federal appellate courts eventually disagreed with Seitz's opinion that the appointments were constitutional.[13] Former Tenth Circuit Court of Appeals judge Michael McConnell, who is now the director of Stanford Law School's Constitutional Law Center, was very polite when he said that her opinion was not quite "frivolous," but it is pretty clear that he thought she did not provide the "counterarguments" to her opinion that she should have. He concluded that there was not any "plausible legal argument to support President Obama's recent recess appointments."[14]

The OLC opinion ignored the fact that during its pro forma sessions, the Senate had indeed conducted business in spite of the declaration in the resolution designating the sessions that no business would be conducted. In fact, the Senate passed an extension of the payroll tax holiday on December 23, 2011, that was signed into law by President Obama during the very period that Seitz was opining that the Senate was in "recess." She didn't explain how that law, or a previous law passed during a pro forma session on August 5, 2011, could be valid if her opinion was correct. As Judge McConnell says, "the Opinion creates an implausible distinction between the legal efficacy of pro forma sessions for various constitutional purposes." In other words, the Senate's sessions were a "recess" when the president wanted them to be (when he wanted to make an appointment) but not a "recess" when he didn't want them to be (when the Senate passed a bill he supported).

As former attorney general Edwin Meese and former OLC lawyer Todd Gaziano (who served in OLC under three different presidents, both Republican and Democratic) said, President Obama's actions were "a breathtaking violation of the separation of powers and the duty of comity that the executive owes to Congress." It was "constitutional abuse of a high order."[15] As a former OLC lawyer, Gaziano is even harsher than Judge McConnell, noting that Seitz's opinion "makes claims that are demonstrably false and is at times, frankly embarrassing." Not only does the opinion fail to prove that Obama's "unprecedented act was constitutional," but it "raises further questions about the legal advice process and the competence of those involved" in preparing it at OLC.[16]

Gaziano says he actually laughed at an argument that Seitz makes on pages 1 and 17 of her opinion, when she says that to defeat the president's recess appointment power, the "Senate may choose to remain continuously in session." In other words, under OLC's new opinion, senators apparently have to "remain in their seat in the Senate chamber at all times" or "at least sleep in their offices, or within range of a 15-minute quorum call."[17] Otherwise, the president apparently has the unilateral authority to make recess appointments anytime there aren't enough senators in the Senate chamber.

Seitz nonchalantly issued an opinion disregarding the serious and substantial legal questions involved and ignoring "90 years of historical practice," making conclusions "unsupported in law or the Constitution" according to Senator Chuck Grassley (R-IA).[18] It was clear that Seitz's opinion, delivered after the president had already acted, was simply written to give Obama political cover and did not provide an objective, professional assessment of the constitutionality of the president's actions.

Holder has effectively eliminated OLC's long and storied role as the office within the Justice Department that has always been willing to question the legality and constitutionality of the actions of the attorney general and the president, as it did over President Bush's warrantless surveillance program, something that almost no one else was willing to do. This eliminated one of the few checks on the president's authority within the executive branch.

As Holder's debasement of OLC demonstrates, his tenure as attorney general has been marked by a dangerous push to legitimize a vast expansion of the power of the federal government that endangers the liberty and freedom of Americans. He has taken such extreme positions on legal and constitutional issues before the Supreme Court that the Justice Department has uncharacteristically lost numerous cases before the U.S. Supreme Court. Historically, the Solicitor General normally wins about 70 percent of the Justice Department's cases; yet in the 2012–2013 term, the department won only about a third of its cases before the Supreme Court. The same thing happened in the prior term—the government lost more cases than it won.

Even more unusual, and further evidence of the outlandish legal opinions he has advanced, is that since January 2012, the Supreme Court has ruled against Holder *unanimously* nine times. So even the liberal justices on the Court, including the two justices appointed by President Barack Obama, Elena Kagan and Sonia Sotomayor, have disagreed with Holder's positions. As George Mason University law professor Ilya Somin says, "when the administration loses significant cases in unanimous decisions and cannot even hold the votes of its own appointees . . . it is an indication that they adopted such an extreme position on the scope of federal power that even generally sympathetic judges could not even support it."[19]

Those decisions are very revealing about the views of the administration and Eric Holder: it is one of unchecked federal power on immigration and environmental issues, on presidential prerogatives, and the taking of private property by the government; hostility to First Amendment freedoms that don't meet the politically correct norms; and disregard of Fourth Amendment protections against warrantless government intrusion. They are views that should alarm all Americans regardless of their political views, political party affiliations, or background.

The overt hostility to religion, particularly the Christian religion, that the Civil Rights Division has shown, was graphically illustrated by Justice in its argument in *Hosanna-Tabor Evangelical Lutheran Church & School v. EEOC*,[20] which dealt with whether antidiscrimination laws applied to church employees. In that case, Holder's lawyers claimed that the federal government had the right to, as the Supreme Court termed it, "interfere" in a church's employment decisions on the hiring and firing of its ministers and religious teachers. The justices of the Court were astounded at the arguments being made by Justice that churches had no more protected rights than private clubs and that the Free Exercise Clause and Establishment Clause of the First Amendment, which provide religious freedom and bar the government from dictating religious practices, did not shield religious institutions from the government.

The Court unanimously told the Justice Department that it could not "accept the remarkable view that the Religion Clauses have nothing to say about a religious organization's freedom to select its own ministers." The Justice Department was pushing a view of the First Amendment that would allow the government to interfere "with the internal governance of the church, depriving the church of control over the selection of those who will personify its beliefs." But the radical position the government took in the case should come as no surprise since one of the principal authors of the brief filed with the Supreme Court was a relatively recent Justice hire: Aaron D. Schuham, formerly of Barry Lynn's Americans United for Separation of Church and State.

In another case it lost nine to nothing, *Sackett v. EPA*, the Justice Department tried to prevent a family from defending itself and contesting a ludicrous order from EPA bureaucrats.[21] The Sacketts owned a small residential lot in Bonner County, Idaho, that was separated from Priest Lake by several other built-on lots. Before beginning construction of their new home, the Sacketts filled in part of their lot with dirt and rock. The Environmental Protection

Agency issued an order to the Sacketts under the Clean Water Act making the claim that their lot was a "wetland" and their actions violated the prohibition against "the discharge of any pollutant" into "navigable waters." The EPA directed them to cease construction, "restore" the lot, and give the EPA access to it. Failure to comply with this administrative order would subject the Sacketts to *a fine of up to $75,000 a day*!

The Sacketts were forced to sue the EPA in federal court after this out-of-control federal agency refused to give them an administrative hearing to contest the order. But the Justice Department actually argued that the Sacketts had no right to go to court to contest the order! Justice claimed the Sacketts would only be able to contest the order when the EPA filed a lawsuit against them for noncompliance. As Senator Ted Cruz says, "DOJ effectively wanted to put the Sacketts into a Catch-22: either the Sacketts complied with the EPA order or they faced fines of up to $75,000 per day while waiting for EPA to sue."[22]

The Supreme Court threw out the Justice Department's outrageous claim that would have deprived the Sacketts of basic due process and access to the courts to contest the EPA's order. The Court disagreed with DOJ's claim that the Sacketts could not initiate a lawsuit but instead would have to wait for the EPA "to drop the hammer" while accruing "$75,000 in potential liability" every day. Contrary to the Department's view, the Court ruled that the Clean Water Act was not "designed to enable the strong-arming of regulated parties into 'voluntary compliance' without the opportunity for judicial review."

As Paul Larkin, a former Justice Department lawyer who argued numerous cases before the Supreme Court says, the "Sacketts are not Fortune 500 companies running factories that daily pour out thousands of gallons of RBS (the acronym for what in the trade is known as Really Bad S#*t) into a river used downstream for drinking water; the Sacketts are private parties who want to build a home on their private property in a partially completed subdivision."[23] Yet Eric Holder unleashed the might of the Justice Department against them to deny their day in court.

While the collection by the National Security Agency of Americans' telephone and Internet records got a great deal of publicity and raised great concern in 2013, in a little-noticed case, Holder's position also posed a serious threat to the privacy of Americans. In *U.S. v. Jones*, the Justice Department essentially tried to convince the Supreme Court that the Fourth Amendment's protections against search and seizure should not prevent the government from tracking any American at any time without any reason.[24]

Justice argued that the police should be able to attach a GPS device to your car without a search warrant or even any reason to believe you committed a crime. Fortunately for those who fear the ever-growing power of the federal government, particularly its abuse of new technology, all nine justices agreed that the Fourth Amendment prevents the government from attaching a GPS to your car without getting a warrant. As the author of the unanimous opinion, Justice Antonin Scalia, said, there was no doubt that the type of "physical intrusion" that occurred when FBI agents attached a GPS to a car sitting in a public parking lot "would have been considered a 'search' within the meaning of the Fourth Amendment when it was adopted."

Even Justice Sotomayor, President Obama's own nominee to the Court, agreed that the government had invaded "privacy interests long afforded, and undoubtedly entitled to, Fourth Amendment protection." But Eric Holder wanted to ignore the Bill of Rights and believed that his agents should be able to track all of your movements in public by attaching a GPS device to your car without permission from a judge. This is a frightening view of government power enhanced by new surveillance technology that would have directly threatened our liberty. Fortunately, Eric Holder's view did not prevail.

The Supreme Court also ruled against Holder unanimously in:

- *Arkansas Fish & Game Commission v. U.S.*,[25] a case in which the Justice Department argued that the U.S. Army Corps of Engineers could temporarily flood and thus destroy the property of landowners (18 million board feet of timber) without having to pay any compensation; Justice Ruth Bader Ginsburg, one of the most liberal members of the Court, wrote an opinion tossing out the Justice Department's argument that the Takings Clause of the Fifth Amendment, which requires the government to provide fair compensation when it takes property for public uses, did not apply to the deliberate and planned flooding caused by the government. If Holder had been successful, the government "would have the ability to tamper with a private citizen's property without paying just compensation."[26]
- *Gabelli v. SEC*,[27] in which the Justice Department claimed that the government should be able to prosecute individuals for violations of the law that occurred years or even decades ago, despite the five-year statute of limitations; such statutes of limitations are imposed by Congress because as the Supreme Court pointed out, they "promote justice by preventing surprises through the revival of claims that have been allowed to slumber until evidence has been lost, memories have faded, and witnesses have disappeared." They are "vital to the welfare of society" and "even wrongdoers are entitled to assume that their sins may be forgotten." In fact, given

the heavy penalties the government can impose in its prosecutions, it "would be utterly repugnant to the genius of our laws" if such prosecutions could "be brought at any distance of time." The Supreme Court dismissed Holder's argument that the government should be able to in essence ignore a statutory limitation and prosecute cases whenever it "discovers" the problem.

- *Arizona v. U.S.*,[28] in which the Court ruled against the Justice Department's claim that President Obama's policy choices should trump state law. The Court did find that three provisions of Arizona's controversial immigration law were preempted by federal immigration law. But Holder lost unanimously on the provision of Arizona's law that he and President Obama had publicly attacked the most vociferously: a provision that requires state law enforcement officials to check on the immigration status of individuals they arrest, stop, or detain if they have a reasonable suspicion that the person is in the country illegally. Holder argued that responding to such inquiries, despite a federal law that *requires* the federal government to respond to requests for immigration status from state officials,[29] would interfere with President Obama's immigration enforcement (or in this case nonenforcement) priorities—which is not to pick up illegal aliens detained by local authorities. This was really a breathtaking argument: Justice was claiming that the president has the ability to override state laws based on the whims of the executive branch. As Justice Alito said, the government's claim that Arizona's provision was "pre-empted, not by any federal statute or regulations, but simply by the Executive's current enforcement policy is an astounding assertion of federal executive power that the Court rightly rejects."

And three other similar unanimous cases where the Supreme Court ruled against the government: one in which the justices rejected the Justice Department's arguments that the Internal Revenue Service could double-tax the income of a company based on a foreign government's characterization of a tax (a clear effort to bend U.S. law to collect more taxes);[30] another that a property owner couldn't defend himself against a fine imposed against him but had to pay the fine first and then sue for compensation;[31] and last, the position that a criminal law banning extortion as it has been understood in American and English law tradition for centuries should be expanded to include attempts to obtain not just money, but intangible benefits like a lawyer's "disinterested legal advice," an argument the Supreme Court said sounded "absurd, because it is."[32]

Eric Holder has had no compunction about trying to manipulate the law, deny basic due process, or make absurd arguments to the Supreme Court. As Ilya Shapiro of the Cato Institute says, what these cases have in common is a view by the Justice Department that "federal power is virtually unlimited: Citizens must subsume their liberty to whatever the experts in a given field determine the best or most useful policy to be."[33]

One other case should be mentioned even though the Justice Department's loss was not nine to zero, but five to four. There has been a great deal of debate about the Supreme Court's decision in *Citizens United v. Federal Election Commission*, in which the Court held that a ban against corporations and labor unions engaging in independent political speech was a violation of the First Amendment.[34] Many believe this was a triumph of First Amendment values over government censorship, while critics have claimed this gives corporations and unions too much power to interfere in the political process, although it should be noted that the ban also applied to nonprofit corporations like the National Rifle Association and the

Sierra Club, or in this case Citizens United, a conservative nonprofit advocacy organization. But what was indeed frightening was one of the arguments that was made by the Holder Justice Department that would have approved government censorship.

In a somewhat unusual occurrence, there were two separate oral arguments before the Supreme Court. In the first argument, on March 24, 2009, Chief Justice John Roberts asked the deputy solicitor general, Malcolm Stewart, a question about the "electioneering communications" provision of federal law that the Court eventually threw out as unconstitutional. This provision banned corporations and labor unions from running an advertisement that named a federal candidate on radio, television, or cable and satellite channels within thirty days of a federal primary or sixty days of the general election, even if the ad had nothing to do with the election.

So if a labor union (or the NAACP or the National Organization for Women) wanted to run a radio ad telling the public to call Senator John Smith to tell him to vote a particular way on an upcoming bill, it would violate federal law if the ad ran within sixty days of the general election if Senator Smith was on the ballot. This particular provision could lead to completely absurd results. As the chief justice pointed out, if Wal-Mart had aired an advertisement selling candidate action figures and it actually used the names of the candidates, it would be committing a federal felony by airing that ad within sixty days of the general election.

Chief Justice Roberts noted that the electioneering communications provision only applied to broadcast ads. He asked Stewart whether Congress could amend the law to expand the ban to books and pamphlets. He specifically proposed the hypothetical of a corporation funding a five-hundred-page book about the American political system and at the end it says "and so vote for X." Roberts wanted to know if it was the position of the Justice Department that

Congress could ban such a book. The shocking answer from the Holder Justice Department, in defiance of the most fundamental First Amendment rights, was that the government "could prohibit the publication of the book."[35] There was a noticeable gasp from the audience when the deputy solicitor general actually said the government had the power to ban books.

Finally, Eric Holder has been part and parcel of the Obama administration's repeated abrogation of the law, showing his disdain for the constitutional division of power between the legislative and executive branches. The Obama administration has been "unilaterally ordering major changes in federal law with the notable exclusion of Congress."[36] Holder has tried to defend his decisions not to enforce the law as the exercise of prosecutorial discretion. But prosecutorial discretion is the ability to decide whether a particular case should be prosecuted based on the specific facts of that case and the applicable law. It does not give a law enforcement agency the ability to simply ignore all violations of a law passed by the legislative branch and signed into law by the president because the head of that agency (or the president) does not agree with the law. That is an utter abuse and a complete violation of the attorney general's constitutional obligation to enforce the law. But it does fit, as George Washington University law professor Jonathan Turley says, "an undeniable pattern of circumventing Congress in the creation of new major standards, exceptions, or outright nullifications. What is most striking about these areas is that they are precisely the type of controversial questions designed for the open and deliberative legislative process."[37]

A prime example of this wholesale nullification of federal laws occurred in 2011. The Obama administration has a habit of announcing controversial decisions during or just before the start of holidays, when Congress is out of town and the news media are not paying attention. So on December 23, the Justice Department announced that it had completely changed its position on the 1961 Interstate Wire Act, which banned gambling over a wire. This law had been interpreted by prosecutors and the courts for years as a complete ban on Internet gambling, from lotteries to online poker. In fact, in 2007 the Justice Department said in congressional testimony that "all forms of Internet gambling, including sports wagering, casino games and card games, are illegal under federal law."[38] The Justice Department collected a record $300 million fine for Wire Act violations in 2010 from the cofounder of PartyGaming, an online poker company based offshore in Gibraltar.

But in a startling Christmas present to the online gambling industry, the Justice Department announced that its long-held interpretation of the law, previously upheld by the courts, was suddenly "wrong" and the only kind of gambling outlawed by the Wire Act was sports gambling. In fact, Justice said that the plans of New York and Illinois, President Obama's home state, to provide online lottery sales were not "within the prohibitions of the Wire Act." Both states had been heavily lobbying Justice to change its opinion. The president of Illinois's state senate said that this change would allow Illinois to "organize the first major poker pool, garner worldwide popularity, and position itself as a 'hub' for multi-state and international iGaming."[39]

This entire episode was bizarre and there really was no real explanation for the Justice Department's complete about-face and reversal of its position on the Wire Act. In addition to benefiting the gambling states, the decision also "produced windfall profits for online lottery and gambling giants like Italy-based Lottomatica and Scientific Games." The Government Accountability Institute, a private nonprofit that investigates government corruption, issued a report pointing out the curious connections between Eric Holder and his law firms and some of these companies.[40] For example, an attorney at Holder's former law firm, Covington & Burling, represented Lottomatica in a $4.8 billion acquisition of GTECH, whose chairman, Donald Sweizer, was a major Democratic Party donor and the former political director of the DNC.[41] With this reinterpretation, Eric Holder transformed the Wire Act "into a vastly different law that potentially allowed billions of dollars' worth of gambling operations on the Internet," and that "radical change [was] made without congressional hearings or debate."[42]

Another example is Holder's refusal to enforce federal drug laws. On October 19, 2009, Holder, through his deputy David Ogden, instructed U.S. attorneys not to prosecute "individuals whose actions are in clear and unambiguous compliance with existing state laws" that legalize marijuana for medical use.[43] But marijuana is classified as an illegal Schedule I drug under the Controlled Substances Act, which bans its sale, possession, and use.[44] Holder held a conference call at the end of August 2013 with the governors of Colorado and Washington, after the states had legalized recreational marijuana use, to inform them that the Justice Department would in essence not preempt their state laws or enforce federal law except to go after drug cartels, prevent marijuana distribution to minors, and block marijuana cultivation on public lands.[45] Holder also announced in August 2013 that he would no longer abide by the federal sentencing guidelines established by the United States Sentencing Commission under the Sentencing Reform Act provisions of the Comprehensive Crime Control Act of 1984, when it came to drug prosecutions of "low-level, nonviolent drug offenders." He would circumvent the minimum, mandatory sentences that Congress believed was necessary to control the drug problem in the United States by undercharging or refusing to prosecute drug offenders.[46]

There is no doubt an ongoing debate about the legalization of marijuana and the proper sentencing for those convicted of drug offenses. But that is an issue that is up to Congress to decide through the legislative process—not by the attorney general, who is only one executive branch official charged with enforcing federal laws passed by Congress. If he can simply decide on his own (or at the direction of the president) not to enforce a federal law for his own reasons, the executive branch then has the ability to "nullify the application of federal law" and "the entire legislative process becomes little more than a pretense."[47] This is a breathtaking and frightening abrogation of our constitutional structure.

Holder's lax attitude on sentencing for drug crimes caused an open revolt among federal prosecutors. In a virtually unprecedented move, on January 27, 2014, the National Association of Assistant United States Attorneys, which represents hundreds of career Justice Department prosecutors, sent a letter to Eric Holder disagreeing with Holder's support for getting rid of mandatory minimum sentences for drug pushers and drug dealers. As the prosecutors told Holder, the mandatory minimum sentencing laws passed by Congress provided "more uniformity in sentencing and, most importantly, crime is now half of what it was in the era before mandatory minimum sentences took hold." These requirements have been the cornerstone of prosecutors' ability to "dismantle large drug organizations and violent gangs" and only "target the most serious criminals." And the primary beneficiaries of this massive crime reduction are those "who were disproportionately crime victims in the past—minority groups, particularly those in the inner city." As former Justice Department prosecutor Bill Otis says, "if something like that had happened in the Bush Administration," it would have been a "Page One story." According to Otis, the fact that so many career lawyers—not political appointees—"revolted against the Attorney General is a development whose importance is difficult to overstate."[48]

We discuss the Civil Rights Division in a separate chapter, but Holder's contempt for the rule of law and his politicization of enforcement in that arena is well documented. His dismissive attitude was illustrated by an appointment he made in December 2013. On December 23, 2013, DOJ's inspector general, Michael Horowitz, sent a memorandum to Holder on the top management and performance challenges facing the Justice Department.[49] Item Six expressed Horowitz's concern over the Voting Section of the Civil Rights Division. Horowitz said that the "non-ideological, non-partisan enforcement of law is fundamental to the public's trust in the Department." Horowitz had identified cases "that the OIG believe risked undermining public confidence in the nonideological enforcement of the voting rights laws" as well as "numerous examples of harassment and marginalization of employees and managers" due to their "perceived ideological political beliefs."

Yet Holder's response to this report was the appointment of Pamela Karlan, a "sharp progressive," as the *New Yorker* calls her,[50] and a "dishonest radical academic," as former Voting Section whistleblower Christian Adams calls her,[51] to be the new deputy assistant attorney general in charge of voting rights. Karlan, who refers to herself as "snarky," has often been mentioned by liberals as a Supreme Court nominee because they consider her "a full-throated, unapologetic liberal torchbearer."[52]

During the Bush administration, Karlan relentlessly attacked the Civil Rights Division's enforcement of the Voting Rights Act, falsely claiming in a law review article in 2009 that "for five of the eight years of the Bush Administration, [it] brought no Voting Rights Act cases of its own except for one case protecting white voters."[53] This was a complete distortion by Karlan, as the Justice Department's own website showed numerous cases filed during that eight-year period on behalf of various minority groups. Karlan, who has made no secret of her opposition to all forms of election integrity measures like voter ID, actually filed a brief on behalf of convicted vote thieves in Alabama, trying to get their convictions overturned.[54] In another example of her intellectual dishonesty, Ed Whelan, another former Justice Department lawyer, pointed out that Karlan was either "hallucinating about an imaginary text or lying" in her criticism of Justice Anthony Kennedy's majority opinion in an abortion case. According to Whelan, he "can't say that [her behavior] bears favorably on her fitness for any position of trust."[55]

As a Justice Department lawyer who formerly worked in the office of the associate attorney general told one of the authors, Karlan's appointment was "a deliberate thumb in the eye of the Inspector General by Holder and the notion of even-handed, apolitical law enforcement." She is probably the best candidate that Holder could find who would be the *least likely* to pay attention to the changes recommended by the inspector general and actually implement a nonideological, nonpartisan enforcement of federal voting laws or to stop the division's harassment of employees with "wrong" political views.

Karlan's appointment was compounded by President Obama's nomination (with Holder's support) of Debo Adegbile to be Karlan's boss as the new assistant attorney general of the Civil Rights Division, a nomination that Carl Rowan Jr. called an "open slap in the face to everyone in law enforcement."[56] During his time at the NAACP's Legal Defense and Education Fund, Adegbile supported racial hiring and college admission quotas, opposed allowing employers to do criminal background checks on job applicants, claimed the government had the right to interfere in the hiring of ministers by religious organizations, and provided legal representation to Wesley Cook, the former Black Panther and Marxist revolutionary who was convicted of the cold-blooded murder of Philadelphia police officer Daniel Faulkner in 1981. Cook, better known as Mumia Abu-Jamal, is probably the most notorious cop killer in the country. Abu-Jamal's guilt was not a close call—he confessed to hospital workers that "I shot the motherf***er, and I hope the motherf***er dies." He did not testify in his own defense—and neither did his brother, who was at the scene of the crime. Yet Adegbile and the NAACP used this case to raise money, making false claims that Abu-Jamal was convicted because of "structural racism" in America. Adegbile's nomination was opposed by a host of police organizations, including the Fraternal Order of Police; the black Democratic district attorney of Philadelphia, Seth Williams; as well as Bob Casey, Pennsylvania's Democratic senator. In a sign of just how radical Adegbile is, a motion to proceed with his nomination failed by a vote of 52 to 47 on March 2, 2014, because a number of Democratic senators voted against him.

Finally, one cannot end a discussion of Eric Holder's arrogant contempt for the rule of law without discussing his decision to violate his constitutional duty to "take care that the laws be faithfully executed" by refusing to defend the Defense of Marriage Act (DOMA) before the U.S. Supreme Court. Again, the issue here is not what one believes about same sex marriage as a matter of public policy. The issue is Holder's dereliction of his duty to defend the constitutionality of laws passed by Congress.

The Justice Department has a long-standing, well-established policy of defending a federal statute unless no reasonable argument can be made in its defense or the statute would infringe on some core presidential constitutional authority. This has been the policy of the department regardless of administration, Democratic or Republican, and is the consensus of experts and high-level Justice Department officials. In a letter that he sent to the Senate in 1980 on the attorney general's duty to defend and enforce legislation, Benjamin Civiletti, the attorney general for the final two years of the Jimmy Carter administration, said that "if executive officers were to adopt a policy of ignoring or attacking Acts of Congress whenever they believed them to be in conflict with the provisions of the Constitution, their conduct in office could jeopardize the equilibrium established within our constitutional system." When confronted with such a choice, "it is almost always the case that [the attorney general] can best discharge the responsibilities of his office by defending and enforcing the Act of Congress."[57] As former Clinton administration solicitor general Drew Days says, this also ensures that the government "speaks with one voice" and it prevents "the Executive Branch from using litigation as a form of post-enactment veto of legislation that the current administration dislikes."[58]

Yet on February 23, 2011, Eric Holder sent a letter to House Speaker John Boehner telling him that despite the fact that the Justice Department had previously defended the constitutionality of DOMA, it would no longer do so because there were no reasonable arguments that could be made for its constitutionality. But the department under Holder had been making precisely such "reasonable" arguments in ongoing litigation for years, claiming that "DOMA is rationally related to legitimate government interests and cannot fairly be described as born of animosity."[59] In the first three years of his administration, President Obama had not treated DOMA as if it was a facially invalid statute; he had expressed ambivalence about a statute overwhelmingly passed by Congress and signed into law by Bill Clinton. Holder suddenly took the position that the Justice Department could no longer defend the law "after previously enforcing the law, leading many to question a decision to abandon the law 'midstream' without any clear advocate with standing to argue the law's merits."[60] And this only happened after increased criticism from the gay community as President Obama was entering his reelection campaign.

Regardless of the question of the legality or acceptance of same-sex marriage, the problem is Eric Holder and the president forswearing their duty to defend laws passed by Congress. The ultimate decision in the DOMA case, *U.S. v. Windsor*, was a narrow 5-4 decision invalidating part of DOMA, but the majority noted that "when Congress has passed a statute and a President has signed it, it poses grave challenges to the separation of powers for the Executive at a particular moment to be able to nullify Congress's enactment solely on its own initiative."[61]

On this issue, Eric Holder also was willing to use federal power to override state sovereignty and defy even the Supreme Court when he announced in January 2014 that the federal government would recognize same-sex marriages performed in Utah despite another Supreme Court ruling. In December 2013, a lone federal judge in Utah, Robert Shelby (a recent Obama appointee), held that Utah's limitation of marriage to heterosexual couples violated the Constitution. After Shelby refused to stay his opinion, the state filed an emergency appeal with the U.S. Supreme Court, which stopped Shelby's judgment from going into effect until a federal appeals court considers the issue.[62] Before the stay was issued, hundreds of marriages were performed; the Supreme Court's stay put those marriages performed in violation of state law in legal limbo.

In announcing that the federal government would recognize those marriages, Holder mischaracterized the Supreme Court's action as an "administrative step" and wrongly cited the *Windsor* decision to justify what he did. The *Windsor* case only held that the federal government has to recognize same-sex marriages that a "state recognizes as marriages;[63] here, the Utah attorney general, Sean Reyes, announced that the state would not recognize the marriages. Noted legal analyst Ed Whelan, a former Justice Department lawyer who worked in the Office of Legal Counsel, says, as "jaded" as he is by "the lawlessness of the Obama administration," even he "didn't expect this." The federal government does not have the power to "treat as marriages those same-sex relationships that the state in which the marriage supposedly took place does *not* recognize as marriages."[64]

The point here is not to debate the appropriateness of same-sex marriage—the point is that this is an issue entirely up to the states and their residents and legislators to decide, not the United States attorney general, who has no authority to override state laws. That is the kind of tyrannical authority that royal governors thought they had in the American colonies prior to the Revolution.

Holder compounded his dereliction of duty by urging that state attorneys general engage in the *same* type of misbehavior. In February 2014, he told a meeting of the National Association of Attorneys General in Washington that they should not defend state marriage laws banning gay marriage—despite the fact that the U.S. Supreme Court has never ruled that such a prohibition violates equal protection. In an interview, a senior state official told the authors that many of the state officials resented having Holder lecture them on their obligations as attorneys general given Holder's own many shortcomings.

After Holder finished his public remarks, the media were cleared out of the room and the doors closed. According to the state official, Holder was then asked by one of the state attorneys general how Holder could make such a recommendation when we have an adversarial-based legal system that depends on both sides of a dispute having vigorous legal representation to make their case, particularly since attorneys general take the position that they are the exclusive representatives of the public? Holder conceded that we have an adversarial court system and admitted that both sides should be represented. He acknowledged that state marriage laws were entitled to a defense. But he said "others" should do that at the expense of the taxpayer, not the state AGs. Holder also falsely claimed that he had worked with the House of Representatives to help it find representation after he told Congress he would no longer defend DOMA.

Eric Holder's actions set a precedent that would allow any future president in essence to veto any legislation signed into law by his predecessor (or to override state laws) by simply deciding not to defend a federal law against legal challenge. If an administration "disagrees with duly enacted laws or finds it politically expedient not to enforce them, it waives the laws out of existence rather than fulfilling its constitutional obligation to take care that those laws be faithfully executed."[65] Why bother going to Congress and trying to persuade its members to repeal laws the president doesn't agree with? What Holder and President Obama did destroys the separation of powers that is the basis of our constitutional system. Whether you are a liberal, a moderate, or a conservative with various points of view on many different issues, everyone should fear having an attorney general who establishes the precedent that prior laws passed by our elected representatives and signed into law by a popularly elected president can be wiped out of existence by one person in a new administration deciding that Justice simply will not defend that law in court. And Holder wants to spread his upside-down view of our constitutional system into the states like an infection.

Federalist No. 47 discussed why the Constitution distributed power between the "legislative, executive, and judiciary departments." James Madison explained that "the accumulation of all powers . . . in the same hands, whether of one, a few, or many . . . may justly be pronounced the very definition of tyranny." Eric Holder has done his best to accumulate that power in the Office of the Attorney General.

CHAPTER 4

THE (UN)CIVIL RIGHTS DIVISION

Civil Rights for Thee but Not for Me

With almost a thousand employees and a 2012 appropriation of $145 million, the Civil Rights Division is one of the largest divisions within the Justice Department. It has seen significant increases in its budget under the Obama administration and has hired many new employees in career civil service positions, primarily radically liberal lawyers. As journalist Byron York says, the division is "bigger, richer and more aggressive than ever, with a far more expansive view of its authority than at any time in recent history.[1]

The extent to which that authority has been misused under the Obama administration was vividly illustrated in a shocking 129-page order released by a federal court in Louisiana in September 2013. It involved the case of five New Orleans police officers who were convicted of civil rights violations over a shooting and subsequent cover-up in the aftermath of Hurricane Katrina.[2] Judge Kurt Engelhardt overturned the convictions because of "grotesque prosecutorial abuse" and the "skullduggery" and "perfidy" of Justice prosecutors. He found that lawyers in the Office of the U.S. Attorney in Louisiana and in the Civil Rights Division had, among other misdeeds, made anonymous postings on the website run by the New Orleans *Times-Picayune* that "mocked the defense, attacked the defendants, and their attorneys, were approbatory of the United States Department of Justice, declared the defendants obviously guilty, and discussed the jury's deliberations."

One of the division lawyers involved was Karla Dobinski. Dobinski was the "taint attorney"—the lawyer assigned to make sure that the defendants' rights were not violated by the division prosecutors using privileged information such as the compelled testimony provided by the officers to internal investigators at the police department. The judge was appalled that the lawyer assigned to ensure that the constitutional rights of the defendants were protected was personally fanning the "flames of those burning to see [the defendant] convicted" before the jury even got the case.

Judge Engelhardt spent ten pages of his order just describing the ethical rules and federal regulations violated by Justice lawyers. He clearly believed that Holder's Justice Department tried to hide what happened because trying to get information out of the department was like "slowly peeling layers of an onion." He was also suspicious that DOJ's reports on the internal investigation were "edited by a supervisor so as to coyly provide less information, rather than more." Reportedly, the supervisors on the case were Deputy Attorney General James Cole (the number-two Obama political appointee at Justice directly under Eric Holder) and an assistant.

The judge noted that an FBI special agent used "shockingly coercive tactics" against defense witnesses. Because of threats of prosecution for perjury over their earlier grand jury testimony by the lead prosecutor of the division, Barbara "Bobbi" Bernstein, three of those witnesses refused to appear at trial on behalf of the defendants. The judge found it highly suspicious that twenty-six months after the trial, not one of those potential witnesses who could have provided exculpatory evidence had "been charged with any crime whatsoever."

Engelhardt pointed the finger of blame in this case directly at Eric Holder. Just like in the incident involving George Zimmerman and Trayvon Martin in Florida, the radical civil rights organizations that are the allies of the administration had clamored for federal prosecutions of the New Orleans police officers. The fact that Dobinski and Bernstein remained employed at the department and that no disciplinary action was taken against them is a sad but telling comment on the behavior that Eric Holder finds acceptable in his prosecutors—if they are liberals who push the kinds of prosecutions that he and the administration's political allies want. As the court noted, this demonstrated a get-a-conviction-at-any-cost attitude by Holder and his minions in the Civil Rights Division:

> The indictment in this case was announced with much fanfare, a major press conference presided over by U.S. Attorney General Eric Holder, and widespread media attention. . . . A DOJ representative said that the indictments "are a reminder that the Constitution and the rule of law do not take a holiday—even after a hurricane." While quite true in every respect, the Court must remind the DOJ that the Code of Federal Regulations, and various Rules of Professional Responsibility, and ethics likewise do not take a holiday—even in a high-stakes criminal prosecution, and even in the anonymity of cyberspace. . . . [T]he Court simply cannot allow the integrity of the justice system to become a casualty in a mere prosecutorial game of qualsiasi mezzo [by any means necessary].

Would that the New Orleans fiasco was an isolated example of Justice's Civil Rights Division abuses.

Under Eric Holder's direction and the supervision of one of the administration's most radical political appointees, Thomas Perez,[3] the assistant attorney general for civil rights from 2009 to 2013, the Civil Rights Division has pursued a militant civil rights agenda intended to help Democrats win elections and implement their progressive version of a socialized America where racial, ethnic, and sexual quotas are required in everything from college admissions to public employment to school discipline.

Perez, with the collaboration of the overwhelmingly liberal career staff in the division, waged a war on religion; abused federal law to restrict the free speech of pro-life activists; went after school districts for having dress codes that don't allow boys to come to class in drag or for implementing voucher programs to help students get out of bad schools; tried to stop states from improving election integrity efforts through voter ID or the verification of the citizenship of registered voters; and arranged a quid pro quo deal to protect an unsupportable race-centric legal theory—disparate impact—used to extort huge settlements from banks and mortgage lenders. The division has been at the forefront of enforcement that is based on liberal ideology and partisan politics, rather than objective law enforcement and the pursuit of justice. Bob Driscoll, a former chief of staff in the Civil Rights Division, says that today "it is more like a government-funded version of advocacy groups such as the ACLU or the NAACP Legal Defense Fund than like government lawyers who apply the facts to the law."[4]

All of this has been quite deliberate. Holder claimed he was "offended" at the way the Bush administration had supposedly transformed the Justice Department, and particularly the Civil Rights Division, which he calls the "crown jewel" of the Department.[5]

Created by the Civil Rights Act of 1957, the division is charged with enforcing federal discrimination laws in voting, employment, housing, immigration, and education. The division is divided into eleven "sections" that have responsibility for different areas, such as the Voting Section. The nearly ninety lawyers and staff in that section enforce the Voting Rights Act, the National Voter Registration Act, and other federal voting laws. At a time in our nation's history when we have less discrimination than we have ever had before, the division is the largest it has ever been and has enormous power to abuse the law and shape the legal environment that governs many different areas of our culture and economy.

A longtime, current employee of the division told one of the authors that in the employee's opinion, the current administration has:

> racialized and radicalized the division to the point of corruption. They embedded politically leftist extremists in the career ranks who have an agenda that does not comport with equal protection or the rule of law; who believe that the ends justify the means; and who behave unprofessionally and unethically. Their policy is to intimidate and threaten employees who do not agree with their politics, and even moderate Democrats have left the department, because they were treated as enemies by administration officials and their lackeys. Another black employee who has worked for the Justice Department for decades said to me that "there is no justice left in Justice under this administration."

From his first day in office, Eric Holder has misused the power of the Civil Rights Division, starting almost immediately with his dismissal of the voter intimidation case against the New Black Panther Party over its actions in Philadelphia in the 2008 election. In March 2013, the inspector general of the Department of Justice, Michael Horowitz, released a report on the operations of the Voting Section of the division that is a disturbing and sad commentary on the mismanagement and misbehavior of the people who work there.[6] The problems exposed in the report are rampant throughout the entire division, problems that have existed for many years but were greatly exacerbated by the Obama administration.

The IG report describes a dysfunctional division torn by "polarization and mistrust," a division beset by unprofessional and unethical behavior, a division in which career civil service employees who are perceived by other employees as conservatives or Republicans or who believe in the race-neutral enforcement of federal discrimination laws are subjected to racist comments, harassment, intimidation, bullying, and even threats of physical violence. It is a division that has experienced other misbehavior by career employees that has gone unpunished, such as perjury and the use of a government credit card to pay for romantic trysts with a mistress.[7] It has engaged in biased hiring practices intended to ensure a staff with a radical, left-wing ideology and has pursued meritless cases, working not on behalf of the American public as a neutral law enforcement agency but to achieve political and ideological objectives.

None of this comes as a surprise. For decades, the division has hired almost exclusively from the ranks of liberal advocacy organizations. The career leadership of the division, like in most government agencies, provides substantive expertise and continuity from one administration to the next. However, the career lawyers in the Civil Rights Division are overwhelmingly liberal and have always manipulated the hiring process to ensure that the staff remains that way. In December 2000, when it became clear that a Republican would be in the White House, the division underwent an unprecedented hiring binge to fill ninety civil service vacancies before the new administration came on board, according to the 2013 IG report.

For example, in a federal government that usually takes months to hire a new employee, the division issued a vacancy announcement on December 19, 2000, that closed on January 2 for eight positions in the Voting Section. Interviews were conducted over a three-day period, January 3–5, 2001, and by January 11, shortly before the inauguration of George Bush, the positions had been filled with individuals who were all "committed to the mission of civil rights," that is, liberals who would fight the new administration. It was very clear the leadership was seeking to prevent the Bush administration from choosing career lawyers who might have a more moderate or conservative view of civil rights enforcement. The former director of human resources in the division told the IG that hiring "had never happened like that before and she believed that the hiring efforts were improper." In fact, a Clinton political appointee "threatened to take control" of the hiring if the section chiefs failed to fill the slots quickly—and they "got the message loud and clear."

These hiring tactics were brought back and increased exponentially under Eric Holder. There were hiring controversies in the Bush administration when Bush political appointees tried to impose a more balanced hiring process that would give experienced lawyers from across the political spectrum a chance to get hired. The former inspector general of the Justice Department, Glenn Fine, a Clinton appointee, issued a partisan report in 2009 thickly laced with bias, inaccuracies, gross exaggerations, and misstatements of both facts and the law. It criticized that hiring, which brought a small number of lawyers into the division who had not worked at liberal civil rights organizations, ignoring the biased hiring that had occurred during the Clinton administration. But then, the conclusion of the report was no surprise given that two of the lawyers who helped write the report were Tamara Kessler, a liberal former Civil Rights Division lawyer who actually worked alongside many of the leading critics identified in the report, and Mark Masling, also a former Civil

Rights Division attorney and self-proclaimed "proud Democrat."[8]

Just one example suffices of how biased Fine's 2009 report was. One of the Appellate Section attorneys who figured prominently in the report—a Clinton political appointee who burrowed into the career civil service and then claimed she was victimized by the Bush political appointees—was promoted to a policy-making counsel position in the division's new front office *on the very first day* of the Obama administration. This is a slot normally reserved for political appointees.

Vowing that they would correct the supposed "abuses" of the Bush administration, Eric Holder and the Obama administration established a hiring system that on its surface appears impartial, but in fact accelerated the practice of hiring only liberal, politically biased, and politically connected lawyers. The new system put an emphasis on experience with civil rights groups, which invariably are liberal and very partisan. It is no surprise, therefore, that 100 percent of all of the lawyers hired by Eric Holder for career civil service positions in the Civil Rights Division have been Democratic activists or ideological liberals and firebrands.

The 2013 IG report found that in the Voting Section alone, 56 percent of those hired since 2009 came from only five organizations: the American Civil Liberties Union, La Raza, the Lawyers' Committee for Civil Rights, the NAACP, and the Mexican American Legal Defense and Educational Fund. The IG report says that the "Voting Section passed over candidates who had stellar academic credentials and litigation experience with some of the best law firms in the country, as well as with the Department" in order to hire those they considered to have a "commitment" to "traditional" civil rights, that is, liberals who support quotas, ethnic and gender entitlements, and a government-imposed racial spoils system. When a division deputy chief, Becky Wertz, was asked to prepare a list of career lawyers who had left during the Bush administration who could be recruited to return, she "could not explain why" she left off the names of the eight lawyers perceived to be "conservatives." Bob Popper, a former deputy chief who finally left the division in 2013 out of frustration, says he was "routinely excluded from hiring decisions" starting in 2009 because he was perceived as a "conservative."

One of the lawyers hired for the Voting Section by the Obama administration was Dan Freeman, a former ACLU attorney with no experience in the voting area. He boasted on his Facebook account that he had started the crowd booing Representative Paul Ryan at President Obama's 2013 inauguration. Although such public displays of political bias are extremely damaging to the reputation of the division and its ability to maintain even the appearance of impartiality, the division did nothing publicly to disavow Mr. Freeman's conduct or to discipline him. Why would it when the political appointees within the division and almost all of the career staff no doubt applauded Freeman's behavior and saw nothing wrong with it?

Another graphic example is Anurima Bhargava, who was hired to be the career civil service head of the Educational Opportunities Section of the division. She is responsible for the appalling motion filed in August 2013 against Louisiana trying to stop its school voucher program, which helps poor kids get out of failing public schools, because it allegedly violated a forty-year-old desegregation order. It is a move that even the liberal *Washington Post* called an attempt "to trap poor, black children in ineffective schools."[9] Even though 9 out of 10 of the students who use the vouchers are black, the division claimed that the program was discriminatory because children leaving the bad schools would change the schools' racial makeup. As the *Washington Post* says, it is "downright perverse" that the Obama administration would "use the banner of civil rights to bring a misguided suit that would block these disadvantaged students from getting the better education opportunities they are due."

But Bhargava has a history of views on racial preferences and racial quotas that appear to be more important than a quality education for poor children, and was hired by the administration from the NAACP Legal Defense Fund precisely because of those views. She pursued numerous cases while at the NAACP seeking to expand the use of racial quotas in public schools. At a forum at the United Nations on minority issues, Bhargava told the attendees that public school systems should use the race, language, immigration status, and religion of students to assign them to schools. It is par for the course for the Holder Justice Department to hire as the head of the division's education section such an appalling racialist who believes it should be legal to discriminate on the basis of race, religion, and other factors in an attempt to create her preferred progressive social outcome.

Since Eric Holder has been in charge, the division has brought numerous cases based on shaky legal theories like the Louisiana voucher case. For example, the division has filed a series of high-profile lawsuits against bankers and mortgage lenders. The law underlying these suits, the Fair Housing Act, requires that the government prove intentional discrimination. In spite of this legal requirement, the division has brought multiple suits based not on evidence of intentional discrimination, but rather on statistical evidence that supposedly shows a "disparate impact" on certain minority groups. These include cases against SunTrust Mortgage, Countrywide Financial, and Wells Fargo.

The banks chose to settle rather than fight the suits, though, out of fear of being labeled "racist" in court even though the dubious "disparate impact" theory "remains on legally unsound ground."[10] Holder also used these settlements to funnel money to liberal, ACORN-type advocacy groups. For example, the settlement with the AIG Federal Savings Bank required the payment of $1 million to an unrelated "qualified organization" (as decided by the Justice Department) to conduct social programs.[11]

Perez was so concerned about the disparate impact theory being challenged in court that he secretly engineered a quid pro quo deal with the city of St. Paul, Minnesota, in 2011 to void such a challenge. The move was so extraordinary that the House Committee on Oversight and Government Reform launched an investigation that detailed Perez's unethical conduct.

St. Paul had a case pending before the Supreme Court, in which the division was not even a party, and which would have determined the validity of the disparate impact theory. Most legal scholars believed the Court was going to rule against the theory, undermining the "entire legal foundation of [Perez's] political campaign of suing banks for discrimination based on dubious statistical evidence."[12]

At the same time, the Justice Department's Civil Division, a completely separate division of the department and not under Perez's authority, was pursuing two claims against St. Paul under the federal False Claims Act that could have netted the American taxpayer $180 million for the city's fraudulent certifications made to obtain federal housing grants. The Civil Division lawyers thought this would be an easy case to win because St. Paul's certifications "were actually more than reckless and that the City had actual knowledge that they were false."[13]

St. Paul's case before the Supreme Court, on the other hand, involved the city trying to "force slumlords to adhere to housing codes, because low-income tenants, including minorities, were living in apartments with rats and inadequate heating."[14] The slumlords were trying to evade their obligations to improve living conditions by claiming that the housing codes intended to protect residents had a "disparate impact" on their minority tenants.

Ordinarily, the Justice Department would have no control over the course of the suit, since it was not a party; the dispute was between St. Paul and private parties. Similarly, Perez had no authority over the Civil Division litigation. However, in an unprecedented action, Perez told St. Paul's lawyers that the Civil Division would agree to drop the False Claims Act claims in exchange for St. Paul dropping the slumlord case. As the *Wall Street Journal* summarized, Perez "intervened to undermine two civil complaints against the City of St. Paul in order to get St. Paul to drop a Supreme Court case that might have blown apart the legal rationale for his dubious discrimination crusade against law-abiding businesses."[15] Perez tried to hide the quid pro quo deal by directing the lawyers in the Civil Division not to mention the deal in their internal case files, and he used his own private email account to secretly arrange the deal with St. Paul's lawyers in violation of the Federal Records Act (he apparently illegally sent hundreds of private emails on division business). Thus, his disparate impact theory stayed alive.

The Civil Rights Division brought questionable cases in other areas as well. For example, Perez launched a series of abusive cases under the Freedom of Access to Clinic Entrances (FACE) Act that were intended to intimidate the pro-life movement. This federal law was passed to prevent physical obstruction or the use or threat of force outside abortion clinics. But the statute specifically protects the First Amendment right of "expressive conduct," including peaceful demonstrations. In 2011, the division tried to get an injunction against a pro-life activist, Angel Dillard, who had merely written a letter to a doctor who was planning on opening an abortion clinic in Kansas. The federal court denied the request because Dillard's activities were protected by the First Amendment. After two years of litigation, in August 2013, the judge dismissed the prosecution, finding that the government had produced no evidence of motive, intent, or wrongdoing that violated the law.

Dillard's letter simply tried to persuade the doctor that her actions were wrong based on "arguments from Scripture, appeals to conscience, and the practical disadvantages and difficulties associated with such a clinic" according to the judge.[16] The Wichita Police Department had concluded there was no threat against the doctor and the FBI had also recommended against a Justice lawsuit. In fact, the FBI told the Justice Department "there was nothing there." The FBI was "frustrated by the suit . . . they felt this was undermining the trust and the relationship that they were trying to develop with people who were not extremists but were still pro-life." DOJ's case, according to the judge, was "speculation piled on top of speculation" and "fatally flawed" because it lacked any proof.

Another egregious FACE Act prosecution was against Mary Susan Pine, who was conducting peaceful sidewalk counseling outside an abortion clinic in Florida, something she had been doing for many years.[17] The government in its complaint contended Pine obstructed access to the clinic, citing a witness who supposedly observed the obstruction. However, the witness turned out to have testimony totally opposite—that Pine did not obstruct anyone at the clinic. The division lawyers did not attempt to preserve videotape evidence from surveillance cameras outside the clinic that would have showed exactly what happened, and the recordings were destroyed by the clinic.

In 2012, a federal judge in Florida threw out the case. The nearly total lack of evidence of any violation of the law and the "negligent and perhaps even grossly negligent" behavior by division lawyers in not preserving crucial evidence in the case led the judge to wonder whether the prosecution of Pine was the "product of a concerted effort between the government and the [abortion clinic], which began well before the date of the incident at issue, to quell Ms. Pine's activities" rather than to enforce the statute. In other words, the judge believed that Pine may have been targeted for her political beliefs. "The Court is at a loss as to why the Government chose to prosecute this particular case in the first place," the judge wrote at the conclusion of his ruling. American taxpayers were forced to pay $120,000 in attorneys' fees and costs to Pine.

Why would Eric Holder bring these frivolous cases? Because a pro-abortion ideology is driving enforcement of the FACE Act, not the objective, unbiased, nonpartisan interests of justice and equal protection under the law. The pro-abortion views of Holder and liberals inside the Justice Department led them to use a federal statute to attack these pro-life activists who were engaged in First Amendment–protected activity. Even though these particular suits were unsuccessful, this misuse of a federal statute intended to stop violence at abortion clinics may have achieved its goal. As the judge observed in the Kansas case, "due to a chilling effect of calls and visits from the FBI, and the filing of the present action by the Department of Justice . . . it is utterly unsurprising that Dillard has ceased political activity she might have otherwise undertaken."

In a similar vein, demonstrating the Obama administration's antipathy to religious freedom, were the division's dubious legal arguments in *Hosanna-Tabor Evangelical Lutheran Church and School v. EEOC*.[18] The Justice Department tried to convince the Supreme Court that the religious freedom clause of the First Amendment did not protect the hiring decisions of a church. This was such an extreme position that all nine justices of the Supreme Court disagreed, finding the arguments made by DOJ "untenable." The Court could not accept "the remarkable view that the Religion Clauses have nothing to say about a religious organization's freedom to select its own ministers." Even the Obama administration's former solicitor general, Justice Elena Kagan, joined a particularly powerful concurring opinion with Justice Samuel Alito rebuking the legal position advanced by the administration.

In another example of the mismanagement of its enforcement responsibilities and the incompetence of too many of its newly hired political lawyers, the division was forced to pay the state of Arkansas $150,000 in attorneys' fees and costs in 2012 for a failed prosecution under the Civil Rights of Institutionalized Persons Act.[19] Once again, the judge found almost no evidence to support the division's claims against the Conway Human Development Center, an institution for developmentally disabled individuals operated by the state of Arkansas. The suit was filed even though there had not been a single complaint by residents of the center or their families. But the suit followed the liberal view on "deinstitutionalization" that believes that all such state facilities should be closed. It is that same ideology that has led to the closing of many state-run mental institutions and the flooding of our streets with the mentally ill.

The federal judge was harsh in his criticism of the division's case, calling into question the basis for the lawsuit and assailing the caliber of the government's witnesses—calling them "unpersuasive . . . [and] not qualified." Concerned parents and guardians opposed the division's lawsuit and the judge found that the government was "in the odd position of asserting that certain persons' rights have been and are being violated while those persons—through their parents and guardians—disagree." This meritless lawsuit was dismissed with prejudice. This case followed another lawsuit the division brought against Arkansas's entire mental health system that was also dismissed because of the division's failure to comply with the basic statutory requirements for filing.

None of this is really a surprise. During the Clinton administration, the division was forced to pay more than $4 million in attorneys' fees and costs in eleven meritless cases the division filed that were thrown out by federal courts. One of these cases demonstrates "the disappointing lack of professionalism" in the division. According to the U.S. Court of Appeals for the Eleventh Circuit:

> A properly conducted investigation would have quickly revealed that there was no basis for the claim that the Defendants were guilty of purposeful discrimination against black voters. . . . We can only hope that in the future the decision makers in the United States Department of Justice will be more sensitive to the impact on racial harmony that can result from the filing of a claim of purposeful discrimination. The filing of an action charging a person with depriving a fellow citizen of a fundamental constitutional right without conducting a proper investigation of its truth is unconscionable.[20]

This did not happen during the Bush administration, when there were adults in charge who kept the radical career lawyers in the division in check—there was not a single such case that the division lost where it had to pay attorneys' fees and costs. But in the Holder Justice Department, the political appointees are as radical if not more so than the career lawyers.

The Holder Civil Rights Division has even twisted federal discrimination laws to go after school districts like the Mohawk Central School District in upstate New York for having a dress code that prevents boys from wearing makeup, nail polish, wigs, and high heels. This administration apparently believes that it is a violation of federal law for high schools to have a dress code that makes distinctions between what is appropriate dress for males and what is appropriate dress for females. Obviously, schools should not allow bullying or violence of any kind. But it is ludicrous to launch federal investigations of schools for having dress codes that differentiate between males and females or to equate such dress codes with sex discrimination.

This unanchored reading of the law on sex discrimination extends to universities. The division (in conjunction with the U.S.

Department of Education) sent a bizarre letter to the University of Montana in 2013 that tells the university how it is supposed to handle sexual harassment allegations. This letter is also intended to "serve as a blueprint for colleges and universities throughout the country"[21] and goes so far that it would make asking someone for a date a federal crime. It lays out a legal rule that directly contradicts Supreme Court rulings that actionable harassment must be objectively offensive to a reasonable person. Instead, DOJ's Orwellian letter dictates that universities must institute a policy that defines sexual harassment as "any unwelcome conduct of a sexual nature."

In 1999 the Supreme Court stated in *Davis v. Monroe County Board of Education* that, for a school to be liable for student-on-student sexual harassment, the conduct in question must be "so severe, pervasive, and objectively offensive that it can be said to deprive the victims of access to the educational opportunities or benefits provided by the school." Needless to say, one could steer a cruise ship through the vast gulf between the actual state of the law and the twisted policy being advanced by the Holder Justice Department.

Under Holder's rule, a single instance of conduct that is "offensive" to one individual would constitute a violation of the law, even if that individual's reaction is totally unreasonable. DOJ also insists that sexual harassment includes "unwelcome" (not just offensive) conduct that is "verbal, nonverbal, or physical conduct."

The breadth of this new mandate, plucked from the mists occupied only by the most radical ideologues, is staggering. Under this definition, a student asking another out on a date could violate the law if the person being asked out found the question "unwelcome" and somehow believed it was the pretext to a sexual advance. If a student was taking a health class where biological reproduction was discussed, the teacher could be found guilty of sexual harassment if a student found the discussion "unwelcome," even if no one else in the class and no reasonable person found it unwelcome or offensive. In other words, under this definition the most trivial conduct could be considered sexual harassment. And, get this—if a university did not take immediate and severe action to punish the "transgressor," it could lose its federal funding.

There is no question that sexual harassment is a serious issue and that schools should take appropriate steps to stop it. But this new DOJ policy is political correctness madness that essentially implements a zero-tolerance policy in colleges for any verbal conduct a hypersensitive listener deems unwelcome. It will have a severe impact on the First Amendment rights of students, restricting not just the dating routines on campus, but also free discussion and discourse on many different issues.

But DOJ's bizarre attitude gets worse, requiring universities to implement what amounts to a "guilty-until-proven-innocent" rule that is completely at odds with impartial justice and fundamental due process. Justice criticizes the University of Montana's procedure for investigating sexual harassment complaints because it has "multiple stages," including an appeals process! The fact that Eric Holder's Justice Department is offended that a student might be able to go through several levels of review and appeal of an adverse decision is something that should scare all of us.

Apparently, Eric Holder would prefer a Star Chamber that immediately slams the door on anyone accused of sexual harassment. How else is one to interpret the directive in the letter that an "appropriate step" by a university would include "taking disciplinary action against the harasser" before "the completion" of the investigation!? Holder appears to want universities to apply the Queen of Heart's admonition in *Alice in Wonderland* to lop off the heads of anyone accused of sexual harassment before there has even been an investigation or hearing to determine whether the accusations are true.

In the *Davis* case, the Supreme Court said it was not outlawing "insults, banter, teasing . . . and gender-specific conduct that is upsetting to students" and that it "trust[ed]" courts would not be misled to impose "sweeping liability." But it is exactly that type of "sweeping liability" that ideologues serving in this administration are now trying to impose by administrative fiat.

In another wacky view of the law that affects higher education, Eric Holder's Civil Rights Division is suing universities over the food they serve in school cafeterias. Contrast this with the 1960s when there was real discrimination in American colleges and the Justice Department fought hard, serious battles to stop such civil rights abuses.

But in 2013, like a scene out of a Monty Python sketch, Holder actually threatened to sue Lesley University in Massachusetts for supposedly violating the Americans with Disabilities Act for not adequately accommodating students with food allergies. Apparently, the school did not have enough gluten- and allergy-free "hot and cold" options in its cafeterias. In the view of Eric Holder, the university was preventing students from equally enjoying "the privileges, advantages, and accommodations of its food service and meal plan system." So according to the Justice Department, what a university chooses to put on (or leave off its menus) could violate federal law and subject it to prosecution by the chief law enforcement agency of the U.S. government.

Faced with expensive litigation, the university unfortunately settled the case with an agreement that not only defines what kind of food it can serve and how its kitchen facilities have to operate, but requires the university to let students "pre-order" their meals and provide them a restricted room to which only allergy "disabled" students have access—it even defines what equipment has to be in the restricted room ranging from a toaster to a freezer.

No one minimizes the problems that some students may have with food allergies and universities should work with students and their families to accommodate such problems when they can. But a federal court in a case called *Land v. Baptist Medical Center* said that a food allergy is not a disability under the Americans with Disabilities Act since it does not substantially limit a student's ability to engage in activity. The idea that this is a federal issue or that the Justice Department should burn up its resources investigating university dining halls is a complete absurdity and contrary to the law. It is another sign of the mindless mission creep that is a hallmark of the Holder Justice Department.

Under this entirely warped view of federal disability law, the Perez-led division actually threatened to sue Princeton, Arizona State, and Case Western Reserve if they dared to participate in an experimental program that would have made the Amazon Kindle available for students to replace traditional textbooks.[22] Perez claimed that allowing students to use Kindles would violate the Americans with Disabilities Act because while the Kindle has a text-to-speech audio feature, the menu that allows you to choose that option requires sight to use. The program was entirely voluntary and no student was forced to participate. According to Princeton, there wasn't even anyone with a visual impairment in any of the three classes that would have been part of the initial program.[23] In essence, Perez took the position that if blind students couldn't use the device, then no student should be allowed to use it. In other words, sighted students needed to be punished under federal discrimination law that was intended to protect the disabled. As Russell Redenbaugh, a former member of the U.S. Commission on Civil Rights, and who lost his sight when he was a child, says, "it's a gross injustice to disadvantage one group, and it's bad policy that breeds resentment, not compassion."[24] Unfortunately, all of the schools gave in to the Justice

Department's intimidation and threats and agreed that no student would be allowed to use electronic books like the Kindle until they were all completely accessible to the blind.

Even in areas of public safety, the division has used federal discrimination laws to try to impose racial hiring quotas and go after fire and police departments to eliminate racially neutral qualification exams. For example, the division pushed the New York Fire Department to hire firefighters who miss 70 percent of the questions on a fire academy entrance exam. It forced the Dayton, Ohio, police department to lower its testing standards because it claimed not enough black recruits were passing the recruitment exam, with the result that Dayton would have to hire individuals who scored an F. This was so outrageous that even the president of the local chapter of the NAACP, Derrick Foward, criticized the division, saying that he did "not support individuals failing a test and then having the opportunity to be gainfully employed."

Eric Holder's Civil Rights Division under Thomas Perez has waged a war on election integrity, trying to stop state voter ID laws or other steps to improve the security of elections. For example, in 2012, the division filed a lawsuit in the battleground state of Florida to stop the state from removing noncitizens from the voter rolls. Even though it is a felony for noncitizens to register or vote in a federal election, Perez claimed that removing aliens was a violation of the National Voter Registration Act (NVRA). Fortunately, the federal court ruled against the division in what was essentially a frivolous claim, holding that the NVRA does not prevent "the revocation of an improperly granted registration of a noncitizen."[25] But it had the intended political effect, because the fear of a Justice Department lawsuit caused county election directors all over the state to refuse to participate in the state program to investigate possible noncitizens and remove them from the registration rolls before the

November election. In this battleground state, every vote (even illegal ones) could have made the difference in who won the presidential contest.[26]

But this also shows the lengths to which Perez was willing to go to try to protect illegal aliens. This is no surprise given his background in private life as the former president of Casa de Maryland, an extreme advocacy organization that opposes the enforcement of our immigration laws. This group has encouraged illegal aliens not to speak with police officers or immigration agents; it has fought restrictions on illegal aliens' receiving driver's licenses; it has urged the Montgomery County, Maryland, police department not to enforce federal fugitive warrants; it has advocated giving illegal aliens in-state tuition rates; and it has actively promulgated "day labor" sites, where illegal aliens and disreputable employers openly skirt federal prohibitions on hiring undocumented individuals. What does it say about Eric Holder and Barack Obama that they believed that someone with such a cavalier and contemptuous view of the rule of law should run the Civil Rights Division and be rewarded for his misdeeds and misuse of federal authority by being nominated to an even higher position as the secretary of the Department of Labor?

But Holder's attitude toward election integrity was made clear in a speech at the LBJ Library at the University of Texas in 2011. In a setting obviously designed to evoke Lyndon Johnson's historic signing of the Voting Rights Act in 1965, Holder railed against voter ID laws and other changes to election procedures designed to protect against voter fraud. As he dismissed the danger of fraud and stolen elections, Holder seemed oblivious to the irony of making such a claim at the LBJ Library, given the infamous Ballot Box 13 and the stolen 1948 election that launched LBJ on his political career.

This was not the speech we should expect from the government's chief lawyer, whose job it is to enforce federal election laws in an objective, nonpartisan manner. Instead Holder was parroting the erroneous and incendiary talking points used by Democratic politicians and racial grievance organizations like the NAACP that falsely compare voter ID requirements and other election reform efforts to the scurrilous and violent actions of a half century ago by state officials who kept black citizens away from the polls.

This comparison to Jim Crow is historically preposterous and insults the heroic work of so many who helped end those injustices. Holder's claim that such practices "remain all too common" shows just how factually challenged he is. Voter ID laws cannot compare on any level to the literacy tests, wholesale intimidation, and violence prevalent in the 1960s. It was also quite ironic to hear Holder refer to the "billy clubs and fire hoses, bullets and bombs" that voters had to confront in that same time period, given that it was his Justice Department that dismissed the voter intimidation lawsuit against the New Black Panther Party and its billy club–wielding thugs.[27]

Holder and Congressman John Lewis (D-GA) make the absurd claim that these election reform efforts by states like Texas and North Carolina are "a deliberate and systematic attempt to prevent millions" of minority and other voters from going to the polls. But the actual experience of states with voter ID laws shows that such claims are merely the product of paranoid fantasies of the left that have infected the attorney general and his entire department. Voter ID laws have been in place in states like Georgia and Indiana for many years and none of the hysterical claims made by opponents have materialized. Turnout of minority voters in those states has not decreased—it has increased, within each state, and in comparison to similar states without voter ID. Voters certainly disagree with Holder—polls show overwhelming support for voter ID across racial, ethnic, and party lines. Apparently, Holder does not see the hypocrisy that at his own Department of Justice headquarters in

Washington, D.C., a government-issued photo ID is required to enter the building, a requirement that he claims is discriminatory when imposed by state governments.

But Holder has launched lawsuits against Texas and North Carolina to stop their voter ID laws, even though the U.S. Supreme Court upheld Indiana's voter ID requirement in 2008 as a constitutional and reasonable requirement. In 2012 Holder's target was South Carolina. Prior to the Supreme Court's decision in 2013 in *Shelby County v. Holder*, part of the Voting Rights Act required a small number of states, including South Carolina, to get approval from the Department of Justice or a federal court for any changes in their voting laws. The Justice Department objected to South Carolina's voter ID law and South Carolina was forced to file a federal lawsuit in 2012 to overturn the objection, spending more than $3.5 million to defend itself. Though the state won, Holder succeeded in delaying the implementation of the voter ID law until after the reelection of his boss in the 2012 election. The South Carolina decision came out so close to the election that the Court did not think South Carolina could implement the voter ID law in time. Since then, the law has been in effect for local and state elections with no problems—none of the supposed "discriminatory" effects that Holder claimed have occurred.

Similarly, Holder has refused to enforce the requirement in the National Voter Registration Act that mandates states clean up their registration lists to remove ineligible voters who have died or moved away. Not a single such lawsuit has been filed since the beginning of the Obama administration, despite the fact that there are many jurisdictions all over the United States where the number of registered voters is larger than the voting age population, according to the Census Bureau. In fact, the Justice Department dismissed with no explanation a pending NVRA lawsuit filed against the state of

Missouri by the Bush administration shortly after Obama came into office. However, former employees within the division have made it clear that Holder imposed a policy of nonenforcement of this requirement because liberals believe maintaining accurate voter rolls is a "voter suppression" tactic and because this provision of the law does nothing to help get more minority voters to the polls to vote for and support Democratic candidates.

One of the most disturbing and troubling problems in the Civil Rights Division, however, is the marked hostility toward race-neutral enforcement of federal discrimination laws. There is no legal question, for example, that the Voting Rights Act, by its very terms, protects all Americans regardless of their race, from discrimination in voting. When the U.S. Commission on Civil Rights was investigating the division's inexplicable dismissal of the New Black Panther voter intimidation case, Perez told the commission in sworn testimony in a hearing on May 14, 2010, that he believes in the race-neutral enforcement of federal voting rights laws.[28] But according to the 2013 IG report, he told the inspector general that he did *not* believe that Section 5 of the Voting Rights Act protected white voters even when they are a racial minority in a particular jurisdiction.[29]

The division applied this racialist theory in rejecting a voting change in Kinston, North Carolina, in 2009. Although white voters are the racial minority in Kinston (black voters make up 65 percent of registered voters), the division blocked a 2008 referendum that changed town elections from partisan to nonpartisan. Despite the fact that black voters overwhelmingly approved the change, the division filed a patronizing objection that, in essence, claimed that the black voters didn't know what they were doing when they voted for the change and wouldn't know whom to vote for if the Democratic Party label wasn't next to the candidate's name on the ballot. The division withdrew its objection based on supposedly "changed circumstances" just two weeks before the U.S. Court of Appeals for the District of Columbia Circuit was set to hear a lawsuit by Kinston residents challenging the objection and the constitutionality of Section 5 of the Voting Rights Act, mooting the case and leading to its dismissal.

But the only "changed" circumstance was a tiny change in the black voter registration level from 65 to 65.4 percent. The real reason Holder withdrew the division's objection was that the facts in this case made the Justice Department look so bad, he didn't want it going to the Supreme Court.

In 2005 the division for the first time successfully brought a Voting Rights Act case against black defendants for discrimination against white voters, in *U.S. v. Brown*, a case arising out of Mississippi. However, from the first moment this matter was raised in the division, liberal career lawyers demonstrated their hostility not only to the concept of suing blacks for discrimination but also to the staff within the division who supported or who worked on the case. And outside civil rights organizations were furious that the case had been filed. They would take their revenge when they took control of the division during the Obama administration.

The 2013 inspector general's report on the mismanagement of the division details the extensive harassment and ostracism of employees who believe in the race-neutral enforcement of the Voting Rights Act or who worked on the *Brown* case. For example, the report describes in great detail the nasty postings and comments made by career staff on "widely read liberal websites concerning Voting Section work and personnel." These postings

> included a wide array of inappropriate remarks, ranging from petty and juvenile personal attacks to highly offensive and potentially threatening statements. The comments were directed

> at fellow career Voting Section employees because of their conservative political views, their willingness to carry out the policies of the CRT division leadership, or their views on the Voting Rights Act. The highly offensive comments included suggestions that the parents of one former career Section attorney were Nazis. . . .[30]

Although the IG report does not identify who the Nazi comments were directed at, they were directed at the parents of the coauthor, Hans von Spakovsky, who worked in the division as a career lawyer during the Bush administration. He was shocked at the hostility with which he was greeted when he was hired. The liberal staff that occupied the division made it clear that solely because of his conservative political views, and regardless of his professional work as an experienced election law attorney, he was considered unqualified to be a career lawyer in the division.

Von Spakovsky is a first-generation American. His mother grew up in Nazi Germany and his father was a Russian who fled the Soviet Union when the communists took control. His father was part of the resistance movement against the Nazis in Yugoslavia during World War II. His parents met in a refugee camp in the American-occupied sector of Germany in 1946 and immigrated to the United States in 1951. Von Spakovsky's mother was arrested by the Gestapo in 1945 when she was a teenager and the fact that she was not killed but survived is a testament to her courage and the grace of God.

Given his parents' terrible experiences, the offensive comments by liberal lawyers about von Spakovsky's parents were especially cruel. And they were made by his fellow employees simply because of his personal political views, his involvement in recommending going forward with the *U.S. v. Brown* reverse discrimination case and approving Georgia's voter ID law, and his publicly expressed belief that the Voting Rights Act protects all voters from discrimination, no matter what their race. Believing in equal enforcement of the law makes you a pariah in the Civil Rights Division, particularly under Eric Holder.

One individual who still works in the division boasted of being part of a "cyber-gang" that was engaged in "cyber-bullying" of conservative employees (the few that exist in the division). Although he admitted that some of his statements "crossed the line" because they included "racist" and "intimidating language," he told the IG that "he did not regret posting the comments."[31]

The viciousness, pettiness, meanness, and unprofessionalism of employees within the division are also shown in the experience of another lawyer in the division. Identified under the alias Arnold Everett in the IG report, the attorney was a former clerk for the chief justice of a state supreme court. Because he was willing to work on disfavored cases, other staff members called him a "hand-picked Vichyite." Because his legal opinions on particular cases differed from those of the radical, liberal lawyers involved in the cases, he was subjected to unremitting hostility. Those same lawyers broke into his computer system and snooped through his work. He was harassed by liberal employees for his Christian religious beliefs (so much for religious freedom). As the IG report concluded, other employees made "unprofessional and disparaging remarks about Everett to each other and to other employees in the Section, mocking his intelligence, his legal acumen, and his personal beliefs."[32]

The terrible conditions and the hostile environment in which Everett was forced to work affected his health and his family. The harassment was limited during the Bush administration because the leadership of the division did its best to stop it. But it resumed with greater intensity during the Obama administration because the political appointees in the division made it clear they also did not like him because of his political views and they had no interest in stopping the harassment. The hostile work environment finally drove him out of the division.

The same thing happened to Bob Popper, the former deputy chief of the Voting Section. He told one of the authors in an interview that "starting in early 2009, his investigations were systematically shut down" because he was perceived as untrustworthy since he was a conservative, despite his extensive experience in voting cases. Popper was hired in December 2005 because of his extensive trial experience and background in voting rights. In his first three years he worked on and appeared in court in numerous cases on behalf of the division, including the New Black Panther Party voter intimidation case. But that changed completely in the Obama administration, whose political managers and their liberal allies in the career staff refused to allow him to appear in court or to work on any substantive matters. As he says, they would not "let [him] anywhere near a courtroom" and gave him "the least substantial and least desired cases available." He was excluded from management decisions and meetings.

Employees who participated in the harassment of conservative employees and whose identities were discovered by the inspector general during the Obama administration were not disciplined in any way. For example, another employee, identified under the alias of Karen Lorrie, actually an employee named Stephanie Celandine Gyamfi, denied under oath that she had publicly posted comments on websites "concerning Voting Section personnel or matters." She did not admit she was responsible until the IG investigators confronted her with evidence that she had done so, but she told the IG that "she did not regret posting comments online, except to the extent that it resulted in questioning from the OIG."[33]

So, rather than being disciplined for her outrageous behavior, she was treated as a hero inside the Voting Section, according to sources inside the division. After Mississippi passed a voter ID statute, she posted on Facebook that the residents there were "disgusting and shameful." Even so, the Obama administration defended her and refused to remove her from cases involving Mississippi or voter ID despite her plain bias, which would bring into question the impartiality of any decision made by the division in cases in which she was involved. That is because the Holder Justice Department had no intention of being impartial and it approved of Gyamfi's behavior toward the few conservatives who work in the division.

The hostility toward staff who favored race-neutral enforcement of civil rights laws culminated in the mistreatment by the Obama administration and Eric Holder of Christopher Coates. He was the most experienced voting rights trial attorney in the entire division and the former chief of the Voting Section. He had received numerous awards for his outstanding work during his career, including from the NAACP. Coates had been instrumental in filing and prosecuting the *Brown* case in Mississippi, and was promoted to head the Voting Section in 2008. He approved filing a complaint against black defendants for voter intimidation in Philadelphia after the 2008 election, the case that came to be known as the "New Black Panther" case. In other words, unlike Eric Holder and other lawyers and Obama political appointees inside the division, he did not believe that some individuals who violate federal law should be given a free pass because of their race. As a result, he was subjected to "overt hostility" and slurs, even being called a "Klansman," according to the IG report.[34]

After the Obama administration came into office, Coates was harassed and mistreated by the new leadership of the division. He was chastised by Loretta King, the acting assistant attorney general at the beginning of the administration, for asking attorney applicants whether "they would be capable of enforcing the Voting Rights Act in a race-neutral manner."[35] The leadership of the division, with the express approval of Attorney General Eric Holder and other senior department leadership, set out to drive Coates, a protected civil service employee and a member of the Senior Executive Service, out of the division. Holder actually held meetings to discuss the removal of Coates, a midlevel management employee many steps below him in the management structure of the Justice Department. And why? Because as Holder told the IG, "the new type of case he understood Coates wanted to pursue were 'reverse-discrimination' cases."[36] He was upset over Coates's prior involvement in the *Ike Brown* case in Mississippi and Coates's approval of the filing of the voter intimidation case against the New Black Panthers.

The Obama administration wanted to ensure, as one email from a liberal lawyer in the Voting Section said, that "the Section be free from enemy hands."[37] The IG report is clear that Coates's "ideology was a factor in the discussions among senior Department and Division officials about removing or reassigning Coates." He was driven out as the chief of the Voting Section because he believes in the equal protection of the law. That is one of the most shameful but enlightening revelations in the entire IG report—that Eric Holder believes discrimination is acceptable—as long as the "wrong" people are being discriminated against.

When, in a hearing before the House Appropriations Subcommittee on Commerce, Justice, Science, and Related Agencies on March 1, 2011, Eric Holder was asked by Representative John Culberson (R-TX) about the "overwhelming evidence that your Department of Justice refuses to protect the rights of anybody other than African-Americans to vote," Holder tried to claim that the Justice Department "does not enforce the laws in a race-conscious way."[38] But Culberson's persistent questioning about the dismissal of the

New Black Panther voter intimidation case by the Civil Rights Division clearly got under Holder's skin. He angrily responded that it was "a great disservice to people who put their lives on the line for my people" to compare what happened in Philadelphia in 2008 to what happened in the South. The "my people" line was very revealing. Holder's slip of the tongue made it very clear that he interprets everything through the prism of how it affects "his" people—black Americans, not all Americans—and that he considers it insulting to "his people" to get upset over the intimidation committed by the jackbooted, paramilitary Black Panthers in Philadelphia (although Holder did admit their attempt to intimidate voters was "inappropriate").

Holder's attitude about "his people" may have begun when he was an undergraduate at Columbia. It was there in 1971 that Holder apparently started carrying around a clipping of a quote from Harlem preacher Rev. Samuel D. Proctor, that he has kept "in wallet after wallet over the ensuing decades," according to J. Christian Adams, a former Justice Department lawyer.[39] The quote:

> Blackness is another issue entirely apart from class in America. No matter how affluent, educated and mobile [a black person] becomes, his race defines him more particularly than anything else. Black people have a common cause that requires attending to, and this cause does not allow for the rigid class separation that is the luxury of American whites. There is a sense in which every black man is as far from liberation as the weakest one if his weakness is attributable to racial injustice.

Adams says that when Holder was asked to explain the passage, he replied, "It really says that . . . I am not the tall U.S. attorney, I am not the thin United States attorney. I am the black United States attorney. And he was saying that no matter how successful you are, there's a common cause that bonds the black United States attorney with the black criminal or the black doctor with the black homeless person."[40]

In other words, Holder apparently believes that a person's skin color is first and foremost his most defining feature and more important than anything else. "Race comes first for Holder," says Adams, a regrettable attitude for the chief law enforcement official of the country. After all, there is a reason that Lady Justice wears a blindfold.

But the purpose of the Civil Rights Division is to enforce the law equally and fairly, without regard to race, in a manner that meets the highest ethical and professional standards. Too many of the employees, and that includes Eric Holder, do not, as the IG report says, "appreciate the importance of public confidence in the impartial legitimate enforcement priorities set by" the division. In fact, they see its authority as a powerful tool that can be used to benefit Democratic candidates and to force their progressive social ideology on public hiring, public education, and many other areas.

They also do not believe that the division's enforcement responsibilities should be pursued in a race-neutral manner that protects all Americans from discrimination. As the IG report says, professionalism means "operating in a manner that consciously ensures both the appearance and the reality of even-handed, fair and mature decision-making, carried out without regard to partisan or other improper considerations."[41] That type of professionalism does not exist today in the Civil Rights Division.

Former Voting Section chief Christopher Coates says that Eric Holder and Tom Perez appear to suffer from the same "deficiency that the old segregationists such as Ross Barnett, George Wallace and Richard Russell suffered from when they refused to enforce the anti-discrimination provisions of the Constitution for the benefit of African-American citizens." According to Coates, "none of these folks in the current Justice Department, including Holder, seem to be capable of understanding the need for race-neutral enforcement of the law when the victims of discrimination are not their 'people.' "[42]

When Tom Perez was asked about the operations of the division during the Bush administration, "he became visibly agitated," claiming that "the whole process of decision-making was completely obliterated! Hiring processes were hijacked! They weren't allowed to bring certain kinds of cases. They weren't allowed to make certain kinds of arguments. I think history will judge the prior administration as the darkest hour in the division's history."[43] Without realizing it, Perez gave a very accurate description of how he and Eric Holder have run the Civil Rights Division of the U.S. Department of Justice.

CHAPTER 5

THE BILLION-DOLLAR *PIGFORD* SCAM

Nothing demonstrates Eric Holder's divisive racial politics and his willingness to suborn justice and the best interests of the public than the multibillion-dollar swindle known as the *Pigford* settlement, which Department of Agriculture employee John Stringfellow calls the "largest scam against federal taxpayers in the history of the United States."[1] Rich Lowry, the editor of *National Review*, said it was "like something out of a Tom Wolfe novel" and that "it would be hard to invent a more damning fable of modern government."[2] In fact, *Pigford* is a prime example of how Eric Holder (and Barack Obama) have used taxpayer funds to buy votes and political support while at the same time using litigation as a cover for providing something that radical black nationalists have demanded for years: "reparations" for black Americans. Although it started in the Clinton administration, it was made exponentially worse by the Obama administration.

The *Pigford* scam started out as a lawsuit filed in 1997 by Timothy Pigford, a fourth-generation black farmer in North Carolina. Pigford believed that he and other black farmers had been discriminated against by the U.S. Department of Agriculture, which they claimed had not extended them loans on the same basis as white farmers, although two different government reports that year (including one by the Government Accountability Office) "found no evidence of ongoing, systematic discrimination."[3] Pigford had gotten some loans from the USDA, but "he was convinced he wasn't getting a fair shot at success, even as white farmers who worked nearby land were getting loans to expand their operations."[4] This lawsuit and a subsequent, highly questionable lawsuit filed by Hispanic, Indian, and women "farmers" quickly "became a runaway train, driven by racial politics, pressure from influential members of Congress and law firms that stand to gain more than $130 million in fees."[5]

In 1999, a federal court turned Timothy Pigford's case into a class-action lawsuit, *Pigford v. Glickman*, which meant that it was now a lawsuit on behalf of all black farmers similarly situated to Pigford who had also been potentially discriminated against, originally about four hundred. The Clinton administration decided to settle the case for a billion dollars and a consent decree was approved by the court. That this was done for political reasons as opposed to the actual evidence in the case was pretty clear—the *New York Times* in its exposé on the scandal quoted a lawyer who said it was "more a political decision that a litigation decision." Bill Clinton had even asked a senior adviser to the Democratic National Committee who was an expert on black voter turnout to get involved to "make sure his home state, Arkansas, benefited."[6]

Even if one acknowledges "that the original Pigford class of about 400 plaintiffs had made a credible case that they were real victims of racial discrimination,"[7] the class expanded exponentially, since the claims process established in the consent decree allowed individuals to make claims with no evidence other than their own assertions that they had suffered any bias or that they were even legitimate farmers. It was almost as if the claims process implemented by the Justice Department was designed to encourage fraud, since individuals could receive *automatic* $50,000 payments by simply filling out a claim form in which they asserted they had "attempted to farm" and had made an "oral" complaint of discrimination to the USDA. According to the judge, claims would be paid with "little or no documentary evidence" and that is exactly what happened. It is estimated that 92 percent of the successful claimants were part of this "attempted to farm" class.[8] Claimants were essentially encouraged to lie—they would get paid if they had just "thought" about farming or tried to grow tomatoes in their backyard.

The number of claimants quickly expanded from the original four hundred black farmers to 14,000 and $1.25 billion was paid out. But claims kept coming even after the original October 12, 1999, deadline passed, so that total is now over 100,000. This, despite the fact that "a 1997 agricultural census found only 18,500 black farmers nationwide."[9] The biggest individual settlement was $13 million, which was paid to New Communities, Inc., a land trust established by Charles and Shirley Sherrod for a communal farm in Georgia. The Sherrods and several other participants in the farm shared in the pay-out. Three days after her case was settled, Shirley Sherrod was hired by the Obama administration to work in the Department of Agriculture. She was fired in 2010 over controversial remarks she made in a speech, but later was offered her job back by the Obama administration.[10]

While there has been no allegation of impropriety with respect to the New Communities claim, there is no question that there was massive, undeterred, and unprosecuted fraud in many of the other payouts made under the *Pigford* settlement. Decisions on USDA loans were made by committees of local farmers in many counties.

Yet the *Pigford* settlement imposed the rule that discrimination was universal, even in places like "Jefferson County, Ark., where numerous discrimination claims came in despite the fact that all the supervisors at that office were black."[11] The *New York Times* analyzed sixteen zip codes in Alabama, Arkansas, Mississippi, and North Carolina and found that "the number of successful claimants exceeded the total number of farms operated by people of any race in 1997."[12] Nearly everyone in two adjoining apartment buildings in Columbus, Ohio, filed claims.[13] Arkansas received hundreds of claims from black women despite the fact that a USDA employee said that in his fifteen years in Arkansas, "he had only ever seen one black female applicant for a loan."[14]

Eight *Pigford* applicants came from a single family—they were all paid off despite their obvious fraud: "Pigford was basically legalized extortion . . . it reached the point where they were just handing money to people," said another USDA employee.[15] Claims coming in from affluent areas like Palm Beach, Florida, and Palm Springs, California, were paid, as well as one applicant who claimed the nonexistent Chicago USDA office had discriminated against them.[16] In fact, *thirty* percent of the payments went to entirely urban areas where there are no farms.[17]

All of this went on to the disgust and chagrin of some of the original *Pigford* plaintiffs, like Abraham Carpenter Jr., a black farmer in Grady, Arkansas. As he complained to the *New York Times*, "why did they let people get away with all this stuff? Anytime you are going to throw money up in the air, you are going to have people acting crazy."[18]

Despite this massive fraud, the FBI and Justice Department prosecutors refused to take action, and almost no cases were prosecuted. The standards for a successful claim were "so low that it was almost impossible to show criminality"[19] and prosecutors were fearful "of the racial politics that would have attended"[20] their cases. The USDA "appears to have turned a blind eye to blatant irregularities" despite the fact that employees such as John Stringfellow said that 80 percent of the claims he reviewed were for individuals who "had never applied to USDA assistance programs, nor farmed at all."[21]

But these mostly fraudulent claims kept rolling in even though the court-imposed deadline had passed. So then-senator Barack Obama—six months after he announced his presidential run—became the sole sponsor of the Pigford Claims Remedy Act of 2007 (Pigford II), which was attached as an amendment to the massive farm bill. Obama's bill extended the deadline for filing claims to 2008 (which would cover the tens of thousands of claims that had continued to come in after the 1999 deadline) and appropriated an additional $1.25 billion in funds for payouts.

Obama's bill came after the head of the Black Farmers and Agriculturalists Association, Gary Grant, promised Obama "all the financial and ballot support the BFAA could marshal in the rural South in exchange."[22] Grant made it very clear that the *Pigford* settlement had nothing to do with farmers—it was all about African-Americans "collecting what [their] grandparents didn't have the opportunity to."[23] In other words, reparations. But Obama's ploy worked:

> Supporters of Obama's presidential campaign argued the then-Illinois senator's move to resolve late Pigford claims would endear him to Southern black voters during the tough Democratic primary race against former Sen. Hillary Rodham Clinton (D-NY). At the time of the bill's introduction in 2007, Obama was finding his footing as a candidate and polls suggested he was struggling to attract black voters. He later won almost unanimously among this group against Clinton.[24]

Former Alabama congressman Artur Davis, who had endorsed Obama, said that while the average voter had never heard of the *Pigford* settlement, "it was critical, however, among some key Democratic constituencies in the South" and that he had "yet to do a town hall meeting" where he was not asked about it. It was "a supremely large issue in the black rural community in the South."[25]

Congress overrode President George Bush's veto of the 2008 farm bill with Obama's amendment but appropriated only $100 million for *Pigford* claims. Obama asked Congress for more money and in February 2010 Eric Holder settled the Pigford II claims for $1.25 billion, contingent on Congress appropriating more money—which it did with the Claims Resolution Act of 2010, in December of that year. Holder heralded the settlement saying that the "plaintiffs can move forward and have their claims heard—with the federal government standing not as an adversary, but as a partner."[26]

In addition to the *Pigford* case, the Justice Department had been vigorously defending a similar lawsuit that had been filed during the Bush administration by Hispanic, Indian, and women farmers. There was almost no evidence that these groups had suffered any discrimination of any kind. Many of their individual claims were "shaky" and federal judges "had already scornfully rejected the [damages] methodology of the plaintiffs' expert."[27] The government's expert, Gordon C. Rausser, a professor at the University of California, Berkeley, had produced a 340-page report showing that Indian farmers "had generally fared as well as white male farmers." In fact, if the Justice Department had gone to court, Rausser said "the government would have prevailed" and he was "astounded" that the case was settled.[28] Neither the Hispanic nor the female claimants had been able to convince the courts to certify them as a class because their claims were too individually distinct—there was no pattern of bias and they had been denied loans "for a variety of reasons, including inadequate farm plans and lack of funds."[29]

But racial politics entered once again and interfered with the resolution of these cases. Members of the Congressional Hispanic Caucus and Democratic senators led by Robert Menendez (D-NJ) "grew increasingly agitated as the plaintiffs' cases appeared to falter" and complained to the White House.[30] They were angry that black farmers were receiving payouts while Hispanic farmers were not and claimed (despite the complete lack of evidence of discrimination by the USDA) that there was "no legitimate reason to delay action for any of the affected groups."[31]

In 2010 three meetings were held in the White House led by Daniel J. Meltzer, Obama's principal deputy White House counsel, with senior Justice and Agriculture officials, including Associate Attorney General Thomas J. Perrelli and Assistant Attorney General of the Civil Division Tony West (who supervised the *Pigford* litigation). West had been profiled by the *San Francisco Chronicle* in 2008 when he was the California finance cochair for the Obama campaign and described as an "Obama power broker."[32] At those meetings, all of the "vehement objections" of "career lawyers and agency officials who had argued that there was no credible evidence of widespread discrimination" were overridden.[33] They were ordered to settle the case and pay out more than $1 billion "to compensate not just the 91 plaintiffs but thousands of Hispanic and female farmers who had never claimed bias in court."[34] And the very same fraud-ridden claims process was put in place to allow payments of up to $50,000 without any proof or documentation. By an "odd" coincidence, the claims process opened in September 2010, just six weeks before the midterm congressional elections.

Eric Holder was asked about the massive fraud in the *Pigford* settlements by Representative Steve King (R-IA) at a Justice Department oversight hearing on May 15, 2013, less than a month after the *New York Times* exposé. This was three years after it had been uncovered by Andrew Breitbart and Daniel Foster at *National Review* (and promptly dismissed by the liberal and progressive media establishment as just conservative anger at remedying proven racial discrimination).[35]

Holder denied the existence of the pervasive and extensive fraud that had been documented—fraud that probably encompasses the *majority* of the payments made. He falsely claimed "that there are steps that we have in place to limit the amount of fraud that goes on there, both in terms of getting sworn statements from claimants, from doing audits," and that the *New York Times* "made the fraud seem more widespread than it actually is."[36] When King asked whether efforts should be made to identify the specific employees at the USDA who had supposedly engaged in such discrimination and cost the American government so much money, Holder answered that he didn't think resources should be spent on that as opposed to compensating those who had been discriminated against. Of course, trying to find the nonexistent federal employees who had supposedly discriminated against the phantom claimants would be very difficult.

Holder's claim that getting a sworn statement from claimants was sufficient to deter fraud was ludicrous, as just about any experienced criminal prosecutor would tell you. His reference to "audits" referred to the fact that Congress had added a requirement to Pigford II that the Government Accountability Office "evaluate the internal controls" in the claims process. As GAO itself pointed out, however, it was limited in its ability to detect fraud in the claims process by the fact that the government had agreed in the settlement Eric Holder was so proud of that "most claims must be evaluated based solely on the information submitted by the claimants."[37] So GAO had "no way of independently verifying that information." In other words, the Justice Department itself had sabotaged the ability of the federal government to stop fraud and deter the scam being perpetrated on the American taxpayer.

Eric Holder agreed to settle what was in essence an unproven—if not frivolous—case, one in which the plaintiffs had been unable to provide any evidence of discrimination. And he set up a claims process that was the same as a prior one in the original *Pigford* settlement that had already been proven to engender massive fraud—which his department refused (with only a few exceptions) to prosecute, even the most obvious cases. Billions of dollars were paid out in taxpayer funds that should never have been paid, and the reason was clearly and obviously a political one. Eric Holder was helping Barack Obama make "reparations" to black constituents and was buying political support and votes not only with his Democratic allies in Congress, but of blacks, Hispanics, Indians, and women all over the country. It was a redistribution of wealth by any means necessary for cynical racial politics at the expense of the average American taxpayer.

In fact, according to the *New York Times*, at least $460 million designated for payment to Indian "farmers" has gone unclaimed because of the small number of Indian farmers who filed claims.[38] Instead of those funds being returned to the U.S. Treasury and the American taxpayer, they are going to be given to Indian nonprofit groups, an enormous funding mechanism for advocacy groups friendly to the president and his political party. According to Rich Lowry of *National Review*, these settlements occurred because "Barack Obama wanted to pander to rural blacks, then he needed to do catch-up pandering to Hispanics."[39] And he and Eric Holder then added women and American Indians for good measure.

CHAPTER 6

THE HOLDER RULE OF IGNORANCE AND DECEIT

In his congressional testimony, Eric Holder has all too often displayed seeming incompetence, a lack of professionalism, a contempt for those questioning him, and a willingness to mislead if not outright lie to Congress. California representative Dana Rohrabacher (R-CA) told one of the authors that for someone to be so unprepared and uncooperative, "he either is the pawn of others engaged in undermining the rule of law, or he is pleading convenient ignorance he is all too fully aware of."

Holder's dismissive attitude toward Congress when it is carrying out its constitutionally mandated oversight function and his contempt for members was on full display in an oversight hearing of the Justice Department before the House Judiciary Committee on May 15, 2013. He was being asked questions by Representative Darrel Issa (R-CA) about a voice mail message left by Holder's subordinate, Assistant Attorney General for Civil Rights Thomas Perez, about a quid pro quo deal Perez arranged to get rid of a Supreme Court case before the Court could issue a decision tossing out the administration's favorite legal theory: "disparate impact."

Perez promised that in exchange, the Justice Department would give up a fraud claim under the False Claims Act worth potentially $180 million to taxpayers. In the voice mail, Perez told Greg Brooker, an attorney in the U.S. attorney's office in Minnesota, not to mention the deal about the Supreme Court case in his internal DOJ "declination" memo, a memo summarizing why Justice would not pursue the False Claims Act case.[1]

Holder got upset over having to answer a series of legitimate and reasonable questions about the deal, about the attempt "to try to keep information out in order to disguise" what was going on (according to Issa), and about the Justice Department's refusal to provides copies of 1,200 personal emails that Perez sent in violation of the Federal Records Act on official Justice Department business, including the quid pro quo deal.[2] Issa's inquiries called into question the ethics of Perez's behavior as well as the Justice Department's unjustified refusal to cooperate, so Holder angrily countered that Issa's behavior in playing Perez's voice mail and raising these questions about Perez was "too consistent with the way in which you conduct yourself as a member of Congress. It is unacceptable and it is shameful."

But what was really shameful was Holder's attempt to cover up Perez's misbehavior. Representative Issa stated that "the American people were denied the Highest Court considering a case" because of the deal Perez engineered and "[t]hat was an undeniable fact." Holder still tried to deny it by saying, "That is incorrect,"[3] even though that is exactly what happened: the city of St. Paul, Minnesota, dismissed its pending Supreme Court case (in which the federal government was not even a party) after being told by Perez that the Justice Department would not purse the False Claims Act claim for reimbursement of upwards of $180 million.

Holder obviously resented being asked tough questions about

controversial actions of the Justice Department, because at the same hearing, he at one point expressed his anger that he was not treated with the respect he thought he deserved as the "Attorney General of the United States." This tirade from Holder came right after Representative Doug Collins (R-GA) expressed his amazement at Holder's "lack of preparation" and his inability to answer basic questions about his recusal from the Justice Department's investigation of a leak to the Associated Press that resulted in a 2012 story about a CIA counterterrorism operation in Yemen that stopped a plot to bomb an American airliner. Holder didn't know when it occurred, even though it was front-page news at the time, and was unable to answer numerous other questions (Holder said he didn't know the answer to various questions, at least fifty-seven times).

As Collins said to Holder: "Did you not think those questions were going to be asked of you today? That when you recused yourself from this . . . did you just honestly think those would not be asked today?"[4] Holder's answer was an unbelievable "I didn't think about whether or not you were going to ask me that question," at which point Collins interrupted him with "You are kidding me? You come to this committee today with these issues like they are right now?"[5] Yet Holder continued to display his ignorance on the matter, telling the committee he couldn't even remember whether he had put his recusal in writing as required by law (he hadn't).

Another area of questioning that Holder expressed ignorance of was the reprehensible behavior of Tracy Schmaler, the director of Holder's Public Affairs Office. Through a Freedom of Information Act request that took the Justice Department nine months to answer, Matt Boyle of the *Daily Caller* obtained a series of emails showing that Holder's public relations director regularly enlisted Media Matters to attack reporters and others covering DOJ scandals.[6] Media Matters is a far-left advocacy group that masquerades as a nonpartisan truth-teller and media watchdog. One of its former staffers, Xochitl Hinojosa, also worked in the DOJ Public Affairs Office at the time.

In essence, Schmaler provided Media Matters with inside information and solicited attacks on former Justice Department lawyers such as J. Christian Adams, Andy McCarthy, and one of the authors, Hans von Spakovsky; as well as bloggers and journalists such as Mike Vanderboegh and William La Jeunesse of Fox News; and members of Congress such as Darrell Issa. Schmaler even sought an article from Media Matters attacking Judson Phillips, one of the founders of Tea Party Nation. All of this was intended to dampen public interest and distract attention from scandals like the dismissal of the New Black Panther Party voter intimidation case or the investigation into Operation Fast and Furious.

Schmaler is the same person who yelled at former CBS reporter Sharyl Attkisson about her covering the investigation into Operation Fast and Furious. Schmaler wouldn't put anything in writing in response to questions from Attkisson and complained about CBS's "unfair and biased" coverage because Attkisson—as opposed to the *Washington Post* and the *New York Times*—was "the only one who thinks this a story" and wouldn't give the administration favorable coverage.[7]

This conduct was reprehensible and unethical, since it involved the use of government resources to abuse private citizens and journalists guilty only of reporting on the Justice Department's malfeasance. It was also unprecedented—there is no evidence that the Public Affairs Office at Justice of any prior administration, Democratic or Republican, ever enlisted outsiders to attack its critics.

But the attacks engineered by Schmaler on Christopher Coates were especially unethical and unprofessional. Coates is the former chief of the Voting Section who was forced out by Holder and

Thomas Perez because he insisted on telling the truth about the New Black Panthers case and the racially discriminatory policies of the Civil Rights Division. At the time Schmaler was soliciting attacks on Coates from Media Matters, he was still an employee of the Justice Department, so Schmaler was directing attacks on one of the department's own employees at a time when he was prosecuting cases for Justice!

That is the kind of behavior one expects from banana republics, not from the chief law enforcement agency of the U.S. government. Schmaler was also potentially violating the federal law that bars retaliation against whistle-blowers like Adams and Coates, who had blown the lid off the false Justice Department claims that no political appointees had been involved in the decision to dismiss the Black Panther case.

Yet at his May 15, 2013, hearing when Holder was specifically asked by Representative Blake Farenthold (R-TX) if the Justice Department was "regularly still consulting with Media Matters for spinning your PR stories?" Holder's unbelievable answer was that "I'm not sure I know what you're talking about."[8] There is no question that the attorney general would have been briefed by his aides about Schmaler's devious machinations with Media Matters once it became public even if he didn't know about it ahead of time.

In fact, there is little doubt that when the story first came out in the *Daily Caller*, it would have been at the top of the media summary that is received by the attorney general and other senior managers every day and which one of the authors reviewed regularly when he worked at the Justice Department. There is also no question that such a revelation would have been a matter of discussion in the attorney general's office by his staff. Unless Holder was suffering from acute memory loss, he knew exactly what Farenthold was talking about.

Unfortunately, Holder doesn't just have a contemptuous attitude toward the members of Congress and a dismissive attitude toward their oversight responsibilities. As an editorial by *Investor's Business Daily* pointed out in 2013, Holder also has a "long history of lying to Congress" about topics ranging from "what he knew about targeting reporters" to Operation Fast and Furious: "As early as the New Back Panthers case, Eric Holder had a problem with the truth."[9]

But this habit of Holder's started long before he ever became attorney general, when Congress was investigating the last-minute pardons issued during the final days of the Clinton administration, including clemency for wanted fugitive Marc Rich. During a hearing by a House committee investigating the pardons on February 14, 2001, he told Congress under oath that "Mr. Rich's name was unfamiliar to me" in 1999 when he helped Jack Quinn, Rich's attorney, get a pardon for Rich.[10]

Yet when Holder was the U.S. attorney for the District of Columbia in 1995, he sued a Swiss company for fraudulently obtaining government contracts by concealing its ties to Rich. The complaint that Holder personally signed specifically talked about Marc Rich and his concealed involvement with the company.[11] When Holder finally settled the case by getting a $1.2 million payment, the *Wall Street Journal* reported on Holder's announcement that the case over the fugitive financier's involvement in the company had been settled.[12] This settlement, "Holder told the *Journal*, ended a broader investigation his office had been conducting into Rich's business interests."[13] Of course, that settlement did not resolve the outstanding criminal charges that caused Rich to flee the United States and were the subject of the pardon signed by Bill Clinton in 2001.

During his 2009 confirmation hearings, Holder repeated his supposed ignorance. But as discussed elsewhere in this book, Holder was well aware of the details of Rich's criminal behavior and the underlying facts of his record. So he blatantly misled Congress on two separate occasions about his involvement in the pardon and his prior knowledge of Rich's criminal activities.

The Justice Department consistently lied to the public and in sworn testimony about the 2009 dismissal of the New Black Panther Party voter intimidation case. When Holder was specifically asked about this on March 1, 2011, before the House Appropriations Subcommittee (responsible for the Justice Department's budget), he falsely claimed that the "decisions made in the New Black Panther Party case were made by career attorneys in the department."[14]

But in a lawsuit by Judicial Watch over the Justice Department's failure to respond to a Freedom of Information Act request for internal communications on the New Black Panther case, federal Judge Reggie Walton specifically found, "The documents reveal that political appointees within DOJ were conferring about the status and resolution of the New Black Panther Party case in the days preceding the DOJ's dismissal of claims in that case, which would appear to contradict Assistant Attorney General Perez's testimony that political leadership was not involved in that decision."[15]

Based on Judge Walton's findings and the internal Justice Department communications discussed in his court order, there is no question that Holder misled Congress about the dismissal of the New Black Panther Party voter intimidation case—testimony that the Justice Department has never corrected.

Holder also misled Congress about his knowledge of Operation Fast and Furious, the reckless Justice Department operation that supplied hundreds of weapons to Mexican criminal and drug cartels, as well as the Justice Department's handling of the contempt citation against him. The House of Representatives on June 28, 2012, held Holder in contempt of Congress for his failure to comply with a congressional subpoena for documents related to the investigation of this reckless Justice Department and ATF operation.[16]

Normally, the Justice Department enforces contempt citations in court. Holder appointed Ronald Machen, the U.S. attorney for the District of Columbia, to supposedly make that decision independently without consultation with anyone else at Justice. Machen reports to Holder, though, so he was not really an independent counsel—Holder refused to appoint a truly independent counsel. Representative Issa asked Holder at a May 15, 2013, oversight hearing whether Machen had made an "independent" decision not to enforce the contempt citation.

Holder answered as follows: "I did not order Mr. Machen not to do anything with regard—I will not characterize it—the contempt finding from this Congress. He made the determination about what he was going to do on his own. So I did not have anything to do with that."[17]

But, in fact, Eric Holder's deputy, James Cole, before the clerk of the House had even transmitted the contempt resolution to Machen, sent a letter to the Speaker of the House of Representatives saying that the Justice Department had "determined" that Holder's response to the subpoena for Operation Fast and Furious documents "does not constitute a crime, and therefore the Department will not bring the congressional contempt citation before a grand jury or take any other action to prosecute the Attorney General."[18]

So it was very clear that Machen had not made an "independent" decision not to enforce Holder's contempt citation; that decision had been taken out of his hands by Holder's own deputy, directly contradicting Holder's sworn testimony to Issa. As Senator Chuck Grassley (R-Iowa) pointed out, Cole was in essence refusing to allow Machen to comply with federal law since 2 U.S.C. §194 says that with regard to any witness who refuses to produce documents or testify before Congress, the appropriate U.S. attorney's "duty . . . shall be to bring the matter before the grand jury for its action." In other words, "it is not optional"—Machen was *obligated* to present the contempt resolution to a federal grand jury.[19]

But Cole's letter came out before Machen could have even "undertaken any such independent assessment" of the contempt resolution and his obligation to present it to a grand jury. So while Holder was blithely telling a congressional committee at his oversight hearing that Machen made an independent decision, the public record showed that Holder's deputy had entirely foreclosed an independent decision, had immediately shut down any Justice Department enforcement, and had ordered Machen to violate federal law. That is why the House of Representatives was forced to go to court on its own to do the job that Machen refused to do.

When Jennifer Rubin of the *Washington Post* questioned the Justice Department about this discrepancy, she was told that Holder "misspoke" and "since he was not involved, he did not recall the details."[20] But as Rubin says, that means that Holder just "made something up at the hearing." She adds that we have seen this routine far too often from the administration, but "when the prevarication repeats over and over again, followed by more prevarication about the original falsehoods . . . you get the sense the truth doesn't matter. What matters is keeping Congress and the media at bay, ducking accountability, and wielding power over other branches of government, the press and political opponents."[21]

When the congressional investigation first started into Operation Fast and Furious, Holder also prevaricated on when he first learned of the operation and gave sworn testimony that is contradicted by other evidence and even himself. On May 3, 2011, when he testified before the House Judiciary Committee during an oversight hearing, Holder was asked by Representative Issa: "When did you first know about the program officially, I believe, called 'Fast and Furious'? To the best of your knowledge, what date?"

Holder responded that he was "not sure of the exact date, but I probably heard about Fast and Furious for the first time over the last few weeks."[22]

Holder changed that answer when he was asked a similar question by Senator Pat Leahy (D-VT), chairman of the Senate Judiciary Committee, in another oversight hearing six months later, on November 8, 2011. Then Holder said that he "first learned about the tactics and the phrase 'Operation Fast and Furious' at the beginning of this year, I think, when it became a matter of public controversy. In my testimony before the House Committee, I did say 'a few weeks.' I probably could have said 'a couple of months.'"[23]

Yet we now know that Holder's deputy chief of staff, Monty Williams, read weekly reports discussing Operation Fast and Furious in 2010, and that just before Marine veteran and Border Patrol agent Brian Terry was killed on December 15, 2010, near Rio Rico, Arizona, Williams made inquiries to U.S. Attorney Dennis Burke about the "Attorney General's participation in announcing the Fast and Furious take-down" at a press conference in Arizona. Gary Grindler, who became Holder's chief of staff in January 2011, had attended detailed briefings on Operation Fast and Furious in 2010 when he was the acting deputy attorney general. Edward Siskel, who was the associate deputy attorney general, was responsible for the ATF portfolio and also "attended detailed briefings on Fast and Furious."[24] Wilkinson, Williams, and Grindler were notified almost immediately about the tie-in between Terry's murder and weapons obtained through Operation Fast and Furious. There were at least seven memos sent to Holder in 2010 discussing Operation Fast and Furious that Holder claims he never read.

In their testimony given to Congress during its investigation, these Justice staffers claimed that they never talked to their boss, Eric Holder, in 2010 about this major law enforcement operation, and did not immediately notify him about the connection between the weapons "walked" across the Mexican border and Agent Terry's death. As the House report concluded, there seemed to be collective "amnesia at Justice Department Headquarters."[25] The House report said Wilkinson's failure to recall details was "simply not credible in light of the timing and circumstances" and that the "documents suggest that there was an immediate and obvious instinct to protect the Attorney General from being associated with an obviously controversial operation." In fact, "Department officials seem to have experienced collective memory loss."[26]

Any Justice Department veteran can tell you that the claims that Holder did not know about this operation are simply not credible. There is no question that the Justice Department is a very large operation and that the attorney general cannot have personal knowledge of everything being done in the department or read every document and memorandum sent to his office. But the job of his staff is to keep him briefed on major operations like Operation Fast and Furious and it is simply not credible that his closest aides, who were without question briefed about this operation, did not tell him about it at all or brief him on the continuing stream of memos they were receiving about the efforts to crack down on drugs and guns along the southwest border.

It is even more incredible that they would not immediately notify Holder about the death of a border agent who was killed with a weapon used in this very Justice Department operation, given the negative consequences, particularly in the public relations arena, that any competent lawyer and senior aide could see flowing from that tragedy. A former senior career lawyer who worked in the solicitor general's office told one of the authors that any competent senior staff would *immediately* notify the attorney general of such a problem.

This is particularly true given that shortly after he took office, Holder "delivered a series of speeches about combating violence along the southwest border" and his vision was crystallized in the "Department of Justice Strategy for combating the Mexican Cartels." Operation Fast and Furious was an integral part of this strategy and it begs credulity to claim that Holder was never briefed about a major operation set up to implement his objectives in the Southwest.[27]

Fast and Furious also demonstrates the studied and deliberate ignorance practiced by Holder to protect his political cronies. This was shown rather directly in questioning by Representative Louie Gohmert (R-TX) when Holder was testifying before the House Judiciary Committee on June 7, 2012.

Gohmert said to Holder: "Did you not ever go back to your office and say when you found out about Fast and Furious, I demand to know who authorized this? Are things so fast and loose in your office that somebody can authorize the sale to international criminals of American guns that are bringing about the death of even American agents, and nobody has to do that in writing?"[28]

This was an obvious question to ask—if Holder was indeed so upset about what happened to Agent Brian Terry and the reckless nature of this operation that he immediately shut it down, as he claimed he did, if he really had not known about it, wouldn't the first question he would ask (or anyone else in his position) be: "Who authorized this?"

Holder avoided answering Gohmert's question by saying, "I asked the inspector general to conduct an investigation. I put an end to the policy that led to the Fast and Furious debacle. I made personnel changes at ATF and in [the] U.S. Attorney's Office. We made changes in the procedures there."[29]

Gohmert countered that Holder wasn't answering his question, which was "[D]id you go back and say, I demand to know who authorized this Fast and Furious program? That was the question." But Holder insisted that he had answered the question. Holder apparently never asked his staff and his top subordinates who had authorized this operation. It is pretty obvious that he either did not want to know or was covering up his own participation in and knowledge of the operation. And his staff was either so incompetent that they did not inform their boss about this major operation and the connected death of a U.S. border agent, or they had convenient memory lapses when they were deposed by congressional investigators.

As explained in the opening chapter and further detailed in the chapter on Holder's mishandling of the national security responsibility of the Justice Department, Holder also lied about the department's investigation of Fox News reporter James Rosen over leaks of information from the State Department about North Korea. But in addition to his false testimony on multiple occasions, Holder's inability to answer basic questions about his actions, Justice Department cases, and the applicable law could only be attributed to incompetence or deliberate ignorance. One of the authors, Hans von Spakovsky, helped prepare high-level Justice Department officials for numerous oversight hearings when he worked at the department. The standard procedure at Justice was to write a voluminous set of briefing papers on every conceivable topic that the official could be questioned about, and particularly on hot topics that were in the news that Justice was involved in. Each briefing paper would be one to two pages long and would provide a complete answer on Justice Department actions and any applicable federal statutes.

The Justice official who was going to testify would then have practice sessions with his aides where they would pretend to be the members of the committee and ask questions of the official in a mock hearing. The pretend hearings were always tougher than the real thing and in four years of doing this kind of work by von Spakovsky at Justice, there was *never* a question from a member of a committee that had not been anticipated ahead of time by the Justice Department staff and for which an answer had not been prepared.

So Holder's ignorance on multiple occasions is a sign either that he is deliberately choosing not to answer the committee's questions, that he has a completely incompetent staff who did not prepare him to answer the most obvious questions, or that he doesn't care enough about his responsibility to respond to congressional inquiries to bother to come prepared to hearings. Given the high caliber of the individuals that prior attorneys general of both parties have had as their staff, it is doubtful that Holder's ignorance is based on incompetent staff. Watching the attorney general's performance and his seeming ignorance on question after question is actually embarrassing to any veteran of the Justice Department.

As former Justice Department prosecutor Andrew McCarthy says, many "things in politics are unpredictable." But "Eric Holder's lack of candor and propensity to politicize justice are not among them." McCarthy says that, "Long before he was confirmed as President Obama's attorney general, he was a key participant, as President Clinton's deputy attorney general, in the shameful pardons of Marc Rich and FALN terrorists. In connection with Rich in particular, Holder gave Congress grossly misleading testimony about his role in the pardon and his knowledge of Rich's sinister background. Nothing about Holder's abysmal performance over the last five years—including his contemptuous misleading and stonewalling of Congress—has been surprising. What is most disappointing is that, knowing what it knew when Obama nominated Holder, the Senate overwhelmingly confirmed him anyway."[30]

As the chief law enforcement official in America, responsible for a legal agency with more than one hundred thousand employees, the attorney general has an uncompromising duty to always conduct himself in an ethical and professional manner. Attorney General Eric Holder has consistently failed in that duty. His misleading testimony to Congress on numerous occasions as well as his failure to provide information and documents to which Congress is entitled are an embarrassment to a long line of lawyers of both political parties who have held that post throughout our history and who carried out their responsibilities in the highest and best traditions of public service.

CHAPTER 7

FAST AND FURIOUS

Imagine if a Drug Enforcement Administration (DEA) official let a kilo of cocaine onto the streets to try to figure out where it was going, but did not make any efforts to follow it after a drug dealer got his hands on it. When dealing with known criminals, federal law enforcement agents know they are never going to see those drugs again—and those drugs could put someone's life in danger from an overdose or other issues that may arise.

The same concept applies to guns. If federal law enforcement agents allow guns to get into the hands of known criminals, and then don't follow them, those weapons will probably end up being used in the commission of crimes—including murders. As such, federal law enforcement frowns upon and rarely ever lets even a smidgeon of drugs or just one gun walk, never mind a couple of thousand, which is what happened in the Fast and Furious scandal.

"Operation Fast and Furious" grew out of a mixture of inept bureaucrats and a cadre of politically motivated anti–Second Amendment Obama appointees. Assigning accountability for the scandal has been difficult, but there are signs the courts may eventually demand the release of records that will allow that to happen.

In Fast and Furious, ATF agents directed people known as "straw purchasers"—low-level illicit weapons purchasers who work for the Mexican drug cartels' smugglers inside the United States—to buy guns at Phoenix, Arizona–area Federally Licensed Firearms dealers. Those guns were then smuggled into Mexico by cartel operatives, after agents let the weapons get into the hands of those cartel operatives by not tracking them.

The cycle of gun walking continued despite protests from street agents for more than a year after it began in late 2009, until U.S. Border Patrol agent Brian Terry was murdered on December 15, 2010, in Peck Canyon, Arizona, by Mexican cartel operatives running a rip crew. A rip crew is a group of bandits who clear corridors in the desert for drug smugglers coming from Mexico into the United States. They are used to eliminate potential competition from other cartels trying to steal drugs en route to a U.S. destination, and from law enforcement officials who may attempt to arrest smugglers.

Two Fast and Furious guns were found at Terry's murder scene, after they had been previously trafficked into Mexico. The revelation sparked what became one of President Obama's first major scandals, one with deadly repercussions that continue to this day. Perhaps even more shocking is, that along with Benghazi, the targeting of conservative organizations by the IRS, and a whole consortium of other scandals that the Obama administration is responsible for, Fast and Furious remains the only one in which President Barack Obama has asserted an official executive privilege claim, to withhold documents about the Justice Department operation that were subpoenaed by the House of Representatives.

The origins of the Fast and Furious scandal date back to the George W. Bush Justice Department, which launched the "Project

Gunrunner" initiative through the Bureau of Alcohol, Tobacco, Firearms and Explosives (ATF) in 2006. The goal of the initiative was to decrease drug and gun trafficking along the U.S. border, crime trades largely driven by the Mexican drug cartels.

In and of itself, Project Gunrunner was not problematic, but incompetent bureaucrats in Arizona's ATF who launched specific investigations as part of it badly mishandled it. Also in 2006, as part of the larger Project Gunrunner, Tucson, Arizona, ATF officials—including Phoenix-based Special Agent in Charge Bill Newell, who ran ATF operations in the state of Arizona and was viewed as a rising star in the agency by officials in Washington—launched an investigation named Operation Wide Receiver.

In Wide Receiver, the beginnings of the gun-walking tactics later employed in a more dramatic and fast-paced way in Fast and Furious were tested. Agents, at Newell's direction, allowed 275 weapons to "walk" in Wide Receiver. According to CBS News, which first broke the Fast and Furious scandal in the news in early 2011 and subsequently uncovered much of the details about Wide Receiver, during Wide Receiver "the vast majority of guns were not tracked and Mexico's government was not fully informed of the case."

"Apparently worried that the gunwalking tactics could be viewed as inappropriate, federal prosecutors in Arizona abandoned the case," CBS News' Sharyl Attkisson wrote of Wide Receiver in early 2013 in a summary of the larger scandal. "Then, in the fall of 2009, Justice Department officials decided to go ahead and prosecute the case."[1]

When President Obama first took office in January 2009, he and his new administration officials announced a series of new initiatives they would be taking to increase activity through the Project Gunrunner program started under the Bush administration. Essentially, they were taking it to the next level—beefing up and expanding tactics used in the past.

On February 25, 2009, Holder gave a press conference to announce the takedown of a drug smuggling ring connected to Mexico's Sinaloa Cartel. At the presser, Holder left some not-so-subtle hints about what he was going to do next. "I met yesterday with Attorney General Medina Mora of Mexico and we discussed the unprecedented levels of violence his country is facing," Holder said. "The Mexican government has been courageous during the last two years to directly confront the drug trafficking cartels and I stand before you today to say that we are ready and willing to continue the fight with our Mexican counterparts against these violent criminal enterprises."[2]

Holder said that the cartels "are lucrative, they are violent, and they are operated with stunning planning and precision." Holder promised that while he was atop the Department of Justice, "these cartels will be destroyed."[3]

Meanwhile, at the end of March 2009, then–secretary of state Hillary Clinton visited Mexico's capital, Mexico City, more than a thousand miles south of the U.S. border. While there, Clinton gave speeches bashing American gun stores and gun owners for the violence.

"Our insatiable demand for illegal drugs fuels the drug trade," Clinton said in a speech that the *New York Times* described as having "unusually blunt language."[4]

"Our inability to prevent weapons from being illegally smuggled across the border to arm these criminals causes the deaths of police officers, soldiers and civilians," Clinton said.

Clinton's campaign in Mexico City included a meeting with then-president Felipe Calderón and television appearances in major media across the United States, including one particularly notable interview with MSNBC's Andrea Mitchell. In that MSNBC hit, Clinton said: "We're going to start tracing these guns, we're going to start cracking down on illegal gun sales, we're going to go after the straw men and women who go in and buy these guns. We're going to use every tool at our disposal."[5]

The nation's top diplomat's trip was much heralded in the press and was an obvious attempt by the political figures at the top of the Obama administration to mislead people into agreeing with her claim that "90 percent" of the "guns that are used by the drug cartels against the police and the military" actually "come from America."

"Our inability to prevent weapons from being illegally smuggled across the border to arm these criminals causes the deaths of police, of soldiers and civilians," Clinton said.

Clinton's claim is actually false. A diplomatic cable uncovered by WikiLeaks shows that 90 percent of the weapons the cartels get come from Central America or from corrupt Mexican military officials. Oftentimes cartels will raid armories in Guatemala. Or crooked Mexican military officials will split up a shipment of new rifles among their troops and the cartels. For instance, if 200 new fully automatic AK-47s came in, a dirty military leader might give 100 to his troops and sell the other 100 to his buddies in the cartel. Then he'll report the missing 100 weapons as an oversight or as stolen—and nobody will ask any questions.

For organized crime purposes, the guns the cartels get from Central America or from corrupt military leaders are better than what cartels could get from America. They're usually fully automatic, military-grade weapons. Weapons they'd be able to traffic into Mexico via straw purchasing rings from Federal Firearms Licensee gun dealers in the United States aren't fully automatic and aren't military grade—they're semiautomatic at best.[6] The ATF's own figures show that only 17 percent of the guns found at Mexican crime scenes have been traced back to the United States.[7]

Despite the inaccuracy of her claim, that political worldview from Clinton, that gun dealers and owners in the United States are responsible for guns getting into criminals' hands in Mexico—a view shared by most of the rest of the Obama administration—dominated Fast and Furious, making its dangerous tactics even more deadly than during Wide Receiver in the previous administration. Essentially the administration needed to find evidence to justify its claims that American gun dealers were chiefly responsible for Mexico's cartel violence.

About a week after Clinton's trip to Mexico, Holder himself made his own—to Cuernavaca, Mexico—a suburb of Mexico City, about forty miles south of the capital—for a firearms trafficking conference. It was Holder's first trip to any foreign country as attorney general.

"I wanted to come to Mexico to deliver a single message: We stand shoulder-to-shoulder with you in this fight against the narcotics cartels," Holder told a roomful of journalists and Mexican politicians. "The United States shares responsibility for this problem and we will take responsibility by joining our Mexican counterparts in every step of this fight."[8]

Holder expanded on his February 25 promise to "destroy" the Mexican drug cartels. He said the way the Obama administration was going to eliminate the organized crime groups in Mexico was by cutting off the supposed flow of weapons from the United States into Mexico—even though that flow, which Clinton had claimed the Obama administration would fight a week earlier, doesn't really exist.

Holder said he and then–homeland security secretary Janet Napolitano were "committed to putting the resources in place to increase our attack on arms trafficking into Mexico."

"Last week, our administration launched a major new effort to break the backs of the cartels," Holder said. "My department is committing 100 new ATF personnel to the Southwest border in the next 100 days to supplement our ongoing Project Gunrunner, DEA is adding 16 new positions on the border, as well as mobile enforcement teams, and the FBI is creating a new intelligence group focusing on kidnapping and extortion. DHS is making similar commitments, as Secretary Napolitano will detail."

Holder said a "topic that has been addressed over the past two days could not be more important." That topic, according to Holder, was "the development of an arms trafficking prosecution and enforcement strategy on both sides of the border."

The president himself visited Mexico City on April 16, 2009, a couple of weeks after Holder's visit. There he and Mexican president Calderón made the same argument Holder and Clinton had made before about weapons trafficking and American gun owners. "In fact, I've asked Eric Holder to do a complete review of how our current enforcement operations are working and make sure we are cutting down on the loopholes that are causing some of these drug trafficking problems," Obama said.[9]

A couple of weeks after Obama returned to Washington, D.C., Napolitano testified before Congress with the same misinformation that Holder, Clinton, and the president were peddling in Mexico City.

"A large number of weapons recovered in Mexico's drug war are smuggled illegally into Mexico from the United States," Napolitano told the Senate Judiciary Committee on May 6, 2009. "Clearly, stopping this flow must be an urgent priority."[10]

Later, in a June 30, 2009, speech, Deputy Attorney General David Ogden promised that ATF and U.S. Immigration and Customs Enforcement (ICE) would work together to battle gun trafficking on the southwest border. He promised ATF and ICE would "ensure coordination between the Departments on firearms investigations."[11]

Each of these political direction changes in law enforcement, and more, led to what Republicans on the House Committee on Oversight and Government Reform, led by Representative Darrell Issa (R-CA), would later describe as the DOJ's development of "a risky new strategy to combat gun trafficking along the Southwest Border."

"The new strategy directed federal law enforcement to shift its focus away from seizing firearms from criminals as soon as possible—and to focus instead on identifying members of trafficking networks," a House Oversight Committee report on Fast and Furious reads. "The Bureau of Alcohol, Tobacco, Firearms and Explosives (ATF) implemented that strategy using a reckless investigative technique that street agents call 'gunwalking.' ATF's Phoenix Field Division began allowing suspects to walk away with illegally purchased guns. The purpose was to wait and watch, in the hope that law enforcement could identify other members of a trafficking network and build a large, complex conspiracy case."[12]

According to the House Oversight report, the Phoenix Field Division of the ATF created a new law enforcement team called "Group VII" to focus on firearms trafficking.

"This shift in strategy was known and authorized at the highest levels of the Justice Department. Through both the U.S. Attorney's Office in Arizona and 'Main Justice,' headquarters in Washington, D.C., the Department closely monitored and supervised the activities of the ATF," the Oversight Committee wrote. "The Phoenix Field Division established a Gun Trafficking group, called Group VII, to focus on firearms trafficking. Group VII initially began using the new gunwalking tactics in one of its investigations to further the Department's strategy."

Those gun-walking tactics had begun as early as November 2009, when agents in the new Group VII in Phoenix began preliminary work on Fast and Furious. The agents' supervisors were attempting to turn what would later be named Fast and Furious, based on early research about it, into what is called an Organized Crime Drug Enforcement Task Force (OCDETF) case.

As ATF special agent John Dodson—an agent who worked on Fast and Furious itself and later became the whistle-blower whose decision to go public with the details of gun walking is the reason why the American people know about this scandal—revealed in his recent book, an OCDETF case "is a funding program that law enforcement agencies apply for and when approved, it basically gives them an unlimited amount of funds to work a case."[13]

Over the course of the next several months, all the way until Terry's death on December 15, 2010, supervisors like Fast and Furious case agent Hope McAllister, Group VII leader Dave Voth, Assistant Special Agent in Charge George Gillett, and Special Agent in Charge Bill Newell directed Dodson, Larry Alt, Lee Casa, Joe Medina, Tonya English, and other ATF agents on the ground to allow guns to walk.

"We had more than probable cause, the legal standard to make an arrest, and in my opinion enough to convict criminally where the standard is proof beyond a reasonable doubt," Dodson wrote about the first time he was ordered to allow criminals to get away with guns, which happened in January 2010. "Worst-case scenario would have been that we start a civil proceeding in which we'd need only to prove something beyond a preponderance of the evidence, a much lower threshold."

That particular incident occurred at the Lone Wolf Trading Company, and at it, Dodson and his fellow agents saw about "15 or so" AK-47 variant rifles walk. "There was no question that he was a straw purchaser and we already had ample evidence that these rifles were going to be trafficked to the border or into Mexico in no time flat," Dodson wrote. "With what we had been able to put together thus far, he was already 'bagged and tagged.' It didn't get much easier than this."

Incidents like this occurred several times over the course of the rest of 2010, despite outcries from Dodson—who, on at least one occasion in May 2010, warned his chain of command specifically that a Border Patrol agent would be killed with these weapons.

Allowing these guns to walk and not arresting the straw purchasers as soon as they walked out the door violated the most basic rules of prosecutions aimed at criminal organizations. An experienced former Justice Department criminal prosecutor told one of the authors that this investigative tactic was nothing short of reckless. When Justice Department prosecutors are trying to break up a drug organization or a mob operation, they arrest low-level members as soon as they purchase or sell drugs or engage in other illegal activities with undercover operatives. Prosecutors then offer them deals in exchange for information about the next level up in the organization or use them to catch their immediate bosses.

The idea is to roll up a criminal cartel starting at the bottom, with the ultimate goal of indicting and prosecuting the leaders who run it. Here ATF could have easily arrested the straw purchasers and then used them to reach the next level up in the drug cartel. Neither the ATF, the Justice Department, nor the State Department ever informed the Mexican government about the operation—which would have been essential if the Obama administration really wanted to trace the weapons across the border to the ultimate recipients in Mexico.

But the incident at the Lone Wolf Trading Company also shows how willing the Justice Department was to deliberately mislead the press and how easily the *Washington Post* was conned in a story it published in 2010 before Operation Fast and Furious became public.

On December 13, 2010, the *Post* ran a story about U.S. gun dealers with "the most traces for firearms recovered by police."[14] The *Post* included "the names of the dealers, all from border states, with the most traces from guns recovered in Mexico over the past two years." The *Post* did not reveal where it got this information, but pointed out that Congress passed a law in 2003 exempting the trace information maintained by the ATF from public disclosure. So the *Post* had to have gotten this information through a leak directly from the ATF and DOJ.

Two of the gun dealers the *Post*'s story assailed were Lone Wolf Trading Company in Glendale and J&G Sales in Prescott, Arizona. Lone Wolf Trading was number one on the list for Mexican traces; J&G was number three.

However, at the time the ATF was apparently leaking this information to the *Post*, both of these dealers were cooperating with the ATF in the Fast and Furious Operation. When Fox News talked to the owner of J&G, Brad DeSaye, about the ATF's disastrous operation, he said that when he questioned the ATF about whether the agency wanted the gun shop to sell to the cartel front men, the ATF said, "Keep selling."

The *Post* actually interviewed DeSaye over his store's appearance in the trace records. DeSaye, to his credit, did not reveal the still-secret ATF operation to the *Post* reporters, even though they were clearly writing a negative story that was potentially embarrassing to DeSaye.

This double dealing by the Justice Department was appalling. It was bad enough that the ATF was running a secret operation that had gone off the rails and was supplying dangerous weapons to violent Mexican drug cartels. But then the agency apparently leaked deceptive information on gun sales that put the gun dealers in a bad light, or at a minimum, misled the *Post* when it should have tried to provide cover for dealers who were following ATF instructions. Indeed, these dealers were showing up in the Mexican trace information because the ATF was telling them to ignore the law and the usual verification procedures and sell guns to the cartels, sometimes dozens in a single day to one person.

This apparent leak by the administration to mislead the *Washington Post* was not a one-time incident. On May 26, 2011, *La Opinión*, the largest Spanish-language newspaper in the United States (based in Los Angeles), published a story about the smuggling of guns from America into Mexico. The spokesman for the Office of the U.S. Attorney in Phoenix again specifically named Lone Wolf Trading, which had sold guns at the express direction of the ATF, as being responsible along with other gun dealers for "a great majority of confiscated weapons in crimes on the other side of the border," without revealing that Lone Wolf had been selling weapons at the express direction of the ATF and the Justice Department. This is the same U.S. attorney's office that "encouraged and supported every single facet of Fast and Furious," according to the joint staff report prepared by Representative Issa and Senator Grassley.

As we now know, several months after Dodson's warning, his fateful prediction turned true: Terry was killed with Fast and Furious guns on December 15, 2010. In an irony that could almost be considered comeuppance to the ATF, the *Washington Post* story was published *the day before Agent Terry was shot.*

Group VII had not made any arrests until then, but within twenty-four hours of Terry's murder, it had arrested Jaime Avila, one of the major straw purchasers in Fast and Furious. But, as Dodson wrote in his book, the "Significant Incident Report" on the matter did not "mention how Avila had blipped our radar and had been identified as a straw purchaser in Fast and Furious back in November 2009."

"It did not say how we had surveilled him many times as he purchased firearms from local gun shops," Dodson wrote. "How we had tracked his many purchases, or listed him in our databases. There was nothing about how we knew, in real time, whenever a weapon he had purchased was recovered at a violent crime somewhere along the border. The only things we hadn't ever done: interdict him, arrest him, interview him, or anything else that might hinder his firearms trafficking, or worse, at least by ATF Phoenix standards, to stop it."

Dodson wrote that such omissions made it clear to him that ATF was "going to cover it up."

After Dodson learned that ATF was going to at least attempt to cover up what would soon become a massive national scandal, he eventually made contact with investigators in the office of Senator Grassley (R-IA), the ranking member of the Senate Judiciary Committee.

Over the next few weeks, Dodson provided those investigators with the information they needed to make an official inquiry of the ATF about the matter. Grassley, who did not have subpoena power because he was in the minority in the Senate, sent a document request about Fast and Furious to the ATF leadership in Washington.

On January 27, 2011, Grassley wrote to acting ATF director Ken Melson. "Members of the Judiciary Committee have received numerous allegations that the ATF sanctioned the sale of hundreds of assault weapons to suspected straw purchasers, who then allegedly transported these weapons throughout the southwestern border area and into Mexico," he wrote in part, detailing gun walking that had—at that point, allegedly—taken place.[15]

Dodson was almost immediately retaliated against by one of his supervisors for speaking out, so Grassley followed up again in a January 31, 2011, letter to Melson to say in part that such retaliation is "exactly the wrong sort of reaction for the ATF."[16] It is also a violation of the Whistleblower Protection Act of 1989, which protects federal employees who report misconduct by federal agencies such as the ATF and the Justice Department.

On February 4, 2011, the DOJ's assistant attorney general for legislative affairs, Ron Weich, responded on Melson's behalf and categorically denied that the ATF let guns walk in Fast and Furious or any other operation. Weich wrote to Grassley that "the allegation described in your January 27 letter—that ATF 'sanctioned' or otherwise knowingly allowed the sale of assault weapons to a straw purchaser who then transported them into Mexico—is false."

"ATF makes every effort to interdict weapons that have been purchased illegally and prevent their transportation to Mexico," Weich added.[17]

After DOJ's denial of gun walking on behalf of ATF, Dodson eventually decided to go public on CBS News with his allegations that guns were being allowed to walk—and that Terry's murder was connected to the gun walking.

He recorded an interview with CBS News' Sharyl Attkisson that aired on March 3, 2011.[18]

That interview, and other matters on Capitol Hill, piqued the interest of House Oversight Committee chairman Representative Darrell Issa (R-CA). Unlike Grassley, Issa was in the majority in the House—and because of his committee chairmanship, had subpoena power.

Congressional investigators from Issa's committee, in April 2011, interviewed various agents involved with Fast and Furious. Then on May 3, 2011, Holder testified before the House Judiciary Committee, on which Issa also sits, where Issa asked him when Holder learned of Fast and Furious. Holder replied that he was "not sure of the exact date, but I probably heard about Fast and Furious over the last few weeks."[19]

The congressional investigation continued for several months afterward, and in early October 2011, documents surfaced that showed the attorney general himself was sent several briefing documents that specifically mentioned Fast and Furious. A memo that Assistant Attorney General Lanny Breuer, the head of DOJ's Criminal Division, sent to Holder on November 1, 2010, included a description of Fast and Furious. A July 2010 memo from the director of National Drug Intelligence Center to Holder lays out how "straw purchasers" purchased more than 1,500 guns under Fast and Furious.[20] According to Carlos Canino, the acting ATF attaché in the American embassy in Mexico, who testified at a hearing on July 26, 2011, this included dozens of .50-caliber sniper rifles—"approximately the same number of sniper rifles a Marine infantry regiment takes into battle." At the hearing, Canino was obviously furious about the operation and made it clear that not only did he not know about it, neither did the Mexican government.

The DOJ initially responded to these documents by saying that Holder does not always read his daily updates, memos, and briefings.[21] But this revelation led to the beginning of what would become a quickly growing surge of calls for Holder's resignation. Representatives Blake Farenthold (R-TX),[22] Raul Labrador (R-ID),[23] and Paul Gosar (R-AZ)[24] called for Holder's resignation because of this. Gosar questioned whether Holder or other DOJ or ATF officials should be considered accessories to Brian Terry's murder.[25]

People like Representative Jason Chaffetz (R-UT), a member of the House Oversight Committee, questioned the accuracy of Holder's May 3, 2011, testimony that he had only learned about Fast and Furious "over the last few weeks."[26]

Holder himself then came out and responded to the allegations that he was being misleading, writing a lengthy letter to Issa that stated in part: "Much has been made in the past few days about my congressional testimony earlier this year regarding Fast and Furious. My testimony was truthful and accurate and I have been consistent on this point throughout. I have no recollection of knowing about Fast and Furious or of hearing its name prior to the public controversy about it."[27]

A few weeks later, then-representative Joe Walsh (R-IL) called for Holder's resignation[28] and he was followed by what became a total of 130 House Republicans by the end of 2012 who demanded Holder resign.[29] Every 2012 GOP presidential candidate similarly demanded Holder resign over Fast and Furious, as did several U.S. senators, including Marco Rubio (R-FL), Jim DeMint (R-SC), and Scott Brown (R-MA).

On October 11, 2012, Issa served Holder himself with a subpoena for documents relating to Fast and Furious. That subpoena, and Holder's refusal to comply with it, set off the biggest oversight battle between Congress and the Obama administration in the latter's more than five years in Washington.[30]

In the meantime, however, when Holder testified before the Senate Judiciary Committee again in early November, he retracted his May 3, 2011, testimony, revising that statement of a "few weeks" to a "couple months."

"I did say a 'few weeks,'" Holder testified at the Senate hearing when asked questions by Senator Patrick Leahy (D-VT), the chairman of the committee. "I probably could've said 'a couple of months.' I didn't think the term I said, 'few weeks,' was inaccurate based on what happened."[31]

Within the next month or so, the Department of Justice—faced with all the evidence that Dodson and others had provided to Congress, and what media outlets were able to uncover—actually retracted the February 4, 2011, letter Weich wrote to Grassley denying that guns were ever walked. The administration admitted that statement was false when it retracted the letter.[32]

A series of hearings and public battles over documents ensued over the course of early 2012. More and more members of Congress kept demanding Holder's resignation, and Holder continued refusing to provide Issa's committee with all the documents pursuant to his subpoena. Negotiations between congressional investigators and Justice Department figures began, and crumbled quickly.

So, Issa's committee prepared contempt resolutions for passage through his committee in June 2012. Shortly before the committee hearing, Ronald Weich, who had sent the false letter to Congress, resigned from the Justice Department. Then just minutes before Issa's committee was beginning its proceedings, President Barack Obama himself stepped in to assert executive privilege over the documents. Obama's executive privilege claim was the lower of two forms of privilege, called deliberative process privilege. The higher form is called presidential communications privilege, but to assert that privilege communications about Fast and Furious would have needed to be to or from the president himself or to or from senior advisers to the president. Since Obama and Holder have claimed they did not know about Fast and Furious, asserting the higher form would have meant the president was being dishonest when he claimed he didn't know about the program.[33]

Then, in late June, as Holder continued refusing to comply with the subpoena, the full House of Representatives took the unprecedented step of voting to hold a sitting cabinet member in contempt of Congress. The vote, on June 28, 2012, was a two-part vote: One contempt resolution was a criminal contempt resolution and the other was a civil contempt resolution. The criminal contempt resolution passed 255-67, with 17 Democrats supporting it. The civil contempt resolution passed 258-95, with 21 Democrats voting for it.[34]

Many House Democrats, including Minority Leader Nancy Pelosi, walked out of the House chamber to protest the vote, even though several of their colleagues voted with Republicans in favor of the contempt vote. It is the first time in the history of the United States that a sitting attorney general has been found in contempt by the House of Representatives.

The criminal contempt resolution was referred to the U.S. attorney for the District of Columbia, Ron Machen, who declined to prosecute Holder.[35] House Republicans, led by Issa, are attempting to enforce the civil contempt resolution with an outside legal team that is suing the Obama administration to have the executive privilege claim overturned and compel document production.

The lawsuit remains ongoing, and is expected to take several years to achieve a final decision—and may end up going to the Supreme Court, depending on what happens in the lower courts. Preliminary decisions from U.S. District Court judge Amy Berman Jackson indicate that she could come down on the side of House Republicans.[36] She refused the Justice Department's request to dismiss the case or to appeal that decision.[37] In quite an ironic twist that is very revealing about Eric Holder, the Justice Department essentially made the same unsuccessful arguments that Richard Nixon's attorney general, John Mitchell, made during the Watergate scandal, when Nixon asserted executive privilege to prevent incriminating documents from ending up in the hands of the Senate, and claimed the dispute was a "political question" the courts should stay out of. As Jackson pointed out in her order, that issue had been decided against the government in *Senate Select Comm. on Presidential Campaign Activities v. Nixon*.[38]

But Senate Majority Leader Harry Reid's recent decision to invoke the nuclear option to force through confirmation of Obama's nominees potentially jeopardizes what may happen on the D.C. Circuit Court of Appeals no matter what final decision Jackson makes on the issue. Part of the reason why Reid invoked the nuclear option, changing long-held Senate rules and precedent, was to get Obama's ideological and political allies whom he nominated for that D.C. appeals court through the Senate.[39]

Obama's executive privilege claim is largely frivolous. Since he asserted deliberative process privilege, the lower form of executive privilege, which allows the president to withhold communications among any executive branch officials, there are restrictions that come with it. Specifically, if there is even the suspicion of government wrongdoing, as Issa has pointed out in his communications to the president, the privilege is invalidated. In the case of Fast and Furious, Obama himself, and Holder, have admitted government wrongdoing occurred.[40]

As such, Grassley said if the court system does not eventually overturn Obama's assertion of executive privilege, "it's going to be the most sweeping abuse of executive privilege in the history of executive privilege."[41]

Issa said that Obama has "asserted an executive privilege that doesn't exist."

"In fact, what's important about these documents is these are the documents related to who knew and helped continue to cover up false statements made to Congress that there were no guns walking," Issa said in late 2013. "In other words, very much like Nixon in Watergate, these are the tapes. These are who knew and when did they know and how long did they debate whether they were going to tell the truth or continue to withhold the truth from the American people and Congress."[42]

Like the lawsuit trying to force the Obama administration to turn over the documents, the deadly consequences of Fast and Furious continue to this day. In December 2013, in a gunfight between Mexican authorities and suspected drug cartel gunmen at a Mexico resort, a Fast and Furious gun was used. CNN reported that five cartel gunmen, including possibly a high-level Sinaloa Cartel chief, were killed in the shootout.[43]

The murders of Mexican police chief Luis Lucio Rosales Astorga and his bodyguard were done with Fast and Furious rifles as well.[44] A Mexican army document obtained by Univision in 2012 showed that Fast and Furious weapons were used in the massacre of Mexican teenagers at a birthday party in Ciudad Juarez in late January 2010. Fourteen young men and women were killed there, and twelve more were injured.[45] In late 2012, a Mexican beauty queen was murdered with Fast and Furious weapons—something that sparked Representative Trey Gowdy (R-SC) to say: "There will be consequences from Fast and Furious that last for the rest of our lives."[46] While Washington has seen many political scandals over the years, this is the first one directly responsible for the deaths of many individuals.

The true number of people killed with Fast and Furious weapons will never be known. Hundreds of the guns remain unaccounted for. In fact, even the Obama administration admits more people are going to die. In a statement to Fox News in response to the December 2013 gunfight in Mexico and the revelation that Fast and Furious weapons were involved, ATF said it "has accepted responsibility for the mistakes made in the Fast and Furious investigation and at the attorney general's direction we have taken appropriate and decisive action to ensure that these errors will not be repeated. And we acknowledge that, regrettably, firearms related to the Fast and Furious investigation will likely continue to be recovered at future crime scenes."[47]

Issa, for his part, puts it more bluntly: "Justice has blood on their hands."[48]

Newly surfacing issues with regard to other ATF operations nationwide indicate that the agency has not learned its lessons from Fast and Furious. Issa, Grassley, and House Judiciary Committee chairman Representative Bob Goodlatte (R-VA) have filed additional document requests relating to a whole new series of troubling allegations. Among them are reports that ATF used mentally impaired persons in undercover investigations—and then misled Congress about that.[49]

About these new allegations, Issa said that he wants to be clear that it is not just a rogue ATF—the Department of Justice and other agencies like the FBI and DEA are clearly involved.

"They're not operating in a vacuum," Issa said. "They always have a U.S. Attorney who's looking at their actions. They usually have a joint task force that includes sometimes ICE [Immigration and Customs Enforcement], which is in a different Department [Homeland Security], DEA [Drug Enforcement Administration], and certainly FBI. They often operate out of FBI facilities. When we say 'ATF,' let's be clear that it is almost always the Department of Justice—including a U.S. Attorney and, in the case of Milwaukee, the same point. These tactics had to be approved by a prosecutor who was working out of there, and it clearly is where some of the responsibility has to lie, with political appointees."[50]

Representative Issa has accurately and very succinctly called Operation Fast and Furious "felony stupid." Not only was it a reckless, out-of-control law enforcement operation that should never have happened, but the Justice Department has done everything it can to cover up the details of the operation, particularly who in the top levels of the department knew about, and approved the operation. The Justice Department's inspector general, Michael Horowitz, said in a memorandum to the attorney general at the end of 2013 that he was concerned over the Justice Department's "reputation for integrity, fairness, and accountability." This was particularly true because the IG had found that in the Fast and Furious investigation, "senior Department and ATF officials shared responsibility for providing inaccurate information in two letters to Congress" and he had "concerns about subsequent representations to Congress by Department officials." This was a very polite way in inspector general–speak of saying that the senior leadership in the Justice Department had lied to Congress.

CHAPTER 8

PROTECTING NATIONAL SECURITY

Amateur Night at the Justice Department

Eric Holder's Justice Department has bounced between a politically correct and suspect view of coping with terrorism to an obsessive quest for leakers of national security secrets. The department's unprecedented and secret pursuit of government leaks to reporters comes at the very same time that the Obama White House itself has been caught leaking sensitive and classified information many times—when it benefited the public image of President Obama and his reelection prospects. Those leaks the Justice Department has no interest in pursuing.

Eric Holder started his tenure by shifting to a weaker, criminal model of terrorism prevention—the kind that miserably failed during the Clinton administration, when he was also in the Justice Department. It was Holder who decided that he wanted terrorists treated like ordinary civilian criminals and read their Miranda rights. In fact, he was so proud of that decision that he sent a letter to Congress on February 3, 2010, noting that failed shoe bomber Richard Reid was "advised of his right to remain silent and to consult with an attorney within five minutes of being removed from the aircraft."[1] Holder seemingly had no concern for the complete loss of the opportunity to interrogate Reid in depth and get information about his trainers, backers, and fellow terrorists, as well as other possible terrorist attacks. As Senator Susan Collins (R-ME), a well-known moderate, said, Holder seemed oblivious to his "mishandling of this terrorist detention in the critical early hours, which likely resulted in the loss of valuable intelligence."

It was Holder who decided that 9/11 mastermind Khalid Sheikh Mohammed and his co-conspirators should be tried in a civilian courtroom in New York City, just blocks from where the twin towers of the World Trade Center once stood. Counterterrorism experts say that would have been a propaganda coup for Al Qaeda and a security nightmare for the city.

Respected former U.S. attorney general Michael Mukasey, who as a federal judge presided over the successful prosecutions of the terrorists involved in the 1993 World Trade Center bombing, said that this decision made "it look like amateur night" at the Justice Department and made the United States "look weak."[2] Mukasey pointed out what Eric Holder doesn't seem to understand: "There are huge differences between the way you're supposed to deal with the guy who tries to stick up a 7-Eleven and a terrorist. It is a mockery of the rule of law to take people who are charged with violating all the rules of war and put them in a situation that's better than the one they would have been in if they followed the rules of war."

Holder was unmoved by the protests of New York officials about the hundreds of millions of dollars for security a trial would cost, or concerns that the city would be a prime target for terrorist acts designed to disrupt the trial. It took an act passed by a Democrat-controlled House and Senate withholding any federal funds to house the terrorists in New York or anywhere else on the mainland to force Holder to reverse his decision and announce that the 9/11 conspirators would be tried by a military commission at the U.S. detention facility in Guantánamo Bay, Cuba. He remained unapologetic about his original decision, showing his contempt for the people's elected members of Congress when he said that he knew how to handle these prosecutions "better than them." He only switched back to military trials because the restrictions imposed on a bipartisan basis by Congress were "unlikely to be overturned in the near future."[3]

None of this should come as any surprise. In June 2008, Holder gave a speech to the American Constitution Society, an organization started by liberal "progressive" lawyers as a counter to the Federalist Society. At the time, Holder was the cochair of Senator Barack Obama's vice presidential search committee. Holder criticized the "disastrous course" of the Bush administration's war on terrorism (not acknowledging that it prevented another terrorist attack on U.S. soil after 9/11) and claimed it was "needlessly abusive and unlawful." In a truly ironic twist, given recent revelations about National Security Agency eavesdropping, he also complained about "secret electronic surveillance" and "warrantless domestic surveillance," as well as the denial of "habeas corpus to hundreds of accused enemy combatants"—that is, terrorists caught on foreign battlefields killing Americans or planning terrorist attacks.

Even earlier in his career, Holder showed a permissive, casual, and dangerous attitude toward terrorists, particularly when doing so could be advantageous for his political patrons. In 1999, when he was the deputy attorney general in the Clinton Justice Department, he recommended that President Clinton give pardons to sixteen terrorists from FALN (Armed Forces of National Liberation). The FALN had carried out "more than 130 bombings, several armed robberies, six slayings and hundreds of injuries" in New York, Chicago, and elsewhere to gain independence for Puerto Rico.[4]

The pardons were delayed because these jailed terrorists, who never applied for or requested clemency, refused to renounce violence. Eventually all but two did so in order to get out of prison. One who received a pardon, Carmen Valentin, even threatened the federal judge who originally handled their cases, Thomas McMillen. At her hearing Valentin told McMillen only her shackles kept her from killing him and that he was "lucky that we cannot take you right now." McMillen said that if the death penalty had been an option, he would have imposed it "without hesitation."[5] The judge pointed out that the FALN terrorists showed no remorse whatsoever for their violent acts. One of them, Ida Rodriguez, told the judge "you're right. Your jails and your long sentences will not frighten us."[6] They were apparently still without remorse when they received their pardons.

When questioned about the pardon recommendation during his confirmation hearing in 2009, Holder admitted that these individuals were "criminals. These were terrorists. These were bad people."[7] But Holder refused to apologize for his decision and still claimed it was reasonable, despite the vehement opposition of the FBI, Justice Department prosecutors, and the victims. It is virtually unprecedented for the Justice Department to recommend pardons unless its own prosecutors on the case agree that clemency is deserved and it is unheard-of to grant clemency to convicted criminals who threaten law enforcement officials, especially judges, with violent retaliation, as the FALN did. Holder never met with the victims of the FALN's acts of violence but met multiple times with advocates for their release; there was also no requirement by the Justice Department that the terrorists "provide information to solve any of their outstanding crimes."[8]

Holder plainly had political motivations. He told the Justice Department's Office of Pardon Attorneys, which reviews all requests for clemency and makes recommendations to the president, to replace its original 1996 report that recommended *against* pardons with one that recommended clemency. Career pardon attorney Roger Adams resisted in numerous memos and a face-to-face meeting, telling Holder of his strong opposition to any pardons "for a group of people convicted of such heinous crimes."[9] Holder was unmoved and told Adams to "draft a neutral options memo instead," which would allow Clinton to grant the pardons without appearing to go "against the Justice Department's wishes."

These pardons were condemned in a House resolution that passed 311-41 and a Senate resolution that passed 95-2.[10] The Senate resolution said the release was "an affront to the rule of law, the victims and their families, and every American who believes that violent acts must be punished to the fullest extent of the law." These unpardonable pardons of terrorists did not prevent Holder's confirmation (neither did his engineering of a pardon for international fugitive Marc Rich, whose wife contributed almost half a million dollars to Bill Clinton's presidential library). But as Joseph Connor, whose father was killed in the FALN bombing of the historic Fraunces Tavern in New York's financial district in 1975, when Connor was just nine years old, said, we should "not tolerate officials who would put our lives in jeopardy by releasing terrorists."[11] Yet we have tolerated just such an official for more than five years.

At the same time Holder was arranging this pardon deal, Hillary Clinton was campaigning for her first term in the U.S. Senate for New York, a state in which the support of Puerto Rican voters is very important. Clinton had "numerous ties to people who were involved with the pardons" and who lobbied Eric Holder and the White House. The pardons were considered "a hot issue" that could have a "positive impact among strategic communities (read voters)."[12] Janet Reno was marginalized by the Clintonites because she was not trusted to make the right political decisions, so Holder had long since become the Clinton White House's chief contact at Justice. It was Eric Holder who helped politicize the pardon process to go easy on terrorists at the cost of national security, before he ever became the nation's first black attorney general, in what former federal prosecutor Andrew McCarthy calls "embarrassingly naked instances of justice succumbing to influence peddling."[13]

From the first moment he was confirmed as the Obama administration's new attorney general, Eric Holder began reshaping the Justice Department's attitude toward terrorism and national security. That included hiring many attorneys who, during the Bush administration, had worked strenuously on a volunteer basis to *help* terrorist detainees in Guantánamo Bay escape justice and to severely weaken the comprehensive security measures that had been implemented by the federal government, including the Justice Department, after the horrific events of 9/11. As of September 2013, at least one hundred of the detainees who were eventually released from Guantánamo have been confirmed by the director of national intelligence to have reengaged in terrorism and another seventy-four are suspected of reengaging.[14] So almost 30 percent of the terrorists these lawyers were so concerned over and wanted released went on to commit even more terrorist attacks and murders.

One of the most controversial hires was Jennifer Daskal for the National Security Division, which was created in 2006 under the Patriot Act to consolidate the Justice Department's counterterrorism operations and prosecutions, as well as strengthen the effectiveness of its national security efforts. Daskal had no prosecutorial experience whatsoever—she was a left-wing activist who had represented Al Qaeda terrorists while working at Human Rights Watch—and yet she was hired to shape DOJ's detention policy and the future of Guantánamo.

The *New York Post* did a profile of her that illustrated her bias:

"Daskal never missed a chance to give Gitmo detainees the benefit of the doubt while assuming the worst about US government intentions."[15] Despite the confessions of 9/11 mastermind Khalid Sheik Mohammed and four of his fellow terrorists, she "refused to accept their guilt." As the *Post* pointed out, Daskal apparently did not hear the outburst from one of the five at the end of his hearing: "I hope the jihad will continue and strike the heart of America with all kinds of weapons of mass destruction." She was "largely responsible for [Human Rights Watch's] exposure of covert CIA operations" that were holding top Al Qaeda operatives and in a 2006 memo she urged the U.N. Human Rights Committee to investigate the United States over its "so-called 'war on terror'" as well as its enforcement of the death penalty and its supposed denial of the right of illegal aliens to organize labor unions.[16]

Daskal was a staunch supporter of another terrorist, Omar Khadr, who was caught on the battlefield in Afghanistan after he launched the grenade that killed Sergeant First Class Christopher Speer. She claimed that prosecuting him would violate his rights as a child because he was only fifteen when he coldly and brutally murdered an American serviceman and that he was simply "a victim of circumstances." As Sergeant Layne Morris, who was wounded in the same attack says, "The fact that [Daskal] took on [Khadr's] case—and has argued the ridiculous things that she has—and is now appointed to the Justice Department, where she brings in those same thought processes and prejudices—it doesn't bode well for the security of our country."[17]

Numerous Justice Department political appointees hired under Holder had similar conflicts of interest due to their (or their law firms') representation of terrorists. One is Tony West, who headed the Civil Division and unfortunately was promoted to become the associate attorney general (the number-three spot in Justice). West proudly volunteered his services to represent the American Taliban, John Walker Lindh, who received a twenty-year sentence after pleading guilty to making war against the United States. Lindh failed to warn CIA agent Mike Spann of the planned uprising by his Taliban brethren in the Qala-e-Jangi prison in Afghanistan in 2001, which led directly to Spann's murder.

Andy McCarthy, the former Justice Department lawyer who prosecuted the terrorists in the 1993 World Trade Center bombing, has pointed out that the many DOJ officials with a conflict from representing terrorists "include Attorney General Holder, whose firm made the terrorists detained at Guantanamo Bay its most lavishly resourced no-fee project . . . boast[ing] about the firm's success in urging federal judges to grant its 'clients'—18 enemy combatants—new 'rights' under the Fifth Amendment and the Geneva Conventions."[18]

Holder refused numerous requests by Congress and news organizations to identify all of the former terrorist lawyers who were working in Justice and had potential conflicts of interest. As Senator Chuck Grassley said, "the administration has made many highly questionable decisions when it comes to national security . . . [and Americans] have a right to know who advises the Attorney General and the President on such critical matters."[19] In Senate testimony in March 2010, Holder compared the Al Qaeda lawyers to John Adams and said he would not "allow their reputations to be besmirched."[20] But he would put them in positions in the Justice Department where their prior representation of terrorists and their demonstrated bias against protecting the nation's security would help shape the Justice Department's implementation of national security policy. It took digging by news organizations like Fox News to find out the names of these lawyers.

Holder's comparison to John Adams is absurd: Adams did not represent members of the British military when we were at war with

England. It is neither unfair nor somehow improper to criticize or question the patriotism and objectivity of lawyers who volunteered to help the enemies of the United States who are dedicated to killing as many innocent Americans as possible and destroying the country. As McCarthy points out, "the Constitution guarantees counsel to people accused of ordinary crimes"—not America's enemies.[21]

Doing pro bono work is part of being a lawyer and that work is a valued part of the legal system. But lawyers can pick the clients they volunteer to help. They can't claim immunity from being criticized for the fact that they volunteered to help cold-blooded murderers and enemies of the United States instead of ordinary, everyday criminals. But lawyers like West and Daskal, and especially the large, wealthy law firms with corporate clients that employ many of these terrorist lawyers, bristle at any such criticism. But if the authors were officers in corporations in need of legal services, we would be wary of employing law firms that provide such pro bono work since it would be the large corporate fees we pay for legal services that would be subsidizing this legal assistance to Al Qaeda.

Jennifer Daskal once said that freeing dangerous terrorists was an "assumption of risk" that must be taken to "cleanse the nation of Guantanamo's moral stain."[22] She and others with similar viewpoints should not have been given the authority to direct policy and make decisions on the prosecutions of terrorists. It would be like hiring mob lawyers for the Organized Crime and Narcotics Task Force or hiring a lawyer who represented the Ku Klux Klan for a job in the Civil Rights Division.

According to McCarthy, since these lawyers have been running the Justice Department:

> [T]here has been a detectable shift in favor of due-process rights for terrorists, a bias in favor of civilian trials in which

> terrorists are vested with all the rights of American citizens, a bias against military tribunals, the extension of Miranda protections to enemy combatants, a concerted effort to publish previously classified information detailing interrogation methods and depicting the alleged abuse of detainees, efforts to subject lawyers who authorized aggressive counterterrorism policies to professional sanction, the reopening of investigations against CIA interrogators even though those cases were previously closed by apolitical law-enforcement professionals, and the continued accusation that officials responsible for designing and carrying out the Bush administration's counterterrorism policies committed war crimes.[23]

When he was speaking to the American Constitution Society in 2008, Eric Holder said that under the Bush administration the "government authorized the use of torture" and "we owe the American people a reckoning." Holder tried to engineer that "reckoning" to the dismay of intelligence and national security experts when he announced in August 2009 that he was asking a special prosecutor, Assistant U.S. Attorney John Durham, to investigate the CIA's handling of about one hundred high-value terrorists captured by American forces on the battlefield.

The investigation was unjustified because during the Bush administration, before Holder was attorney general, a task force of long-term, *career* Justice Department prosecutors in the Eastern District of Virginia conducted an in-depth, exhaustive investigation into the allegations that CIA interrogators had abused their prisoners. They concluded that the CIA had expressly followed the rules laid out by the Justice Department in legal memoranda issued by the Office of Legal Counsel on the use of enhanced interrogation techniques. Though the popular press and critics called the techniques "torture," they were not torture under applicable federal law or presidential authority.[24]

In every case during the first review save one involving a CIA contractor,[25] the career prosecutors—not Bush political appointees—determined that there were no violations of the law and no evidence of abuse by CIA interrogators. The prosecutors drafted extensive "declination memos" summarizing the facts and the findings of their investigations with regard to each prisoner, as well as the applicable statutes and case law, and detailed their conclusions and recommendations that there were no crimes to prosecute.

Seven former CIA directors, covering thirty-five years of Democratic and Republican administrations including the Nixon, Reagan, Clinton, and both Bush administrations, sent a letter to Barack Obama protesting Holder's decision to reopen the criminal investigation. They said that Holder's decision would create "an atmosphere of continuous jeopardy" for CIA employees and would "seriously damage the willingness of many other intelligence officers to take risks to protect the country." As they pointed out, "Those men and women who undertake difficult intelligence assignments in the aftermath of an attack such as September 11 must believe there is permanence in the legal rules that govern their actions."[26] Leon Panetta, the director of the CIA at the time, was so upset over Holder's decision that he engaged in a "profanity-laced screaming match" at the White House.[27]

Holder admitted that he did not read the "detailed memos that prosecutors drafted and placed in files to explain their decision" before he decided to reopen the investigations.[28] It is almost unbelievable that Holder would make a decision on a matter so sensitive and important, involving the nation's ability to obtain crucial intelligence information to prevent more horrendous attacks like 9/11, without bothering to read his own prosecutors' analysis of the facts, the evidence, the applicable law, and their recommendations to decline prosecution. This, combined with his prior statements before he even became attorney general, makes it clear that the decision to launch a new investigation was part of an ideological crusade against the CIA rather than an objective law enforcement decision.

One of the authors worked for three different assistant attorneys general at the Justice Department and not one of them would have ever considered making such a critical decision without having first reviewed the detailed legal and factual memoranda sent to them by their lawyers. Indeed, they would have considered a failure to do so to border on malpractice, as well as being potentially unethical. Greg Katsas, who was acting associate attorney general during the George W. Bush administration, said in an interview that the "declination memos should have been the first thing [Holder] read. He effectively overruled professional career prosecutors who had been studying the facts of these cases for months if not years. And he did so without so much as even considering the reasons for their decision. Hard to explain that decision on anything but nakedly political grounds."

Fortunately for the CIA case officers wrongfully retargeted by Holder, Leon Panetta took advantage of a quirk in the CIA's authorizing statute and quickly announced that he would use agency funds to pay for their legal defense. The Central Intelligence Agency Act of 1949 specifically allows the director of the CIA to use its appropriated funds "for objects of a confidential, extraordinary, or emergency nature," and he alone deems whether it is in the public interest to do so. This provision was upheld in a Supreme Court decision in 1974 in which a taxpayer tried to claim that exempting the funds of the CIA from general government accounting, audit, and use regulations was unconstitutional. His case was thrown out.[29]

But having their legal costs paid for did not make up for the legal liability and risk these CIA employees faced for the two years that the Justice Department's special prosecutor reinvestigated them. Or for all of the time away from their jobs and the consternation and fear caused by having to deal with another set of investigators and lawyers examining every aspect of how they had conducted their jobs of trying to get vital information from vicious, coldhearted killers who were still targeting innocent Americans.

In the end, no doubt to Holder's disappointment, special prosecutor John Durham made exactly the same decision that had been made by the prior task force of career prosecutors—that the Justice Department should not "initiate criminal charges in these matters."[30] Marc Thiessen, who worked in the Bush White House, said the "CIA created a well-run, highly disciplined interrogation and detention regime, where clear guidelines were established, the safety of the detainees was ensured, invaluable intelligence was uncovered and any deviations from approved techniques were stopped, reported and addressed. Now the special prosecutor assigned by Holder to investigate that regime has affirmed—once again—that this program operated completely within the law."[31]

But Holder was not apologetic for putting these CIA officers through this unneeded, expensive, and repetitive investigation, although he claimed that he appreciated "the work of and sacrifices made by the men and women in our intelligence community on behalf of this country. . . . They deserve our respect and gratitude for the work they do."[32] But Holder's actions spoke louder than his belated words at the end of this investigation—too bad he didn't actually show real respect and gratitude for the work of the CIA by not mounting a crusade against them to start with.

Marc Thiessen probably said it best when he pointed out that the lives of these CIA employees "will never be the same. They have spent much of the decade since Sept. 11 under threat of prosecution, fighting to defend their good names even as they worked to keep us safe. As a result of the witch hunt that Holder unleashed, some of our most talented, capable counterterrorism officials have left government service—and countless others, who might have contemplated such service, have chosen other careers instead. The damage this investigation has done is incalculable."[33]

At the same time that Eric Holder was trying to unravel our intelligence operations against terrorists, he was also conducting an abusive, high-profile prosecution of a politically unpopular defendant, Blackwater Worldwide. Blackwater was a private contractor who provided security for State Department and other government employees in Iraq and was a favorite boogeyman of left-wing advocacy groups. Five of its employees were charged by the Justice Department with manslaughter and "firearms violations" arising out of a shooting that occurred in Baghdad, Iraq, on September 16, 2007.[34]

After receiving a message of an IED explosion near a compound where U.S. officials were meeting with Iraqi officials, the Blackwater team took up positions in Nisur Square, a traffic circle just outside the International Zone, to secure an evacuation route for the American officials. They got into a firefight in which fourteen Iraqis were killed and others wounded. The media painted this as an overreaction by the Blackwater guards, who claimed they had been shot at by insurgents. Those media accounts failed to acknowledge the fact that State Department investigators who went to the scene after the firefight found shell casings from AK-47s—the favorite weapon of Iraqi insurgents—which tended to confirm the claim that the Blackwater team had been shot at. None of the contractors were equipped with AK-47s.

No one minimizes the seriousness of what happened or the fact that civilians were killed. But the "firearms violations" charges were particularly ridiculous—the Justice Department apparently objected to the Blackwater guards being equipped with automatic weapons and grenade launchers in a country flooded with automatic weapons and grenade launchers routinely used by terrorists and insurgents to attack American forces and their Iraqi allies.

In a startling and unusual action, federal judge Ricardo Urbina dismissed the indictment against the five Blackwater guards in 2009 in a ninety-page opinion, preventing the case from even going to trial. His scathing criticism of Holder's prosecutors, including lawyers from the National Security Division, made it clear that they had engaged in gross prosecutorial misconduct. That misconduct included withholding "substantial exculpatory evidence" from the grand jury that indicted the defendants, such as the fact that within "five seconds" of the Blackwater team pulling into its position in the square, they "started taking fire."[35] The prosecutors also presented evidence summaries to the grand jury that were "distorted versions of the testimony on which they were based."

The worst abuse of the prosecutors, however, was their use of sworn statements that the guards had given immediately after the incident to State Department investigators. The guards were required to make the statements as part of their contract with Blackwater and the State Department. The use of such testimony, just like the use of the compelled testimony of police officers to internal department investigators, is strictly barred from being used in subsequent criminal prosecutions. In the case of *Garrity v. New Jersey*,[36] the Supreme Court concluded that using such compelled statements violates the Fifth Amendment privilege against self-incrimination.

According to Judge Urbina, the Justice Department was forced to acknowledge that "its investigators, prosecutors and key witnesses were exposed to (and indeed, aggressively sought out) many of the statements given by the defendants to State Department investigators." This was due to their "zeal to bring charges" against Blackwater, and in that "zeal," the trial team "repeatedly disregarded the warnings of experienced, senior prosecutors, assigned to the case specifically to advise the trial team" that the evidence they were using was "thoroughly tainted." The excuses offered by the Justice Department prosecutors for their abusive behavior "smack of post hoc rationalization" and were simply implausible, according to the judge. In fact, they were "all too often contradictory, unbelievable and lacking in credibility."[37]

The question this case raises is "whether prosecutors felt they could get away with such abusive behavior because Blackwater was such a politically unpopular defendant." Eric Holder had made clear his attitude and Blackwater, which had political ties to Republicans, had been made "a whipping boy to further undermine public support for the Iraq war."[38] The dismissal of the indictment was another black eye for the Holder Justice Department but more evidence of how prosecutors under his authority were willing to abuse their power for political reasons.

It is true that a federal appeals court in 2011 sent the case back to Judge Urbina saying that he needed to review the evidence against each defendant individually to see "what evidence—if any—the government presented against him that was tainted."[39] After his specific findings of wrongdoing by the government during remand, the Justice Department brought new charges against four of the defendants through a new grand jury in October 2013. But those new charges and the appeals court decision don't change the fact that Holder's prosecutors were willing to use tainted evidence to bring charges in violation of their ethical duty as prosecutors and to ignore the evidence of some of the witnesses in the case that the "Blackwater convoy was under fire."[40]

Finally, a discussion of the Justice Department's handling of national security matters cannot be had without pointing out the totally contradictory and hypocritical approach that Holder has applied to the investigation and prosecution of leaks of classified information. At the very same time that the Justice Department has prosecuted more leak cases against low-level government employees and contractors "than all prior administrations combined,"[41] it has been "overlooking and rewarding politically beneficial leaks"[42] by high-level individuals in the administration, particularly the White House, that make the president and the administration look good politically as being tough and successful in fighting terrorism. And Eric Holder, when questioned by Congress about its leak investigations, gave "deceptive and misleading"[43] testimony, although "it would be less kind and more accurate to say that [what Holder said] would rise to be a lie by most people's standards," according to Representative Darrell Issa (R-CA), chairman of the House Committee on Oversight and Government Reform.

In fact, the Obama administration, which came into office promising more transparency, has implemented the most aggressive effort to control the dispersal of government information "since the Nixon administration," according to former *Washington Post* executive editor Leonard Downie, who was one of the editors at the newspaper during the Watergate investigation.[44] David Sanger, the chief Washington correspondent for the *New York Times*, says that "[t]his is the most closed, control-freak administration I've every covered,"[45] although Sanger himself benefited from a controlled leak by the administration on the Stuxnet virus, engineered by the United States to damage Iran's nuclear program.

The revelation of information about the Stuxnet virus shows how the administration leaked "classified, or highly sensitive information in what appears to be a broader effort by the administration to paint a portrait of the President of the United States as a strong leader on national security issues," according to Senator John McCain (R-AZ).[46] Stuxnet was the first malicious software designed to attack the computer-assisted industrial control system of a nuclear plant.[47] It caused Iranian centrifuges being used to enrich uranium to spin out of control and explode.

The *New York Times* story on June 1, 2012, by Sanger reported that President Obama had secretly ordered the cyberattacks on the computer systems running Iran's nuclear enrichment facilities, and included highly sensitive details such as the code name for the operation and even a detailed description of a White House Situation Room meeting, something that could only have come from a high-level administration official.[48]

On June 8, 2012, Holder asked Rod Rosenstein, the U.S. attorney for Maryland, to investigate the Stuxnet leaks. But State Department emails obtained by Freedom Watch through the Freedom of Information Act detail extensive cooperation between the White House and the State Department with Sanger "during the period that he broke confidential national security information."[49] The emails were only turned over after a lawsuit and after the State Department had told Freedom Watch that it had no relevant documents.

According to the emails, the State Department arranged official background interviews for Sanger with State Department officials; then–National Security Council advisor Tom Donilon also talked to Sanger. In fact, a public affairs official at the State Department made it clear in an email that the White House was "cooperating" with Sanger and that Sanger had spoken to Hillary Clinton and "scores of people," including "over at NSC and other agencies. We have been cooperating with him on this project and the chats have all been on background."[50]

So while the Justice Department investigation has been concentrating on retired Marine General James Cartwright over the Stuxnet virus leak,[51] the real question is whether the Justice Department will simply ignore the officially sanctioned leaks that were made by Obama political appointees at the State Department, the National Security Council, and the White House and that Holder is no doubt aware of. Given the general criticism over the president's lack of action against Iran in 2012, the reason for the Stuxnet leak was "obviously to make President Obama and his administration look strong" in the lead-up to his reelection, according to Freedom Watch's Larry Klayman. Before Sanger published—with the active help of the Obama administration—the details of one of the most successful cyberattacks in history, designed to stop a country officially designated as a sponsor of terrorism from developing a nuclear bomb, it "was clearly one of the most tightly held national security secrets in our country," according to Senator McCain.[52]

Another highly publicized leak investigation that upset the entire Washington and New York media community shows Eric Holder's tendency to ignore leaks by high-level administration officials while prosecuting politically unimportant individuals. On May 7, 2012, the Associated Press reported on a CIA counterterrorism operation that had intercepted a plot by the Al Qaeda affiliate in Yemen to bomb a U.S. airliner using a more advanced version of the bomb that failed to explode over Detroit on Christmas Day 2009.[53] The 2012 bombing was intended to coincide with the one-year anniversary of the killing of Osama bin Laden.

Unfortunately, the leak also disclosed that the CIA had been able to stop the plot because of information from a double agent inside Al Qaeda, a Saudi Arabian intelligence agent who had to be rushed to safety after the AP agreed to hold its story for a week. Eric Holder called it "if not the most serious, it is within the top two or three most serious leaks that I have ever seen. It put the American people at risk, and that is not hyperbole." According to Holder, it "required very aggressive action."[54]

That "very aggressive action" involved the Justice Department violating its own regulations and federal law when it secretly seized—and failed to notify the AP—telephone records for a two-month period for twenty separate AP phone numbers, including the main AP number in the press gallery of the House of Representatives, its office numbers in New York City, Washington, D.C., and Hartford, Connecticut, as well as the cellular, work, and home telephone numbers of individual reporters.[55] The president of the AP, Gary Pruitt, did not learn about the seizure until May 2013, a year later, when he was notified by the Justice Department; he immediately sent a letter back to Eric Holder protesting the scope of the seizure and the failure of prior notice or negotiation with the AP, calling it a "massive and unprecedented intrusion."

The original Yemen story involved only five reporters and an editor, yet the Justice Department didn't subpoena the records of just those individuals to try to find the government official who had leaked information about the bombing plot to the specific reporters working on the story. Instead, it seized all of the AP's telephone records from its general numbers for two months, involving more than one hundred reporters, and which would "reveal communications with confidential sources across all of the newsgathering activities undertaken by the AP during a two-month period, provide a road map to AP's newsgathering operations, and disclose information about AP's activities and operations that the government has no conceivable right to know."[56] Fifty news organizations signed a letter protesting the Justice Department's actions.[57]

The congressional inquiry about the AP investigation was answered by Deputy Attorney General James Cole, since Holder told Congress that he had recused himself from the case. But Cole did not explain why the Justice Department violated its own regulations requiring prosecutors to negotiate with the news media before issuing any subpoena unless the responsible assistant attorney general determines that such negotiations would pose a substantial threat to the integrity of the investigation. In fact, Cole falsely claimed Justice had complied with all applicable legal requirements.

Reporters are also protected under the Privacy Protection Act, which prohibits the federal government from using search warrants to seize the work product of journalists unless there is probable cause to believe they have committed a criminal offense. According to the signing statement of President Jimmy Carter, who signed the Privacy Protection Act into law, government officials must either "request voluntary compliance or use subpoenas—with advance notice and the opportunity for a court hearing—instead of search warrants when they seek reporters' materials as evidence."[58]

Cole, whose response was called as "amateurish as it was unilluminating" by the *Washington Post*,[59] told Congress that the Justice Department had conducted more than 550 interviews before it seized the AP's phone records, so its investigation was not exactly a secret. And since the AP's phone records are maintained by its telephone carriers, there was no possibility of these records being destroyed if the AP had gotten advance notice, as it should have, that the Justice Department was seeking these records through a subpoena. There was no reasonable claim that notifying the AP would compromise the integrity of the leak investigation; the only effect of failing to give the AP notice was that it prevented the AP from fighting the Justice Department in court.

Apparently, the AP records did lead the Justice Department to one of the leakers. In September 2013, the FBI announced that an FBI contractor, Donald Sachtleben, had agreed to plead guilty to disclosing to the AP that "there was a foiled al-Qaeda plot on the first anniversary of Osama bin Laden's death."[60] His leak was prompted by the false claims made by the White House that "there was no credible terror threat on the anniversary of bin Laden's death."

But Sachtleben wasn't responsible for the worst part of the Yemen plot leak. The most damaging information, that there was a Saudi undercover agent who had infiltrated the Yemen Al Qaeda affiliate, "was actually disclosed by Richard Clarke, a former official in the Clinton administration," and by President Obama's own homeland security adviser John Brennan.[61] The original AP story said nothing about the government having a double agent inside Al Qaeda.

On May 7, 2012, after the AP story and just before the network evening newscasts, Brennan "held a small, private teleconference to brief former counter-terrorism advisers who have become frequent commentators on TV news shows."[62] Brennan told the advisers that the Yemen plot was never a real threat because Washington had "inside control" over it.[63] Just after the conference ended, Clarke told ABC's *World News Tonight* that the bombing plot "never came close because they had insider information, insider control," and a few hours later on ABC's *Nightline* he surmised that since the government was saying the plot "never came close because they had insider information, insider control," that implied "that they had somebody on the inside who wasn't going to let it happen."[64] It was Clarke's revelation gotten directly from Brennan that led to headlines the next day that the United States had a spy inside the plot.

Despite Brennan's direct responsibility for the Yemen leak, "unnamed White House officials vehemently denied" that Brennan improperly disclosed classified information[65] and he was confirmed to be the new head of the CIA. So once again, the Holder Justice Department went after a low-level FBI contractor who leaked information to counter a misleading story put out by the Obama administration, and ignored the leak of the most damaging information by a political appointee of President Obama, who leaked that information specifically to shape the media spin about the efficacy of the administration's fight against terrorism.

Anther Justice Department investigation into a leak about North Korea, while not as damaging to America's intelligence gathering, shows the willingness of Holder to skirt and bend, if not break, federal law. This is also a case in which Holder gave "deceptive and misleading" testimony to Congress, a habit of his that has helped lead to his being the first attorney general in American history to be held in contempt by the House of Representatives.

On June 11, 2009, James Rosen, the chief Washington correspondent for Fox News, published a story about North Korea.[66] Rosen reported that U.S. intelligence believed that North Korea would respond to a UN Security Council resolution condemning the country's nuclear and ballistic missile testing program in four different ways, including launching another missile. Rosen quoted an unnamed source but said he was withholding details "to avoid compromising sensitive overseas operations."

Holder ordered the FBI to open an investigation that led to the indictment of Stephen Jin-Woo Kim, a Lawrence Livermore National Laboratory employee who was on a detail to the State Department, and who eventually pleaded guilty to disclosing national defense information. Kim was one of ninety-six individuals who had accessed the relevant classified intelligence report on North Korea on June 11, the day the story came out, but the only one who had spoken with Rosen that same day by telephone, as well as having prior telephone calls and email exchanges with Rosen. The FBI had found all of this evidence by seizing Kim's official State Department telephone and email records.

The FBI also believed that Kim met with Rosen face-to-face on June 11. This was based on the electronic system that tracked the State Department badges of both Kim and Rosen and showed them leaving and returning to the State Department building at 2201 C Street, NW in Washington, D.C., at almost the same time.[67]

But the FBI also had emails between Kim and Rosen because the agency had secretly obtained a search warrant in May 2010 for Rosen's personal email account. The Privacy Protection Act bans the government from obtaining a search warrant for a reporter unless "there is probable cause to believe" the reporter is committing a crime, so the affidavit filed in the Justice Department's warrant application claimed that "there is probable cause to believe that the Reporter [Rosen] has committed a violation" of the Espionage Act "at the very least, either as an aider, abettor and/or co-conspirator of Mr. Kim."[68] The only factual basis the FBI revealed for that assertion was that Rosen flattered Kim, "exploited" his vanity, and was very "persistent" in seeking information about the North Korean situation, actions all reporters do routinely when they try to convince a source to provide them with information.

The search warrant application, which was personally reviewed and approved by Eric Holder under applicable DOJ policy, also requested that the federal court issue an order preventing the email provider from notifying Rosen of the search warrant. It alleged that disclosure would endanger the life and safety of an individual, potentially cause flight from prosecution, destruction and tampering of evidence, intimidation of potential witnesses, or otherwise seriously jeopardize the investigation. Since Rosen could not destroy or tamper with emails on his email provider's server and the FBI had already seized all of Kim's telephone and email records, the claims made by the agent were clearly false. And no one can seriously argue that any of the other claims—such as that Rosen would flee—would apply, either.

Two separate judges refused to grant the Justice Department a warrant, with each separately concluding that DOJ "was required to notify Mr. Rosen of the search warrant."[69] But Justice appealed the decision and convinced the chief judge of the Federal District

Court for the District of Columbia, Royce C. Lamberth, to issue the warrant. The Justice Department didn't move to unseal the search warrant records until November 7, 2011. However, due to a series of errors by the court clerk, the search warrant was not unsealed until May 16, 2013, when the clerk started receiving media inquiries as the story broke.[70]

The day before, however, on May 15, Eric Holder testified before the House Judiciary Committee and was specifically questioned about the Justice Department's leak investigations. He made no mention whatsoever of the warrant that had been issued for Rosen's emails. When Representative Hank Johnson (D-GA) asked Holder about the seizure of the AP's phone records and possible prosecution of the press for publishing stories based on classified information, Holder responded:

> With regard to potential prosecution of the press for the disclosure of material, that is not something that I have ever been involved, heard of, or would think would be a wise policy. In fact my view is quite the opposite. . . . The focus should be on those people who break their oaths and put the American people at risk, not reporters who gather this information. That should not be the focus of these investigations.[71]

This testimony was not true. Holder claimed that prosecuting the press was "not something that [he had] ever been involved, heard of, or [thought] would be a wise policy" and yet he had *personally approved the application for a search warrant*[72] that claimed Fox reporter James Rosen was a co-conspirator or aider and abettor of criminal activity, which would make Rosen just as guilty of violating the Espionage Act as the government official who disclosed the classified material. If Holder did not believe this to be true, and if he had no intention of ever prosecuting Rosen, it was unethical for him to approve such a false claim based on a false premise in a sworn affidavit that was filed with the court.

When the House Judiciary Committee learned about the Rosen investigation by Justice after Holder's hearing, it tried to question him in a letter about "the obvious clash between his testimony and the truth." But Holder refused to respond. Only after weeks of delay did Holder finally send a response on June 19, 2013, that "failed to answer any of the Committee's questions."[73] In fact, Holder admitted in his letter that even though the Justice Department had had no intent to prosecute Rosen, the department claimed he had committed a crime precisely because such a claim was necessary "in order to proceed under the Privacy Protection Act." His response did not "ameliorate" the committee's view that his testimony was "deceptive and misleading" and it took no comfort in the claim made by Holder that the department "never intended to prosecute Mr. Rosen when it labeled him a criminal suspect."

In fact, as the committee pointed out, the legislative history of the Privacy Protection Act makes it clear it was intended to prevent the government from searching the files of journalists for evidence against third parties. Holder's view, that the government can search the files of a journalist as long as the government makes a pretextual showing that the journalist is involved in criminal activity, "runs exactly counter to the purpose of the PPA."[74]

There is no question that leaking classified information is a serious violation of the law that can endanger the national security of the country and the lives and safety of intelligence agents and the general public. But going after government officials is a different prospect than going after journalists engaged in First Amendment activity. The government protects classified material through strict internal controls, limiting access, and prosecuting officials who leak the information—not prosecuting the reporters who publish the leaks. Holder's approval of a secret investigation of James Rosen is exactly the kind of abusive government action that will have a deterrent effect on reporters and particularly their sources. It is also completely unacceptable to classify reporters doing their jobs as criminals as Holder did in the FBI affidavit.

As Michael Clemente, an executive vice president at Fox News, said, naming a reporter as "a criminal coconspirator for simply doing his job as a reporter" is "downright chilling."[75] First Amendment lawyer Charles Tobin added that "search warrants like these have a severe chilling effect on the free flow of important information to the public."[76]

The administration obviously realized it had a problem even with the generally liberal press, which has treated Barack Obama and Eric Holder with kid gloves during his presidency, after news about the AP and Rosen investigations came out. Holder held seven meetings with representatives of about thirty very concerned news organizations, after which he announced a "new" set of guidelines that would supposedly restrict Justice Department investigations into leaks involving reporters.[77] But the guidelines still allow prosecutors to obtain a search warrant for a journalist's phone and email records if he is the target of a criminal investigation—which is exactly how Holder improperly convinced a federal judge to issue a warrant against Rosen before these "new" guidelines. The guidelines also require news organizations to be notified of such a warrant unless the attorney general believes it would harm the leak investigation—which was also exactly what the law was prior to these "new" guidelines. Yet Justice failed to notify the AP and in fact asked the judge to *delay* notification. These "new" guidelines were obviously just face-saving propaganda created by the Justice Department PR shop that were intended to satisfy the media that Holder was taking steps to assuage their concerns even though they made no significant changes in Justice policy and helped mask Holder's violation of the legal rights of the AP and James Rosen as well as prior internal DOJ guidelines.[78]

But while the Justice Department aggressively has gone after accused low-level leakers of classified information, it has ignored the leaks of classified and sensitive information by the White House and senior administration officials. Senator Dianne Feinstein (D-CA), the chairwoman of the Senate Intelligence Committee, herself said that the White House has been behind recent national security leaks and that President Obama must understand "that some of this is coming from their ranks."[79]

At the same time that his administration threatened to prosecute a former member of SEAL Team Six, Matt Bissonnette, for his firsthand account of the May 2011 raid that killed Osama bin Laden, President Obama's Justice Department ignored what is probably the most blatant and outrageous leak directly engineered by the Obama White House—detailed classified information about the mission by Team Six that found and killed Osama bin Laden. In fact, the reason we know it was SEAL Team Six is that Vice President Joe Biden identified them publicly at a dinner of the Atlantic Council at the Ritz-Carlton Hotel in Washington, D.C., on May 3, 2011.[80] This meant that every member of Al Qaeda knew which American military unit to target and where to look for them, since they are based in Norfolk, Virginia. In fact, Karen Vaughn, the mother of one slain member of SEAL Team Six, said she was called by her son after Biden's leak to tell her to delete all information about their family on "social media, Facebook and Twitter." She said that she "never heard [her son] that afraid in his life. He told me: 'Mom, we're picking up chatter. We're not safe. You're not safe. Delete everything.' "[81]

It was only three months after bin Laden's death that fifteen members of SEAL Team Six were among the thirty-eight service members killed in an attack on a Chinook helicopter in Afghanistan by Taliban fighters using rocket-propelled grenades, and who were "waiting on three sides for the aircraft as it approached. The Chinook was a sitting duck as it hovered in the sky. The evidence is overwhelming and disturbing: SEAL Team 6 members were ambushed."[82]

The White House not only required the CIA and the Pentagon to give special briefings to the makers of the movie *Zero Dark Thirty*, screenwriter Mark Boal and director Kathryn Bigelow, but according to documents obtained by Judicial Watch through a lawsuit and a Freedom of Information Act request, even revealed the classified name of the identity of a "planner, SEAL Team 6 Operator and Commander."[83]

Classified information and "scads of details" were released by the White House and the Pentagon to the filmmakers and the public about the bin Laden mission.[84] In fact, while the administration was leaking this information, the Justice Department was in court arguing against attempts by organizations like Judicial Watch to obtain information about the bin Laden raid under the Freedom of Information Act. Even liberal columnist and Obama supporter Maureen Dowd admitted that this leaking to the filmmakers was done so it would "give a home-stretch boost" to the president's tough reelection campaign.[85]

In other words, "at exactly the same time that it was telling a court that the mission is too secret to permit such disclosure, the White House launched a coordinated campaign of selective media leaking that had only one purpose: to glorify the president."[86] In essence, the "Obama administration strategically leaked details of the bin Laden raid for political advantage," says one criminal defense lawyer who represents military clients.[87] He adds that "using strategic leaks for political gain, while complaining that a witness to events wrote about what he personally saw and did, really is the height of hypocrisy." Those officially sanctioned leaks led directly to the imprisonment of the Pakistani doctor who helped locate bin Laden for U.S. forces.

Then–Secretary of Defense Robert Gates was so concerned about these leaks coming out of the White House that he went to meet with Tom Donilon, Obama's national security adviser. According to David Sanger of the *New York Times*, Gates told Donilon that he had "a new strategic communications approach to recommend." When Donilon asked what it was, the defense secretary angrily responded: "Shut the fuck up."[88]

One final example of Holder's selective investigation of leaks: on May 29, 2012, in the lead-up to the reelection of Barack Obama, the *New York Times* wrote a story disclosing the existence of the president's secret "kill list." This was a list of Al Qaeda and Taliban terrorist targets personally selected by the president to be killed or captured.[89] The details given in the article, which include discussions President Obama had with advisers as well as descriptions of counterterrorism meetings in the White House Situation Room, make it very clear that the "leak" of this highly classified operation came from the Obama White House.

But according to the House Judiciary Committee, it "is not aware of any Justice Department investigation into the leak of the targeted kill list." Why would there be? This leak was obviously orchestrated by senior Obama aides in the White House for political theater as the president was campaigning, so he could show how tough he was in the war on terror. Holder allowed political considerations to intrude on his duty as the chief law enforcement officer of the United States to go after leaks of classified information.

Through his hiring of biased, hostile lawyers and his treatment of terrorists as ordinary criminals; his orchestrated, ideological attack on the intelligence community; and his highly selective prosecutions of government leaks, Eric Holder has weakened the national security operations of the Justice Department as well as helped President Obama manipulate the president's power as "an odious instrument for propaganda" according to Glenn Greenwald, a former columnist for *The Guardian*. Holder has helped the president ensure "that all embarrassing or incriminating information remains suppressed, and the only thing the public learns—and the eager, grateful press amplifies—are the informational crumbs doled out by the White House in order to glorify the leader. That's the very definition of state propaganda."[90]

Joe Connor, whose father was killed in a criminal conspiracy by the FALN terrorists Holder helped pardon at the end of the Clinton administration, told one of the authors that he testified against Holder's confirmation in 2009 because it was clear to him that even in matters of national security, "Holder puts political gain above the safety of the American people he is sworn to protect," and that he "did not have the values, judgment or character to be our attorney general." That has been shown, according to Connor, by Holder's "insistence on trying al-Qaeda terrorists (who killed my father's godson among the thousands on 9/11) including KSM in U.S. civilian courts, his nonexistent investigation of the Benghazi terror attacks, and his quite literal playing of Russian roulette by providing weapons to Mexican narco-terrorists that resulted in agent Brian Terry's murder." Conner says that "Holder's malfeasance, though thoroughly reprehensible, is no surprise." He asserts that Holder's misconduct as attorney general has proven that what he, Connor, said back in 2009 was right.[91] This is a damning indictment by someone whose family was twice victimized by terrorism.

CHAPTER 9

CORRUPTION ABROAD

Prosecuting American Businesses but Not the Administration

Nothing quite shows the unbridled hypocrisy of the Obama administration and prosecutorial abuse by the Holder Justice Department as does the attempted prosecutions of American companies under the Foreign Corrupt Practices Act (FCPA). The FCPA was passed by Congress in 1977 to prevent companies from bribing officials of foreign governments in "obtaining or retaining business."[1] But Congress designed the law to stop high-level bribery and corruption of foreign government officials; it was not meant to cover the low-level payments and gifts that are often routinely required in many Third World countries "to grease the wheels of bureaucracy."[2] Yet that is the type of corruption the Justice Department has pursued under dubious legal theories. When it has actually been forced to go to court by defendants unwilling to give in to the department's intimidation tactics, the Justice Department has often lost. DOJ's prosecutions have been dismissed due to prosecutorial abuse and other misdeeds by Eric Holder's prosecutors.

For the first two decades after it became law, the FCPA was a little-used statute. In 2000, there was just one prosecution under the law by the Justice Department. However, Lanny Breuer, Holder's subordinate and the politically appointed assistant attorney general of the Criminal Division, proclaimed that the FCPA would "be a focus for the Criminal Division" and one of its "top priorities." As Mike Koehler, a leading expert on the FCPA, has said, Breuer spoke about the FCPA with almost "religious fervor."[3] Breuer said that the United States was "in a unique position to spread the gospel of anti-corruption, because there is no country that enforces its anti-bribery laws more vigorously than we do."[4] By 2010, Breuer was bragging about the government reaching a record twenty-three settlements with companies that altogether netted $1.8 billion in fines.

But at the very same time that the Holder Justice Department and Lanny Breuer were stepping up their enforcement of their version of the FCPA, the federal government itself was engaging in the very type of corruption that the law was intended to stop. As the *New York Times* reported in April 2013, "for more than a decade, wads of American dollars packed into suitcases, backpacks and, on occasion, plastic shopping bags have been dropped off every month or so at the offices of Afghanistan's president—courtesy of the Central Intelligence Agency."[5] The tens of millions of dollars that flowed into Afghanistan was called "ghost money" by Khalil Roman, President Hamid Karzai's deputy chief of staff from 2002 to 2005, because "it came in secret, and it left in secret." While the intent of the payments was to buy influence with Karzai, lawmakers, warlords, and bureaucrats, American officials quoted anonymously in the *New York Times* said that the cash has fueled corruption and that the United States was "the biggest source of corruption in Afghanistan."

Neither Breuer nor Holder has ever commented publicly on the fundamental unfairness of the Justice Department's push to "spread the gospel of anti-corruption" by punishing those in the private sector whose actions don't even come close to the outright bribery engaged in by the U.S. government. Apparently, the rules that apply to ordinary American citizens don't apply to government bureaucrats or the White House. Breuer and Holder are not spreading "the gospel of anti-corruption" to their boss, Barack Obama, or other parts of the federal government like the Central Intelligence Agency. These prosecutions have been particularly ironic when one compares the tens of millions of dollars in cash bribes paid by the administration to the "defining feature" of enforcement against private industry under Breuer—allegations over relatively minor "items as bottles of wine, watches, cameras, kitchen appliances, business suits, television sets, laptops, tea sets, and office furniture."[6]

What is almost as bad is that the Justice Department has threatened and intimidated many companies into settling claims under the FCPA. In fact, the Criminal Division's "success" in recent years has relied almost entirely on settlement agreements with corporations, exchanging an agreement "not to prosecute" for payment of a fine. These "Non-Prosecution Agreements" were reached by "risk-averse corporate actors" under "dubious legal theories that have never been subjected to judicial scrutiny."[7] Breuer defended the settlements by saying that without its new policy of avoiding criminal prosecutions with settlements, the government "faced a stark choice when it encountered a corporation that had engaged in misconduct—either indict or walk away."[8]

Well, of course. That is the choice government prosecutors *should* have—to indict or walk away. As Mike Koehler says, "Bringing criminal charges against a person (natural or legal) should not be easy. It should be difficult. Our founding fathers recognized this as a necessary bulwark against an all-powerful government, and there is no legal or policy reason warranting a change from such a fundamental and long-lasting principle."[9]

Insulating its behavior from judicial scrutiny makes it much easier for Justice Department prosecutors to abuse their authority because it puts them "in the role of prosecutor, judge and jury all at the same time."[10] Even former attorney general Alberto Gonzales has criticized these settlements, saying that "the more that American companies elect to settle and not force the DOJ to defend its aggressive interpretation of the Act, the more aggressive DOJ has become in its interpretation of the law and its prosecution decisions."[11]

In fact, when the Holder Justice Department has been forced into court, it has often suffered embarrassing defeats. Cases have been lost because of abusive behavior by its prosecutors and the FBI agents involved in the investigations, as well as accusations that the Justice Department withheld evidence and tried to mislead juries and courts. But while the targets of the Justice Department's unjustified prosecutions have been acquitted or had their convictions overturned, fighting the most powerful law enforcement agency in the country has ruined their businesses and bankrupted their personal lives.

One of the most graphic examples of these abusive FCPA prosecutions is the case that Lanny Breuer called "the largest single investigation and prosecution against individuals in the history of DOJ's enforcement of the FCPA." In what came to be known as the "Africa Sting" case, the Justice Department tried to prosecute twenty-two executives and employees in the military and law enforcement industry for supposedly trying to bribe the minister of defense of an African country. The prosecutions resulted from an FBI sting operation called Operation Landslide, in which FBI agents and a federal informant posed as the representatives of an allegedly corrupt Gabonese minister named Ali Bongo.[12]

The informant was Richard Bistrong, described as "a drug-addled former law enforcement equipment salesman."[13] Bistrong "had a $15,000 monthly cocaine habit and routinely had sex with prostitutes." The vice president of a police equipment company, he had been fired in 2007 when the company discovered that he had been bribing foreign officials and had accepted $1.3 million in kickbacks from suppliers.[14] After he pleaded guilty to a violation of the FCPA, he agreed to help the FBI in Operation Landslide. He tried to interest executives at other companies in a $12 million contract to supply equipment for the presidential guard of Gabon. Bistrong worked with a supposed Frenchman named Pascal Latour, who was really an FBI agent whose French accent was so bad it was described by a defense attorney "as sounding like Inspector Clouseau's in the 'Pink Panther' movies."[15]

As in prior sting operations like Abscam, which inspired the recent movie *American Hustle*, the FBI set up surveillance equipment in hotel rooms where Bistrong's meetings took place. But even though the sting was intended to catch executives who were willing to pay bribes to get the fake African business, neither Bistrong nor Latour ever "uttered the words 'bribe' or 'kickback'" in their description of the deal—they simply talked about the commission that would be required.[16] What further hurt the government's case was a series of embarrassing text messages eventually turned over to the defendants in which the FBI agents and Bistrong talk about sex, prostitutes, and booty calls, as well as their excitement about going to Las Vegas, where they were going to close "the deal."[17] One of the texts from FBI agent Michael Dubravetz told Bistrong he was going "to have a good time in Vegas the two days before" Bistrong got there and that he would probably be married by then "to a woman of ill repute!"

In the press conference announcing the indictments and the arrests in Las Vegas, Lanny Breuer could not contain his excitement, joking that "this is one case where what happened in Vegas doesn't stay in Vegas." He was right, but not in the way that he expected—what didn't stay in Vegas was the misbehavior of the FBI agents involved in the sting and the abusive behavior of the Justice Department prosecutors. The text messages revealed that the FBI agents and Bistrong "basked in the positive press" of Breuer's press conference, saying it was "like an atomic mushroom cloud" and speculating on who would play them in a movie based on the sting.[18]

Ultimately, after two lengthy, expensive trials, all of the defendants were either acquitted or had the indictments dismissed by the judge or the Justice Department because of the weakness of the government's case, and doubts raised about the credibility of Bistrong, the FBI, and DOJ. In fact, in a very unusual occurrence, one of the jury foremen, a nonpracticing attorney, posted an anonymous blog describing the many problems with the government's case. The jury "with near unanimity found nearly all of the prosecution witnesses to be evasive and combative." Moreover, the jury believed that the defendants in the case "had acted in good faith and the FBI/DOJ in bad faith." The jurors were concerned, as any reasonable person would be, that Bistrong, the government's main witness, had "freely admitted on the stand more illegal acts than the entire group of defendants was accused of, yet was able to plead only one count of conspiracy to violate the FCPA." "Prolonging this prosecution" would be "a waste of government resources," the jury foreman said.[19]

When the final charges were dismissed by the Justice Department after their stinging losses in court, Judge Richard Leon of the U.S. District Court for the District of Columbia called these prosecutions "a long and sad chapter in the annals of white-collar criminal enforcement." He criticized the "government's very, very aggressive conspiracy theory that was pushing its already generous elasticity to its outer limits." By the time of the second trial, "that elastic snapped in the absence of the necessary evidence" to support the government's claims. He also criticized the way the Justice Department had investigated the case and handled its informant, Richard Bistrong. Judge Leon accused government prosecutors of "sharp practices that have no place in a federal courtroom," which is a very critical comment by a federal judge.[20] However, such "sharp practices" seem to have become a common occurrence with government prosecutors and their "win-at-all-costs" attitude since Eric Holder became the attorney general.

Judge Leon also pointed out that "unlike takedown day in Las Vegas" and the big public relations campaign conducted by Breuer and the Justice Department, there would be "no front page story in the *New York Times* or the *Post* . . . reflecting the government's decision today to move to dismiss the charges against the remaining defendants in this case." Neither Lanny Breuer nor Eric Holder held a press conference to announce that their big prosecution had failed and that the claims they had made with great public fanfare were invalid. Nor did they make any public apologies or offer to reimburse the defendants for the enormous amounts they had spent defending themselves from an unjustified prosecution. And there is no indication that any of the lawyers or FBI agents involved were ever disciplined for their misbehavior.

Michael Madigan, a lawyer who represented one of the defendants, criticized the Justice Department for not recognizing that this "case was flawed from Day 1, both by its choice of a snitch (a despicable, dishonest 30 yr cocaine addict who admitted to taking kickbacks and stashed millions of dollars in Swiss bank accounts to avoid U.S. taxes), the 'it's all just a game' commentary from the agents who disrespected the rule of law, and the structuring of the 'sting' in its documents and taped conversations to make the Defendants think it was a legal transaction they were being asked to participate in." His client, John Godsey, wanted to know "how our Justice system could have gone so awry and where he goes to get his reputation and two full years of his life back!"[21]

The lawyers representing another defendant, Lee Allen Tolleson, blamed the government for pinning "its entire investigation on a despicable character, Bistrong, who manipulated Federal Agents throughout the investigation, in order to save his soul for his misdeeds. . . . Now, where does Lee go to get back his good name? He is from a small Arkansas town with a GED and has a home education. His family has been devastated financially by this process. Two things have kept him grounded: his faith in God and his family." [22]

Even with all of the travails suffered by the defendants, there was some poetic justice and final embarrassment for the Justice Department at the end of the case. Despite the Justice Department's request that Richard Bistrong, their cocaine-addicted informant, not receive any jail time for his violation of the FCPA, Judge Leon gave him an 18-month prison sentence. So the only person who ever went to jail in the Africa Sting case was the Justice Department's own informant and center of the fraudulent sting![23] Not quite the movie ending that the FBI agents and Bistrong imagined.

If this was the only "corruption" case involving the FCPA that Eric Holder had lost, one could put it down to the random throw of the dice one gets when conducting government prosecutions. Prosecutors sometime lose even good cases because of events they cannot necessarily control. But the Africa Sting case was just one of a number of similar cases that illustrate bad lawyering and misbehavior by Eric Holder's prosecutors working under Lanny Breuer. The Justice Department garnered a similar result in a criminal prosecution in Houston against John O'Shea, the general manager of the American subsidiary of ABB Ltd., an international company headquartered in Zürich, Switzerland, that provides technology and equipment in the utility industry.

The Justice Department claimed that O'Shea had made illegal payments through an intermediary to "foreign officials" at the

Comisión Federal de Electricidad, a Mexican utility supposedly owned by the Mexican government, in exchange for contracts with ABB.[24] But the Justice Department's case was so poorly put together that the federal judge assigned to the case, Lynn Hughes, dismissed it before it could even be considered by a jury. Judge Hughes was stinging in his criticism of the government, including that the Justice Department's key witness against O'Shea, the company's Mexican representative, Fernando Basurto, knew "almost nothing."

According to the judge, Basurto's answers "were abstract and vague, generally relating gossip."[25] The Justice Department couldn't even prove that the employees of the Mexican utility were foreign government officials, as is required under the FCPA. Judge Hughes said that the Justice Department "is supposed to know before it brings the indictment that it can prove" the governmental status of the individuals that the defendant supposedly bribed. Furthermore, the government and Basurto did not produce financial records that they were obligated to give O'Shea's lawyers. There was no real evidence that O'Shea had done anything other than pay the commissions due to Basurto as the sales representative of his company in Mexico, which the judge likened to "sort of like being a public relations officer."[26]

O'Shea was acquitted and the Justice Department's shoddy case thrown out, but the damage to O'Shea and his family was horrendous. He had been arrested "in the early morning darkness by armed federal agents who took him away in handcuffs," a completely unnecessary procedure for an accusation of financial improprieties and no violence.[27] There is absolutely no reason why the Justice Department could not have contacted O'Shea and his lawyers to notify them of the prosecution and the indictment. However, such a more temperate procedure would not have had the same publicity value for the Justice Department.

The business that O'Shea had conducted in Mexico was to provide an upgrade of the country's massive, outdated power grid. He was a married grandfather with two children who, because of this abusive prosecution, lost his job, his house, his savings, and many of his friends. There were sobs from his family members in court when Judge Hughes dismissed the charges and O'Shea said "it is like starting over."[28]

The unsuccessful prosecution of O'Shea illustrates another problem with the Justice Department's stepped-up use of nonprosecution settlements in FCPA cases. O'Shea's employer, ABB, was too intimidated by the Justice Department to fight the dubious charges in court and was apparently afraid of bad publicity. As a result, it settled with the Justice Department, agreeing to pay a hefty penalty and fine. The employee it fired and abandoned, John O'Shea, who had supposedly engaged in bribery, bankrupted himself fighting these false criminal charges in court and won, showing just how invalid and unfounded the case against ABB was.

After the acquittal, O'Shea's lawyer, Joel Androphy, made a key point that appears to have escaped Eric Holder and Lanny Breuer. Mexico is a country in which corruption is endemic and bribery is an accepted part of the culture, as it is in many other Third World countries. That is why the federal government and the CIA have a long history of paying bribes in foreign countries. As Androphy said, "deflecting blame for bribery in corruption-ridden countries onto unknowing business executives is both Cervantian and unfair." He hoped that O'Shea's victory would "encourage others wrongfully accused under the FCPA to fight the charges against them."[29]

As in other cases, none of the prosecutors at the Justice Department, including Eric Holder, ever apologized to O'Shea and his family for the hell they put him through. No press release was issued notifying the public and the media of the acquittal in the same way that the original indictment had been trumpeted by the Public Affairs Office of the Justice Department.

Shockingly, despite the obvious problems with the government's main witness, Fernando Basurto, Justice Department prosecutors tried to use him *again* in an entirely separate FCPA case that also involved the same Mexican utility, the Comisión Federal de Electricidad. In late 2010, the Justice Department indicted the Lindsey Manufacturing Company, Keith Lindsey (its president and CEO), and Steve Lee (its CFO), for supposedly paying bribes to utility officials through the commissions the company paid to its Mexican sales representative, who was also indicted along with his wife, Angela Maria Gomez Aguilar.

The trial took five weeks and the jury deliberated for only one day, convicting all of the defendants. Lanny Breuer himself boasted about the verdict in a Justice Department press release, calling the convictions an "important milestone" because Lindsey Manufacturing was "the first company to be tried and convicted on FCPA violations"; and he promised that it would "not be the last."[30]

However, a federal judge in California, A. Howard Matz, overturned the convictions and threw out the government's case, just like Judge Hughes had in Texas. Matz "excoriated the FBI agent and prosecutors in charge of the case for lying and withholding evidence, as well as misleading the jury and court."[31]

Judge Matz acknowledged an important point that is well known to government lawyers and private defense attorneys: DOJ lawyers are given enormous leeway in their conduct by judges. That is why it is so important that only the most ethical, professional, ideologically unbiased individuals are hired by the Justice Department—it is too easy for an unethical lawyer to take advantage of that leeway and use the enormous power of DOJ to ruin the lives of innocent Americans. As Matz said, "when faced with motions that allege government misconduct, most district judges are reluctant to find that the prosecutors' action were flagrant, willful or in bad faith."[32]

But in the Justice Department's prosecution of Lindsey Manufacturing, Judge Matz concluded:

> The Government team allowed a key FBI agent to testify untruthfully before the grand jury, inserted material falsehoods into affidavits submitted to magistrate judges in support of applications for search warrants and seizure warrants, improperly reviewed e-mail communications between one Defendant and her lawyers, recklessly failed to comply with its discovery obligations, posed questions to certain witnesses in violation of the Court's rulings, engaged in questionable behavior during closing argument and even made misrepresentations to the Court.[33]

It turned out that neither Keith Lindsey nor Steve Lee had ever had "anything to do with" their Mexican sales representative's wife, who was also a defendant in the government prosecution. They had "never met her or communicated in any way with" her—their supposed co-conspirator. Moreover, the government prosecutors tried to use Fernando Basurto, the flawed witness from the failed O'Shea case in Texas, as a witness against Lindsey Manufacturing. Basurto gave testimony that directly conflicted with testimony from the O'Shea case and Judge Matz became very angry at the prosecutors' suggestion to jurors that Keith Lindsey or Steve Lee "had any connection to Basurto or even knew anything about him." The prosecutors' claims "were not only misleading, but contrary" to the court's prior findings. The judge could not understand why the government had brought Basurto into the case:

> I think it's fair to say that in [his] testimony, Mr. Basurto testified before us about his role in an entirely different con-

> spiracy involving this company known as ABB. None of the defendants who is in this courtroom have been accused of any involvement in that conspiracy. None of the defendants in this courtroom have been accused of having any role whatsoever in that case. This case, in short, does not involve ABB. That's the other case.[34]

The only purpose served by bringing in Basurto was to try to prejudice the jury with stories about the corruption endemic in Mexico, even though he had absolutely no connection with Lindsey Manufacturing and knew nothing about the government's made-up case against the Lindsey defendants.

The long list of wrongdoing by the FBI agents and Justice Department prosecutors in this case cataloged by the judge is shocking and shows once again the apparent win-at-any-cost attitude that seems to have infected the Holder Justice Department. One of the prosecutors inserted a false statement into the affidavit of an FBI agent without consulting the agent, a false statement that was crucial to proving the government's case about payments supposedly being transferred between two organizations. That false statement was also used to obtain search warrants, resulting in what the judge called "unauthorized warrantless searches."

There were no transfer payments, yet the prosecutors also made the same claim to the grand jurors who issued the original indictments of the Lindsey defendants when they presented the testimony of one of the key FBI agents in the case, Susan Guernsey. Judge Matz detailed the "unfounded and erroneous portions" of Guernsey's grand jury testimony, saying that "perhaps she was [just] sloppy, or lazy, or ill-prepared by the prosecutive team."[35] But the prosecutors apparently realized she would be a poor witness and that the Justice Department's investigation was "terribly flawed," and so they did everything they could to keep Guernsey outside the courtroom and off the witness stand. They even refused to turn over her grand jury testimony to the defense, as well as exculpatory evidence from other witnesses, as was their obligation.

In another move that showed the depths to which the prosecutors were willing to sink in order to win the case, prosecutors put on another FBI agent, Dane Costley, to testify. Through his testimony, the government introduced a chart as an exhibit that supposedly showed that part of the payments made by Lindsey Manufacturing to another company, named Grupo, owned by defendant Enrique Aguilar, was used to pay the tuition of a private school of a Mexican utility executive. But Judge Matz discovered *after the trial was over* that in the O'Shea case, the Justice Department had "attributed the source of that very tuition payment" to a different company—not Lindsey Manufacturing. Since one of the very same prosecutors who had been involved in the O'Shea prosecution was on the trial team for the Lindsey case, this could not have been an inadvertent error. The court said the misleading link demonstrated "how far the government was willing to go" to obtain a conviction.

Matz was shocked at the behavior of the prosecutors over this conflicting testimony. He cited a prior Supreme Court case about how "serious questions are raised when the sovereign itself takes inconsistent positions in two separate criminal proceedings against two of its citizens." But this flatly contradictory testimony by government witnesses showed "just how far the Government was willing to go."

In an action reminiscent of the NSA eavesdropping scandal, the prosecutors obtained recordings from the U.S. Bureau of Prisons of the privileged telephone conversations and copies of emails between Ms. Aguilar and her defense lawyers. She was being kept in prison to prevent her flight back to Mexico (she had been arrested on a shopping trip in the United States). DOJ had obtained a warrant for her telephone conversations with her husband, who was still in Mexico and was being sought by federal authorities. But prosecutors also obtained the attorney-client communications and the emails, which were not covered by the warrant, and then lied to the court when they claimed they had been authorized to obtain all "communications" that Aguilar made from prison.

The Lindsey defendants would not have suffered through this outrageous prosecution if Eric Holder's prosecutors had been doing their jobs in the ethical and professional way they should have been. Prosecutors can certainly lose cases they believe are valid and credible and that had a thorough and effective investigation because they are, for some reason, unable to convince a jury that a particular defendant is guilty. The vagaries of the criminal justice system are something all lawyers are familiar with.

But according to Judge Matz, the government should have known from the very beginning that it did not have a credible case. The grand jury transcripts that the government improperly withheld from the defense lawyers "show that at the investigative stage the Government failed to consider a number of factors pointing to [the] innocence" of Lindsey Manufacturing and its executives.[36]

Some may question whether the prosecution simply made a series of unintentional errors. But there was no doubt in the mind of Judge Matz of the shamelessness of the government's actions:

> [H]ow could a prosecutor's insertion of a false statement in an FBI agent's affidavit not be flagrant? How could a prosecutor's failure to detect and correct numerous unfounded misstatements of an agent testifying under oath before a grand jury not be flagrant? How could the prosecution's obtaining of privileged communications between a Defendant and her attorney,

> followed by a misrepresentation about whether the Court had approved it, not be flagrant? Perhaps the Government's failures . . . were inadvertent, as the prosecution contended . . . but even those acts were clearly wrongful. They demonstrate, at best, that the Government was reckless in disregarding and failing to comply with its duties.[37]

The consequences of this "flagrant" misbehavior by Eric Holder's prosecutors were a "severe ordeal" for Keith Lindsey and Steve Lee. As Judge Matz pointed out, the "charges were filed against them as a result of a sloppy, incomplete and notably over-zealous investigation, an investigation that was so flawed that the Government's lawyers tried to prevent inquiry into it." The government attributed "motives, statements and conduct" to them "that were wholly unfounded or were obtained unlawfully." Even though the "financial costs of the investigation and trial were immense, the emotional drubbing these individuals absorbed undoubtedly was even worse." In fact, the judge indicated that "the very survival of that small, once highly respected enterprise has been placed in jeopardy."[38]

After this very embarrassing end to a case that Lanny Breuer had touted as "historic," the Justice Department at first filed an appeal. But in May 2012, it voluntarily withdrew its appeal without explanation and dropped its attempt to get $24 million from the company "in the form of asset forfeiture."[39] Although the judge threw out the case because it said that the Government team committed many wrongful acts and "should not be permitted to escape the consequences of that conduct," there is no indication that the Justice Department ever took any steps to discipline the lawyers or FBI agents involved in "flagrant" lies, misdeeds, and prosecutorial misconduct.

But then, that is no surprise in the Holder Justice Department.

What is also no surprise is that nowhere on the DOJ website can you find any mention of the dismissal of these (and other) FCPA prosecutions that the Justice Department has lost. As some have pointed out, President Obama has "championed transparency and open government." If that were really true, then the Justice Department and Eric Holder would "keep citizens informed of all FCPA developments—*not just those that cast the DOJ in a favorable light.*"[40] But informing the public of the numerous cases in which courts have found prosecutorial misconduct by Eric Holder's prosecutors would not be helpful to the image that Eric Holder has tried to cultivate with the public about his conduct as attorney general, or the historical view of his boss, Barack Obama, and his administration.

CHAPTER 10

WHAT IS TO BE DONE?

> The power to enforce the law, which carries with it the equally salient power not to enforce the law, is a president's most imposing domestic weapon—rivaled in importance only by the awesome authority (and potential for global mischief) inherent in a president's status as commander-in-chief of the U.S. Armed Forces.[1]
>
> —Andrew McCarthy, lead federal prosecutor against 1995 World Trade Center bombers

The evidence is clear that Eric Holder and his political subordinates have politicized the Justice Department to an unprecedented degree—"worse than John Mitchell under Richard Nixon," one former Justice Department lawyer told the authors. This is quite a criticism given that many DOJ veterans believe the department reached its nadir under Mitchell. But Mitchell seems like an amateur by comparison to how Holder has corrupted the law enforcement duties of the Justice Department to carry out the political objectives of Barack Obama and to implement his radical ideology.

The many cases in which judges have accused DOJ prosecutors of engaging in prosecutorial abuse during Holder's tenure show, unfortunately, how this high-level corruption has also seeped into the lower levels of the department. The political hiring into the civil service–protected career ranks that has gone on in parts of DOJ, such as the Civil Rights Division, guarantees that radical ideologues will continue to trouble the department long after Holder and his unethical, biased political appointee subordinates have left. Most political appointees leave when an administration ends, but appointees and their political allies who have burrowed down into career positions will be there for decades.

In 2001, one of the authors encountered such burrowed-in former Clinton administration political appointees when he first went to work at Justice as a career lawyer. They did everything they could to stop the implementation of the new administration's policies and law enforcement priorities, sabotaging, leaking, and generally engaging in unprofessional behavior that would get you fired if in the private sector. But as career employees, it was virtually impossible to fire them because of the civil service protections of federal law—even when they were totally incompetent. One longtime career lawyer in the Civil Division said that because it was so hard to fire even bad staff, he would regularly get them out of his area by promoting them—at which point they would become someone else's problem.

We cannot expect any help in remedying the unprofessional and politicized behavior of high-level Justice Department lawyers from the internal office at the department that is supposed to be the watchdog against unprofessional behavior: the Office of Professional Responsibility (OPR). OPR reports directly to Eric Holder, who has encouraged, directed, and approved this behavior. OPR's own website says it is "responsible for investigating allegations of misconduct involving Department attorneys that relate to the exercise of their authority to investigate, litigate or provide legal advice." But OPR is filled with biased lawyers who are often barely competent, and is headed by a hyper-Democratic loyalist, Robin Ashton, whom Holder installed on Christmas Eve 2010.

As one of the authors discovered when he worked at the Justice Department, besides being populated overwhelmingly by liberal Democrats, OPR is also full of lawyers that many in the Justice Department view as lacking the general level of professional competence found elsewhere in the frontline divisions within Justice. OPR has demonstrated on numerous occasions that it is incapable of handling politically charged issues in an even-handed manner. Nowhere was this shown more so than in the report it released in 2009 on its investigation of John Yoo and Jay Bybee, the Bush administration lawyers in the Office of Legal Counsel who wrote the memos analyzing the legality of the "enhanced interrogation techniques" that were used with certain terrorism suspects. OPR accused Yoo and Bybee of "unprofessional misconduct" for supposedly not providing "thorough, candid, and objective" legal advice.[2]

But the error-filled OPR report and its erroneous finding were flatly rejected by David Margolis, the Justice Department's most senior career official, a veteran lawyer with many decades of experience at Justice under many different administrations.[3] Attorney General Michael Mukasey (who was not at DOJ when the Office of Legal Counsel memos were written) and Deputy Attorney General Mark R. Filip also blasted OPR for attempting to deny basic due process to Yoo and Bybee by not giving them the opportunity to review the initial draft report.[4] This injustice was only corrected after Mukasey and Filip personally intervened to demand that OPR follow its own well-established procedures.

That initial draft report by OPR was leaked to the news media in "an unethical attempt to smear the reputations of [Yoo and Bybee] while they were under a gag order and unable to reply," an acute demonstration of the reprehensible behavior of the personnel in OPR.[5] Unfortunately, the same ambush tactic of not allowing an opportunity to review a draft report was used in OPR's prior investigations of the U.S. attorney firings and the faux scandal over supposed "politicized" hiring in the Civil Rights Division during the Bush administration.

In their memos, Yoo and Bybee had carefully outlined in great detail the legalities of a complex question in a very unsettled legal area shortly after the most devastating terrorist attack the United States had ever suffered. The men operated under what General Mukasey astutely characterized as "enormous time pressure" as the Bush administration was quickly "trying to formulate a plan to ensure that the Sept. 11, 2001 attacks would not be repeated." Yet OPR ignored this reality.

Indeed, the OPR lawyers assigned to the investigation made little effort to disguise their own left-leaning prejudices. It was thus no surprise that, as General Mukasey and Mark Filip noted, OPR's "investigation" was "based on factual errors, legal analysis by commentators and scholars with unstated potential biases, unsupported speculation about the motive of Messrs. Bybee and Yoo, and a misunderstanding" of significant interagency practices.

Some of OPR's criticisms were laughable. For example, the OPR attorneys accused Yoo and Bybee of professional misconduct for not citing a particular case from the Ninth Circuit Court of Appeals—an unpublished opinion. But the Ninth Circuit's own rules specify that unpublished opinions can't be cited by lawyers for any purpose. To do so would be an ethical violation. These types of repeated errors throughout the OPR report demonstrated a lack of basic competence by the OPR lawyers—the exact charge made by OPR against Yoo and Bybee.

To bolster its claim that Yoo and Bybee had "advanced novel legal theories" and "ignored relevant authority," the OPR attorneys prominently cited Professor David Luban of Georgetown University as an "expert." But they failed to mention that Luban isn't a lawyer, has never practiced law, has a doctorate in philosophy, and was a longtime critic of the Bush administration and the war on terror.

The OPR report even criticized Yoo and Bybee for not considering the moral implications of these issues, something that was very revealing about the biases of the OPR investigators and their lack of understanding of the duties of a lawyer. Yoo and Bybee had been tasked with providing pure legal analysis—not moral and social critiques. The Office of Legal Counsel is supposed to give legal advice "shorn of any policy preference or shading," as General Mukasey and Mr. Filip noted, so that senior policy makers at Justice and in the White House receive legal analysis that does not "mask discretionary policy preferences as legal requirements."

In other words, Yoo and Bybee were tasked with analyzing the legal issues involved—it was up to the White House and the president to decide the moral and policy questions about "enhanced interrogation techniques." Through its report, OPR was trying to criminalize the rendering of frank legal opinions on a complex and difficult issue of the law, and to damage the professional reputations of government lawyers who were valiantly performing their duties under the most difficult of circumstances, an outrageous and spiteful miscarriage of justice that was fortunately stopped by David Margolis. Even the release of the final report showed the "political nature" of the whole OPR attack on the former Bush administration lawyers—the Justice Department failed to release the highly critical letter that had been written by Mukasey and Filip on the OPR investigation.

None of the problems with the OPR report should have been a surprise. After all, the OPR's lead lawyer in the investigation was Tamara Kessler. She had also led the OPR investigation into the claims of "politicized" hiring in the Civil Rights Division during the Bush administration, despite the fact that she was a former Civil Rights Division lawyer who was friends with many of the individuals unfairly criticizing the Bush administration. That report was also laced with the same bias, inaccuracies, gross exaggerations, and misstatements of fact and law found in the OPR report on Yoo and Bybee.[6]

These reports were supervised by the head of OPR, H. Marshall Jarrett, a Holder protégé. Holder rewarded him with a reassignment to lead the Executive Office for U.S. Attorneys, a much more powerful position within the Justice Department, even though his behavior, according to the *Wall Street Journal*, made "him unfit for such a job."[7] Eric Holder saw an opportunity to put in a loyalist, someone who would make sure that, unlike in the Bush administration, there would be no critical reports filed about Holder during his tenure. This was also particularly important because at the time OPR was conducting an investigation into the dismissal of the New Black Panther Party voter intimidation case and the Civil Rights Division's hostility to race-neutral enforcement of the law.

Eric Holder had made no secret of his desire for a report that cleared his personnel of any wrongdoing. In the middle of this open investigation and only one week after he appointed Robin Ashton as the new head of OPR in December 2010, he told the *New York Times* that "there is no 'there' there" and that the Black Panther investigation was over a "made-up controversy."[8] Thus, Holder was improperly and unethically signaling to the lawyers in OPR and his new subordinate what their conclusion should be in their investigation—never mind what the facts uncovered.

It is true that Ashton was a career Justice Department lawyer and not a political appointee in the literal sense. But according to lawyers who worked with her at DOJ, she was also a highly political person who was so upset over George Bush's reelection in 2004 that she angrily vented her frustration to her colleagues in the Executive Office for U.S. Attorneys (EOUSA), where she was a deputy director. She requested that she be "detailed" to the office of Senator Patrick Leahy of Vermont, one of the fiercest and most partisan Democrats in the Senate.[9] The Justice Department acquiesced to her request and paid Ashton's salary while she worked in Leahy's office, helping him attack the Bush administration's Justice Department. As one Justice Department lawyer who worked with Ashton told one of the authors, "You don't do a detail with Patrick Leahy if you're not a committed, solid Democrat whose political loyalty Leahy would never question."

Ashton's bad reputation went beyond partisan grievance. Two former directors of EOUSA were interviewed in 2006 by the House Judiciary Committee during its investigation of the firing of nine U.S. attorneys. According to someone familiar with the entire transcripts of those interviews, the directors were scathing in their criticism of Ashton. They described Ashton as someone who treated subordinates like chattel while doing everything possible to ingratiate herself with her bosses, often claiming credit for work that others had done.

"Given her partisan instincts and the loyalty she feels to Eric Holder," one former DOJ lawyer told one of the authors at the time of her appointment, "there is no way that Robin Ashton will allow any report to come out that criticizes Eric Holder or his deputies." In fact, that prediction has turned out to be true. Despite all of the scandals enveloping Eric Holder's tenure as attorney general, the only public reports listed on the OPR website are reports critical of the Bush administration. No investigation has ever been opened by OPR over the complaints that Holder and other senior deputies have lied to Congress and made misrepresentations to other bodies, such as the U.S. Commission on Civil Rights, despite the fact that lying under oath is one of the most serious charges of misconduct that can be made against an attorney.

The New Black Panther Party report, which was completed under Ashton's watch, was a complete "whitewash of the malfeasance at the Civil Rights Division," according to J. Christian Adams, the whistle-blower and former Civil Rights Division lawyer who had filed the original voter intimidation lawsuit against the Panthers.[10] Ashton's report repeatedly accepted "versions of facts that defend Obama administration positions while dismissing facts to the contrary," without making any effort to verify the accuracy of the claims made against Holder and his subordinates.[11] So Holder got what he wanted out of Ashton. As Adams says, "the media entirely ignored" all of the mistakes, shortcomings, and misrepresentations in her report on the New Black Panthers and instead just reported that OPR had "cleared" Holder and other lawyers of any wrongdoing.[12]

The problems with the OPR lawyers and the conflict of interest inherent in having OPR's director report directly to the attorney general prompted the inspector general of the Justice Department, Michael Horowitz, in 2013 to ask that the Office of the Inspector General (OIG), rather than OPR, be given authority to investigate the misconduct of Justice lawyers. In his listing of top challenges facing the Justice Department, Horowitz said that the public's confidence in the department properly addressing employee misconduct could not be improved without eliminating the statutory limitation preventing the IG from handling these claims.

As Horowitz pointed out, the "institutional independence of the OIG . . . is crucial to the effectiveness of our misconduct investigations."[13] Unlike the IG, "OPR does not have that statutory independence," since the "Attorney General appoints and can remove OPR's leader," which power Eric Holder took great advantage of to ensure his inviolability as well as that of his minions inside the Justice Department.

OPR also keeps almost all of its investigations secret. Even though it files an annual report with Congress giving overall numbers of its investigations, it refuses to disclose the names of attorneys who have been found guilty of misconduct, in order "to protect the privacy of the Department attorneys," as if the public, judges, and defense lawyers have no right to know the details of government employees found guilty of wrongdoing.[14] This is an abuse of privacy standards and is information that should be made public. So OPR does not have the "strong record of transparency" that the IG has, and which Horowitz says is "vital to ensuring the Department's accountability and enhancing the public's confidence in the Department's operations."

The limitation on the IG has never been lifted and OPR remains the office at Justice responsible for investigating employee, and particularly lawyer, misconduct. So it is clear that there is no independent office inside the Justice Department that is willing to confront Eric Holder or any of his other top political subordinates over their wrongdoing and that of other lower-level lawyers. As long as they have the "correct" ideology and are carrying out the political directives and objectives of Holder and the Obama administration, they are protected, no matter what the law or professional codes of conduct require.

Lifting the statutory limitation on the IG could help alleviate some of these problems—as long as you have an IG who is willing to do something about such problems. Unfortunately, that is not always the case. The prior IG, Glenn Fine, was a Clinton administration appointee who demonstrated his bias on repeated occasions.[15] He released a joint report with OPR on the supposedly "politicized" hiring in the Civil Rights Division during the Bush administration just before Eric

Holder's confirmation hearing. That biased report was filled with inaccuracies, gross exaggerations, and misstatements of both facts and the law. Fine refused to investigate evidence with which his office had been provided about the politicized hiring that had occurred in the Civil Rights Division during the Clinton administration, when Holder was the deputy attorney general; particularly a successful effort to fill open career slots in the final days just before the swearing in of President George W. Bush on January 20, 2001. In fact, the IG who replaced Fine, Michael Horowitz, did investigate this particular claim and found that there was a concerted effort by Clinton political appointees to "fill vacant positions . . . on a highly expedited basis so as to be completed prior to the change in administration." The motivation was "to hire attorneys who favored the enforcement philosophy of the outgoing administration and to keep the hiring decision out of the hands of the incoming administration."[16]

The timing of Fine's report seemed aimed at providing maximum political benefit to Fine's fellow Democrats in their effort to get Holder quickly confirmed without any opposition, despite Holder's misfeasance during his prior stint at Justice, particularly when it came to pardons. So giving the Office of the Inspector General the ability to investigate unprofessional conduct will work only if you truly have an independent IG willing to fulfill his or her duty. That has not always been the case, as the difference between Fine and Horowitz demonstrates.

One abuse that can be somewhat alleviated is the ability of the Justice Department to conspire with its political allies and agree to collusive settlement agreements and consent decrees with advocacy groups. These voluntary settlements of litigation are intended to get around limitations on statutory authority, to "short-circuit normal agency rulemaking procedures, to accelerate rulemaking in ways that constrain the public's ability to participate in a meaningful fashion, and to do an end-run around the inherently political process of setting governmental priorities."[17]

The Reagan administration demonstrated how to do this in 1986. Reagan's attorney general, Edwin Meese III, was very concerned about the "Carter Administration's abuse of consent decrees, and the courts' willingness to hold the government to agreements that bound the Reagan Administration to its predecessor's unwise policy choices."[18] Meese issued a memorandum implementing a policy intended to severely limit the ability of Justice lawyers to agree to such collusive, secret settlements.[19] Meese pointed out that the executive branch has "misused" such settlements and "forfeited the prerogatives of the Executive in order to preempt the exercise of those prerogatives by a subsequent Administration." They were also used to provide "an unwarranted expansion of the powers of the judiciary," since they allowed judges to approve settlements that went far beyond what the government was required—or allowed—to do. And they often gave judges the ability to order the executive branch to spend money to support the requirements of the settlement, usurping the role of Congress in deciding how to spend taxpayer funds.

Meese's memorandum specified that the Justice Department could not enter into agreements that limited or interfered in the ability of federal agencies to "revise, amend, or promulgate regulations." It also could not agree to make any commitment to spend "funds that Congress has not appropriated and that have not been budgeted," or to lobby Congress to seek a particular appropriation. DOJ could not agree to divest federal agencies of the authority to make decisions that were committed to the agency "by Congress or the Constitution." Finally, DOJ could not agree to a consent decree or settlement agreement that provided relief or a remedy that went beyond what a federal statute or regulation authorized or beyond what a court could order if the case had gone to trial and judgment.

Unfortunately, the Clinton administration "substantially relaxed the Department's policy"[20] after it decided it did not want to be legally bound by the lines drawn in the Meese memorandum.[21] The Obama administration and Eric Holder have clearly entirely ditched Attorney General Meese's approach because it limits the administration's ability to expand federal power or to help its liberal allies in the advocacy world. The only way to stop this is to implement the restrictions in a federal statute that cannot be "relaxed" by the attorney general. An attorney general could certainly try to ignore such a federal law, but its existence would provide a cause of action to those wanting to challenge a settlement that the Justice Department agreed to that violated the law—and judges would be aware that they could not approve such settlement agreements.

The secrecy of the backroom deals that Holder and his cronies have entered into could also be limited through action by Congress in the same statute that implements the Meese guidelines. It could require agencies like the EPA to publish copies of lawsuits they are involved in on their website and in the *Federal Register* in the same way proposed new regulations are published so that the public and other watchdogs become aware of the litigation. If the federal agency and the Justice Department decide to settle the lawsuit or enter into a consent decree, they should be required to publish the proposed settlement in the same manner, with a restriction that they can't actually agree to the settlement for some period of time, such as sixty days, in order to give the public, businesses, and anyone else who will be affected by the settlement time to file public comments with the agency, DOJ, and/or the court—just as happens with proposed regulations. And the federal agency should be forced to file a pleading in the court explaining whether or not it has taken into account those public comments in revising the settlement agreement, and if not, why not.

In essence, Congress should require that all of the rules—including the extensive time limits—that apply to agency regulatory rule-making in the Administrative Procedure Act will apply to any potential regulatory rule-making that is done through litigation. These are the kinds of requirements that have been proposed in a bill introduced in Congress in 2013, the Sunshine for Regulatory Decrees and Settlements Act.[22]

Congress should also implement legislation that specifically says that one administration cannot bind a future administration through these types of settlement agreements and consent decrees. In other words, if the federal government wants to modify or end such an agreement "on the grounds that it is no longer in the public interest," courts should be directed to review that request de novo[23]—meaning as if it is a brand-new case, without requiring the government to be bound by what happened previously in the litigation.

Another change that Congress could make to increase the transparency of these types of settlements—and particularly the payment of attorneys' fee by DOJ to advocacy organizations—would be to require much more detailed information from the Justice and Treasury departments about such payouts. One of the little-known costs that taxpayers unwittingly pay is the Judgment Fund, administered by the Treasury Department. This fund is used to pay "judicially and administratively ordered monetary awards against the United States" when it loses lawsuits, as well as settlements by the government of threatened or actual lawsuits. It is a permanent, indefinite appropriation that literally pays out with little notice billions of dollars for mistakes, errors, and claimed violations of federal law committed by federal agencies and federal employees.

The Treasury Department does file a yearly report with Congress and maintains a Web page that can be searched. But the cryptic and limited information available in the report and on the Web page is not sufficient to identify what it was that the government did wrong, how the case was settled and why, and who is benefiting from these government payments. The name of the federal agency that was a defendant in the litigation or claim is identified, but not the plaintiff—or the attorneys—who brought the action. The statute or regulation that was the basis of the claim is listed, but there is not even a brief description of what exactly the dispute was about or what violation was supposedly committed by the federal government.

No copy of the complaint, judgment against the government, or settlement agreement is made available. This could easily be provided through a hyperlink that would allow anyone to click on these documents and obtain the details of the lawsuits. Taxpayers deserve to know all of the details of how the Judgment Fund is being spent, something that is not currently possible. There is no ability, for example, to determine whether government agencies are engaging in collusive litigation with certain plaintiffs and advocacy organizations, settling claims that should not be settled, and making payments to plaintiffs and their attorneys that are not reasonable under the applicable law and facts.

There was a bill introduced in Congress in 2013 by Representative Cory Gardner (R-CO) and Senator Deb Fischer (R-NE) that would accomplish this, the Judgment Fund Transparency Act of 2013, but it has not moved.[24] That is unfortunate because this is really not a partisan issue. Regardless of their party affiliation, members of Congress should be interested in requiring greater transparency of payments made to cover liability arising from the actions of federal employees and federal agencies. But then, perhaps Senator Harry Reid and others like him don't really want the public to know what the Holder Justice Department is doing or how much it is paying off its political friends and allies (and their lawyers) using taxpayer money.

Unfortunately, however, none of these changes could have done anything to prevent many of the other problems that have been caused in the Justice Department by Eric Holder's contempt for the rule of law, his willingness to push unwarranted prosecutions, his politicized decision making, his readiness to mislead and ignore Congress, and his disastrous policies, on issues from civil rights to national security, that have endangered the freedom, prosperity, and safety of the American people. A number of veterans of the Justice Department that the authors spoke with were unable to suggest any structural or statutory changes that can prevent a bad attorney general from abusing the power that office conveys.

Edwin Meese III has a very gentlemanly policy, which has been followed by most attorneys general over the years, of not commenting on the performance of specific attorneys general, and he was unwilling to provide an assessment of Eric Holder in an interview. But when asked about the possibility of structural or statutory changes to the Justice Department, he said that there really was no substitute for "making sure good people are elected who will appoint good people to offices within the executive branch," like the Office of the Attorney General.[25]

Congress has the ultimate power of impeachment, but has almost never exercised it generally and has never exercised it at all with regard to the attorney general. In fact, only nineteen federal officials have been impeached in the entire history of the country, eight of them federal judges. The last one was former Louisiana federal judge Thomas Porteous in 2010.[26] Of course, Eric Holder is the first attorney general to be held in contempt by the House of Representatives.

Meese said that his experience at the Justice Department showed him that bad behavior within the department is an "aberration and exception to the general rule." The Justice Department is "by and large a well-run operation and most of the divisions are not ideological in their law enforcement."[27] The real checks on the behavior of the department, according to Meese, are "Congress, through both appropriations and congressional oversight hearings—which it needs to vigorously exercise—and public opinion." He says that public opinion is a very important factor in itself that can be used to promote professional, nonbiased behavior at the Justice Department.

Even liberal commentators have criticized Holder, with the *New Republic* saying that Holder's reputation "is more damaged than he ever could have imagined."[28] The Office of Attorney General "has a fundamental conflict embedded in its mandate: It is required to both take orders from and investigate the White House."[29] Many attorneys general, like Griffin Bell, Edwin Meese, and Michael Mukasey, have handled this potential conflict with professionalism and the highest regard for the best interests of the public and their sworn duty to uphold the Constitution and the laws of the United States. Others, like Eric Holder, have put the interests of their political master—and their particular political views—first.

This has meant that while Barack Obama and his attorney general have publicly tried to "maintain the veneer of respect for legal processes," they have in reality worked to "stretch or break the rules whenever necessary to achieve the desired outcome—social justice being a higher form of legitimacy than society's rule of law."[30] In fact, both the president and the attorney general seem to have taken to heart President Andrew Jackson as their exemplar. In *Worcester v. Georgia* in 1832, the U.S. Supreme Court upheld the independence of the Cherokee Indians.[31] Jackson ignored the Supreme Court's decision, forcing a treaty on them that led to the forcible removal of the Cherokees from Georgia, what became known as the Trail of Tears. Jackson is said to have responded, "John Marshall has made his decision; now let him enforce it!"[32] Holder and Obama have shown the very same contemptuous attitude toward laws passed by

Congress that they don't want to enforce. And Holder has aggressively used the enormous power and plentiful resources of the Justice Department to abuse the liberty and economic rights of Americans, to manipulate racial politics to drive a wedge of hostility deep into the heart of our society, and to exploit the administration of justice as a political tool to benefit his president and his political party.

Under Eric Holder, the Justice Department has become:

> "[A] sort of full employment program for progressive activists, race-obsessed bean counters (redundant I know), and lawyers who volunteered their services during the Bush years to help al-Qaeda operatives file lawsuits against the United States."[33]

There is no way to know how long it will take to repair the damage that Eric Holder has done to the management and operation of the Justice Department. One thing we do know for sure—it will take a great deal of work by a new attorney general who is willing to take on the activists that Holder will leave embedded within the career civil service ranks of the department. And it will take political willpower and steadfastness of a kind that is rarely seen in Washington.

Whether that happens at all will depend on who is president, because it is the president who decides on the character, attributes, and competence of the individual chosen to be the head of the largest law enforcement organization in the United States. And it is the president who decides whether his administration—and his attorney general—will fulfill their obligation to "faithfully execute" their duty to enforce the law and "preserve, protect and defend the Constitution of the United States."

NOTES

Chapter 1: Justice in Charge

1. "Journalists or Criminals? Attorney General Eric Holder's Testimony before the Committee and the Justice Department's National Security Leak Investigative Techniques," Committee on the Judiciary, House of Representatives, July 31, 2013, Executive Summary.
2. Ibid.
3. "Krauthammer's Take: Holder Won't Be Punished," *National Review Online*, July 31, 2013.
4. Bill Otis, "The Bordering on Silly Defense of Eric Holder," crimeandconsequences.com, June 2, 2013.
5. Matthew Boyle, "Holder Less than Candid on Fast and Furious," *Daily Caller*, Oct. 4, 2011.
6. Matthew Boyle, "Holder Claims His Testimony Was Accurate Pushes Back Against 'Inflammatory Rhetoric,'" *Daily Caller*, Oct. 7, 2011.
7. Matthew Boyle, "During Senate Testimony Holder Changes Misleading Testimony from May Hearing," *Daily Caller*, Nov. 8, 2011.
8. "Justice Withdraws Inaccurate Fast and Furious Letter It Sent to Congress," NPR Blog, The Two Way, Dec. 2, 2011.
9. Mackenzie Weinger, "Ted Cruz, Eric Holder Mix It Up At Hearing," *Politico*, Jan. 29, 2014.
10. Daniel Klaidman, "Attorney General May Probe Bush Torture Policy," *Newsweek*, March 13, 2010.
11. Joel Gehrke, "Attorney General Holder Can't Explain Constitutional Basis for Obama's Executive Orders," *Washington Examiner*, Jan. 29, 2014.
12. Interview with Senator Ted Cruz, Jan. 20, 2014.
13. Bridget Johnson, "Holder Confirms Obama Ready to Use Executive

Order on Guns 'in Absence of Meaningful Action' by Congress," PJ Media, Jan. 29, 2014.

14. Dylan Byers, "Jill Abramson: 'This is the most secretive White House I have ever dealt with,'" *Politico*, Jan. 23, 2014.
15. Daniel Klaidman, "Attorney General May Probe Bush Torture Policy," *Newsweek*, March 13, 2010.
16. Andrew Longstreth, "Making History with Obama," *American Lawyer*, June 5, 2008.
17. Keith Herbert, "Likely Obama Pick's NY Roots," *Newsday*, Nov. 22, 2008.
18. Longstreth, "Making History with Obama."
19. Ibid.
20. Ibid.
21. Ibid.
22. Wil S. Hylton, "Hope. Change. Reality.," *GQ*, Dec. 2010.
23. Javier C. Hernandez, "Poised to Scale New Heights," *New York Times*, Nov. 30, 2008
24. Hylton, "Hope. Change. Reality."
25. Longstreth, "Making History with Obama."
26. Hernandez, "Poised to Scale New Heights"; Charles C. Johnson and Ryan Girdusky, "As College Student, Eric Holder Participated in 'Armed' Takeover of Former Columbia University ROTC Office," *Daily Caller*, Sept. 30, 2012.
27. Hylton, "Hope. Change. Reality."
28. Interview with Craig Donsanto, Dec. 19, 2013.
29. Daniel Klaidman, "Attorney General May Probe Bush Torture Policy," *Newsweek*, March 13, 2010.
30. Ibid.
31. Annie Groer, "Sharon Malone, Eric Holder's Wife, to Appear in PBS Special 'Slavery by Another Name,'" *Washington Post*, Feb. 10, 2012.
32. Dayo Olopade, "Eric Holder's War," *American Prospect*, Jan. 31, 2010, citing *Essence*.
33. Daniel Klaidman, "Independent's Day," *Newsweek*, July 11, 2009.
34. "Eric Holder Profile", NPR *All Things Considered*, Sept. 30, 1997.
35. *Grutter v. Bollinger*, 539 U.S. 306 (2003).
36. John Fund, "Infinite Affirmative Action?" *National Review*, March 6, 2012.
37. Eddie Dean, "Almost Blue—Carl T. Rowan, Jr. Walks a Self-Assigned Beat of D.C. Police Corruption," *Washington City Paper*, Jan. 23, 1998.
38. *U.S. v. Popa*, 187 F.3d 672, 673-674 (D.C. Cir. 1999).
39. Popa, 187 F.3d at 675.

40. Popa, 187 F.3d at 677.
41. Interview with Eugene Volokh, Jan. 4, 2014.
42. Eugene Volokh, "One-to-One Speech vs. One-to-Many Speech, Criminal Harassment Laws, and Cyberstalking," 107 *Northwestern University Law Review* 731, 744 (2013).
43. David S. Cloud and Gary Fields, "Aided by Millions in Gifts, an Insider Gets His Client Presidential Absolution," *Wall Street Journal*, Jan. 29, 2001.
44. Siri Agrell, "Holder Likely to Reform Justice Department" *Globe and Mail*, Nov. 19, 2008.
45. Andrew Longstreth, "Making History with Obama," *American Lawyer*, June 5, 2008.
46. Ibid.
47. Wil S. Hylton, "Hope. Change. Reality.," *GQ*, Dec. 2010.
48. David Johnston, "The New Team: Eric H. Holder Jr.," *New York Times*, Nov. 11, 2008.
49. Longstreth, "Making History with Obama."
50. Ibid.
51. Hylton, "Hope. Change. Reality."
52. Ibid.
53. "FY 2013 Budget Summary," U.S. Department of Justice.
54. "Total Discretionary Budget Authority and Authorized Positions—FY 2003—FY 2013," U.S. Department of Justice.
55. That would not be possible today because in 1967, Congress passed the Federal Anti-Nepotism statute to prevent the hiring of relatives by federal officials. See 5 U.S.C. § 3110. This is sometimes referred to as the "Kennedy Act." See *Association of Am. Physicians & Surgeons v. Clinton*, 813 F.Supp. 82, 87 n.8 (D. D.C. 1993), rev'd, 997 F.2d 898 (D.C. Cir. 1993).
56. "DOJ Seal—History and Motto," www.justice.gov/jmd/ls/dojseal.htm.
57. Interview with Christopher Coates, Jan. 28, 2014.

Chapter 2: Gibson Guitar's Green Raid

1. Andy Meek, "Gibson CEO Fires Back over Federal Raid," *Memphis Daily News*, Aug. 26, 2011.
2. Deborah Zabarenko, "Gibson Guitar CEO Slams U.S. Raids as 'Overreach,'" Reuters, Oct. 12, 2011.
3. Meek, "Gibson CEO Fires Back Over Federal Raid."
4. Zabarenko, "Gibson Guitar CEO Slams U.S. Raids as 'Overreach.'"
5. "Gov't Says Wood is Illegal if U.S. Workers Produce It," Gibson Press Release, Aug. 25, 2011.

6. Craig Havighurst, "Why Gibson Guitar Was Raided by the Justice Department," NPR, Aug. 31, 2011.
7. James C. McKinley Jr., "Gibson Guitar Settles Claim Over Imported Ebony," *New York Times*, Aug. 6, 2012.
8. Letter of July 27, 2012, from Jerry Martin, U.S. Attorney for the Middle District of Tennessee, to Donald A. Carr, Pillsbury, Winthrop, Shaw Pittman.
9. As the settlement agreement explained, a fingerboard is also called a fretboard and "is the piece attached to the neck of the guitar, immediately under the strings." There are even pictures of fretboards and fingerboard blanks and it is probably the first time in the history of the Justice Department that a settlement of criminal charges had to explain the construction of a guitar.
10. Paul J. Larkin Jr., "Gibson Guitar: Settling Away Bad Publicity," The Foundry at The Heritage Foundation, Aug. 7, 2012.
11. "Now the Gibson Guitar Raids Make Sense," *Investor's Business Daily*, May 23, 2013.
12. Anita Wadhwani, "Gibson Guitar CEO to Face Feds over Raid on Factory," *Tennessean*, Sept. 15, 2011.
13. Ibid.
14. Larkin, "Gibson Guitar: Settling Away Bad Publicity."
15. "Now the Gibson Guitar Raids Make Sense," *Investor's Business Daily*, May 23, 2013.
16. Eric Felten, "Guitar Frets: Environmental Enforcement Leaves Musicians in Fear," *Wall Street Journal*, Aug. 26, 2011.
17. Ibid.
18. Wadhwani, "Gibson Guitar CEO to Face Feds over Raid on Factory."
19. See http://www2.gibson.com/Products/Electric-Guitars/Les-Paul/Gibson-USA/Government-Series-II-Les-Paul.aspx.
20. See www.justice.gov/enrd/.
21. Kimberly A. Strassel, "Greens Gone Wild," *Wall Street Journal*, April 9, 2013.
22. Ibid.
23. *Evans v. U.S.*, 694 F.3d 1377, 1381 (Fed. Cir. 2012).
24. See *Preseault v. Interstate Commerce Commission*, 494 U.S. 1 (1990) and *Preseault v. U.S.*, 100 F.3d 1525, Fed. Cir. 1996)(en banc). In 2014, the Supreme Court ruled against the government again in *Marvin M. Brandt Revocable Trust v. U.S.*, 572 U.S. ___(2014).
25. Cecilia Fex, "The Elements of Liability in a Trails Act Taking: A Guide to the Analysis," 38 *Ecol. L. Q.* 673, 676 (2011).
26. Ibid.

27. *Ladd v. U.S.*, 713 F.3d 648
28. Thor Hearne interview with Hans von Spakovsky, Dec. 30, 2013.
29. *Hash v. U.S.*, No. 1:99-CV-00324-MHW, 2012 WL 1252624 (D. Idaho April 13, 2012).
30. Thor Hearne interview with Hans von Spakovsky, Dec. 30, 2013.
31. "Environmental Litigation: Cases Against the EPA and Associated Costs Over Time," U.S. Government Accountability Office, GAO-11-650, Aug. 2011.
32. "GAO Report Exposes Millions in Environmental Litigation Fees for First Time," U.S. Senate Committee on Environment and Public Works, Press Release, Aug. 31, 2011.
33. 5 U.S.C. § 553.
34. 5 U.S.C. § 553(b)(2).
35. "A Report on Sue and Settle—Regulating Behind Closed Doors," U.S. Chamber of Commerce, May 2013, p. 5.
36. Ibid, p. 12.
37. Julian Hattern, "Greens, Industry Spar Over 'Sue and Settle,'" *Hill*, Nov. 22, 2013.
38. "A Report on Sue and Settle—Regulating Behind Closed Doors," U.S. Chamber of Commerce, May 2013, pp. 6–7.
39. Ibid, p. 3.
40. "Presidential Memorandum—Flexible Implementation of the Mercury and Air Toxics Standards Rule," Office of the Press Secretary, White House, Dec. 21, 2011.
41. "EPA Admits Error in Proposed Mercury MACT Rule," *Power Magazine*, May 25, 2011.
42. Ibid.
43. "Potential Impacts of Future Environmental Regulations," North American Electric Reliability Corporation, Nov. 2011.

Chapter 3: A Contempt for the Constitution and the Rule of Law

1. Testimony of Jonathan Turley, U.S. House of Representatives, Committee on the Judiciary, Dec. 3, 2012.
2. Carrie Johnson, "Some in Justice Department See D.C. Vote in House as Unconstitutional," *Washington Post*, April 1, 2009.
3. See *Adams v. Clinton*, 90 F. Supp. 2d 35, 46-47 (D. D.C. 2000), aff'd 531 U.S. 941 (2000); Kenneth R. Thomas, "The Constitutionality of Awarding the Delegate for the District of Columbia a Vote in the House of Representatives or the Committee of the Whole," Congressional Research Service RL 33824, Jan. 24, 2007.

4. Testimony of John P. Elwood, Deputy Assistant Attorney General, Office of Legal Counsel, Department of Justice, U.S. Senate Judiciary Committee, May 23, 2007.
5. Johnson, "Some in Justice Department See D.C. Vote in House as Unconstitutional."
6. Edward Whelan, "Look Who's Politicizing Justice Now," *Washington Post*, April 5, 2009.
7. Carrie Johnson, "D.C. Vote Memo Called Informal," *Washington Post*, April 3, 2009.
8. Whelan, "Look Who's Politicizing Justice Now."
9. Ibid.
10. Dan Eggen and Paul Kane, "Gonzales Hospital Episode Detailed," *Washington Post*, May 16, 2007.
11. Evan Perez, "A Pick for Sensitive Justice Post," *Wall Street Journal*, Dec. 22, 2010.
12. "Lawfulness of Recess Appointments During a Recess of the Senate Notwithstanding Periodic Pro Forma Sessions," Memorandum Opinion for the Counsel to the President, Assistant Attorney General Virginia A. Seitz, Office of Legal Counsel, U.S. Department of Justice, Jan. 6, 2012.
13. As this book was being written, the issue was before the U.S. Supreme Court in *National Labor Relations Board v. Noel Canning*.
14. Michael McConnell, "The OLC Opinion on Recess Appointments," www.advancingafreesociety.org, Jan. 12, 2012.
15. Edwin Meese III and Todd Gaziano, "Obama's Recess Appointments are Unconstitutional," *Washington Post*, Jan. 5, 2012.
16. Todd Gaziano, "Whitewash on Illegal Appointments Won't Work," The Foundry, Heritage Foundation, Jan. 12, 2012.
17. Ibid.
18. Lachlan Markay, "Grassley Not Buying DOJ's Non-Recess Appointment Apologia," The Foundry, Heritage Foundation, Jan. 12, 2012.
19. Seth McLaughlin, "Obama Administration has Lost Two-Thirds of Supreme Court Cases," *Washington Times*, June 26, 2013.
20. 132 S.Ct. 694 (2012).
21. 132 S.Ct. 1367 (2012).
22. Sen. Ted Cruz, Ranking Member, Senate Judiciary Subcommittee on the Constitution, Civil Rights and Human Rights, "The Legal Limit: The Obama Administration's Attempts to Expand Federal Power," Nov. 2013.
23. Paul J. Larkin Jr., "*Sackett v. EPA*: Supreme Court Takes Up Property Rights Case," Heritage Foundation Foundry, Jan. 9, 2012.
24. 132 S.Ct. 945 (2012).

25. 133 S.Ct. 511 (2012).
26. Ted Cruz, "The Legal Limit."
27. 133 S.Ct. 1216 (2012).
28. 132 S.Ct. 2492 (2012).
29. 18 U.S.C. § 1373(c).
30. *PPL Corp. v. Commissioner of Internal Revenue*, 133 S.Ct. 1897 (2013).
31. *Horne v. USDA*, 133 S.Ct. 2053 (2013).
32. *Sekhar v. U.S.*, 133 S.Ct. 2720 (2013).
33. Ilya Shapiro, "Why Obama Keeps Losing at the Supreme Court," Bloomberg, June 6, 2013.
34. 558 U.S. 310 (2010).
35. Transcript of *Citizens United v. Federal Election Commission*, Case No. 08-205 (March 24, 2009), pp. 28–30.
36. Testimony of Jonathan Turley, U.S. House of Representatives Committee on the Judiciary, Dec. 3, 2012.
37. Ibid.
38. Nathan Vardi, "Department of Justice Flip-Flops on Internet Gambling," *Forbes*, Dec. 23, 2011.
39. Matt Smith, "Stop Eric Holder's Online Gambling Push," *Daily Caller*, May 21, 2012.
40. Wynton Hall, "Eric Holder's DOJ Legalizes Online Gambling; Donors and Friends Make Big Money," Breitbart, Aug. 7, 2012.
41. Ibid.
42. Testimony of Jonathan Turley, U.S. House of Representatives Committee on the Judiciary, Dec. 3, 2012.
43. Letter of Deputy Attorney General David Ogden to Selected United States Attorneys, Investigations and Prosecutions in States Authorizing the Medical Use of Marijuana, Oct. 19, 2009.
44. The Controlled Substances Act has been upheld by the Supreme Court in *Gonzales v. Raich*, 545 U.S. 1 (2005).
45. Evan Perez, "No Federal Challenge to Pot Legalization in Two States," CNN, Aug. 30, 2013.
46. Sari Horwitz, "Holder Seeks to Avert Mandatory Minimum Sentences for Some Low-Level Drug Offenders," *Washington Post*, Aug. 11, 2013.
47. Testimony of Jonathan Turley, U.S. House of Representatives Committee on the Judiciary, Dec. 3, 2012.
48. Bill Otis, "Hundreds of Career Prosecutors Revolt Against Holder," www.crimeandconsequences.com, Jan. 30, 2014.
49. "Top Management and Performance Challenges Facing the Department of Justice—2013," Memorandum from Michael E. Horowitz for

the Attorney General, the Deputy Attorney General, Office of the Inspector General, U.S. Department of Justice, Dec. 11, 2013, reissued Dec. 23, 2013.

50. Jeffrey Toobin, "A Sharp Progressive Joins the D.O.J.," *New Yorker*, Dec. 20, 2013.
51. J. Christian Adams, "Meet the Dishonest Radical Academic Eric Holder Tapped to Oversee Federal Election Law," PJ Tatler, Dec. 20, 2013.
52. "Peter Baker, "Favorites of Left Don't Make Obama's Court List," *New York Times*, May 25, 2009.
53. Pamela S. Karlan, "Lessons Learned: Voting Rights and the Bush Administration," 4 *Duke J. Const. L. & Pub. Pol'y* 17, 28 (2009).
54. John Fund and Hans von Spakovsky, *Who's Counting? How Fraudsters and Bureaucrats Put Your Vote at Risk* (New York: Encounter Books, 2012), p. 108.
55. Ed Whelan, "Pamela Karlan, Anti-Textualist Fantasist," *National Review Online*, Oct. 20, 2013.
56. Carl Rowan Jr., "Adegbile Utterly Unfit for Justice's Civil Rights Post," *Washington Times*, Jan. 22, 2014.
57. "The Attorney General's Duty to Defend and Enforce Constitutionally Objectionable Legislation," 4A O. O.L.C. 55 (1980).
58. Drew S. Days III, "In Search of the Solicitor General's Clients: A Drama with Many Characters," 83 K.Y.L.J. 485, 502 (1995).
59. Defendant's Motion to Dismiss at 25, *Smelt v. U.S.*, Case No. 09-00286 (C.D. Cal. 2009).
60. Testimony of Jonathan Turley, U.S. House of Representatives Committee on the Judiciary, Dec. 3, 2012.
61. *U.S. v. Windsor*, 570 U.S. ___(2013), Slip Op. at 12.
62. "Supreme Court Puts Utah Same-Sex Marriage on Hold," CBS News, Jan. 6, 2014.
63. Ed Whelan, "AG Holder's Lawless Action on Marriage in Utah," Bench-Memos, *National Review Online*, Jan. 10, 2014.
64. Ibid.
65. Elizabeth H. Slattery and Andrew Kloster, "An Executive Unbound: the Obama Administration's Unilateral Actions," Heritage Foundation Legal Memorandum No. 108 (Feb. 12, 2014).

Chapter 4: The (Un)Civil Rights Division

1. Byron York, "Obama's Zealous Civil Rights Enforcer," Townhall.com (Aug. 9, 2010).
2. *U.S. v. Bowen*, Case. No. 10-204 (E.D. LA. Sept. 17, 2013).

3. Perez was confirmed as the new secretary of the Department of Labor in July 2013 despite his radical record.
4. Byron York, "Obama's Zealous Civil Rights Enforcer Gets Busy," *Washington Examiner*, Aug. 6, 2010.
5. Wil S. Hylton, "Hope, Change, Reality.," *GQ*, Dec. 2010.
6. "A Review of the Operations of the Voting Section of the Civil Rights Division," Office of the Inspector General, U.S. Dept. of Justice, March 2013.
7. Chuck Neubauer, "Taxpayers Financed Justice Official's Romantic Travel," *Washington Times*, Oct. 5, 2011. This employee was not asked to pay back the money he embezzled and he was given a bonus to agree to an early retirement.
8. Hans A. von Spakovsky, "Revenge of the Liberal Bureaucrats," *Weekly Standard*, January 23, 2009.
9. "Justice Department Bids to Trap Poor, Black Children in Ineffective Schools," *Washington Post*, Sept. 1, 2013.
10. "DOJ's Quid Pro Quo with St. Paul: How Assistant Attorney General Thomas Perez Manipulated Justice and Ignored the Rule of Law," Joint Staff Report, House Committee on Oversight and Government Reform, April 15, 2013, p. 62.
11. *U.S. v. AIG Federal Savings Bank*, Case No. 10CV178 (D. Del. March 19, 2010).
12. "The Ambitious Mr. Perez," *Wall Street Journal*, April 17, 2013.
13. "DOJ's Quid Pro Quo with St. Paul: How Assistant Attorney General Thomas Perez Manipulated Justice and Ignored the Rule of Law," Joint Staff Report, House Committee on Oversight and Government Reform, April 15, 2013, p. 14.
14. "The Ambitious Mr. Perez," *Wall Street Journal*, April 17, 2013.
15. Ibid.
16. *U.S. v. Dillard*, Case No. 11-1098 (D. KS Aug. 15, 2013)
17. *U.S. v. Pine*, Case No. 10CV80971 (S.D. Fla. Jan. 13, 2012).
18. 132 S.Ct. 695 (2012),
19. *U.S. v. Arkansas*, 794 F.Supp.2d 935 (E.D. Ark. 2011).
20. *U.S. v. Jones*, 125 F.3d 1418 (11th Cir. 1997).
21. Letter of May 9, 2013, to President Royce Engstrom, University of Montana.
22. Byron York, "Why Did Feds Claim Kindle Violates Civil Rights?," *Washington Examiner*, Aug. 3, 2010.
23. Ibid.
24. Ibid.
25. *U.S. v. Florida*, Case No. 4:12cv285 (N.D. Fla. June 28, 2012). See also *Arcia v. Detzner*, Case No. 12-22282 (S.D. Fla. Oct. 4, 2012), in which

the court dismissed a similar lawsuit filed by private parties concluding that under their theory of the NVRA, a state would be prohibited from removing from its voting rolls anyone who was improperly registered, such as noncitizens, minors, fictitious individuals, and individuals who live in other states, which "would produce an absurd result" (Slip Op. at 14).

26. For a description of the problems caused by illegal voting, see John Fund and Hans von Spakovsky, *Who's Counting?*.
27. "Attorney General Eric Holder Speaks at the Lyndon Baines Johnson Library & Museum," Dec. 13, 2011, available at www.justice.gov/iso/opa/ag/speeches/2011/ag-speech-111213.html.
28. Hearing on the Department of Justice's Actions Related to the New Black Panther Party Litigation and its Enforcement of Section 11(b) of the Voting Rights Act, U.S. Commission on Civil Rights, May 14, 2010, pp. 32–33.
29. A Review of the Operations of the Voting Section of the Civil Rights Division, Office of the Inspector General, U.S. Dept. of Justice, March 2013, p. 90.
30. Ibid., p. 127.
31. Ibid., pp. 129–30.
32. Ibid., pp. 119–20.
33. Ibid., p. 129.
34. Ibid., pp. 123, 129–30.
35. Ibid., pp. 160–61.
36. Ibid., p. 166.
37. Ibid., p. 163.
38. Andrew Ramonas, "Texas Lawmaker Says Civil Rights Division Only Protects Black Voters," MainJustice, March 1, 2011.
39. J. Christian Adams, "What's In Eric Holder's Wallet? His Real Race Card," PJ Media, July 12, 2013.
40. Ibid.
41. A Review of the Operations of the Voting Section of the Civil Rights Division, Office of the Inspector General, U.S. Dept. of Justice, March 2013, p. 258.
42. Interview with Christopher Coates, Jan. 28, 2014.
43. Hylton, "Hope. Change. Reality."

Chapter 5: The Billion-Dollar *Pigford* Scam

1. Daniel Foster, "Pigford's Harvest," *National Review*, Feb. 21, 2010.
2. Rich Lowry, "The Obama/Clinton Reparations," *National Review*, April 30, 2013.

3. Sharon LaFraniere, "U.S. Opens Spigot After Farmers Claim Discrimination," *New York Times*, April 25, 2013.
4. Foster, "Pigford's Harvest."
5. LaFraniere, "U.S. Opens Spigot After Farmers Claim Discrimination."
6. Ibid.
7. Daniel Foster, "*Pigford* and Discrimination," *National Review*, April 20, 2013.
8. Foster, "Pigford's Harvest."
9. Ibid.
10. Helena Andrews, "Shirley Sherrod Says She'll Never Work for the Government Again," *Washington Post*, Jan. 14, 2014; http://www.ruraldevelopment.org/shirleydirector.html.
11. Foster, "Pigford's Harvest."
12. LaFraniere, "U.S. Opens Spigot After Farmers Claim Discrimination."
13. Ibid.
14. Gary Hewson, Peter Schweizer, and Andrew Breitbart, "The Pigford Shakedown: How Black Farmers' Cause Was Hijacked by Politicians, Trial Lawyers & Community Organizers—Leaving Us with a Billion Dollar Tab," Breitbart, Dec. 6, 2010, p. 11.
15. Ibid.
16. Ibid.
17. LaFraniere, "U.S. Opens Spigot After Farmers Claim Discrimination."
18. Ibid.
19. Ibid.
20. Foster, "Pigford's Harvest."
21. Ibid.
22. Ibid.
23. Ibid.
24. Kevin Bogardus, "CBC Upset Over Obama's Stance on Black Farmers," *Hill*, April 23, 2009.
25. Ian Swanson and Kevin Bogardus, "As Champion of the Black Farmer, Obama Could Win Southern Votes," *Hill*, Sept. 19, 2007.
26. "Department of Justice and USDA Announces Historic Settlement in Lawsuit by Black Farmers Claiming Discrimination by USDA," Press Release, U.S. Department of Justice, Feb. 18, 2010.
27. LaFraniere, "U.S. Opens Spigot After Farmers Claim Discrimination."
28. Ibid.
29. Ibid.
30. Ibid.
31. "Senators Urge Settlement in USDA Discrimination Lawsuit by Hispanic Farmers," Press Release of Senator Robert Menendez, June 20, 2009.

32. Joe Garofoli, "Obama Power Broker New Face of Black Politics," *San Francisco Chronicle*, March 1, 2008.
33. LaFraniere, "U.S. Opens Spigot After Farmers Claim Discrimination."
34. Ibid.
35. For a discussion of this, see Conor Friedersdorf, "How Did Progressive Journalists Get Pigford So Wrong?," *Atlantic*, May 2013.
36. "Oversight of the United States Department of Justice," Judiciary Committee, U.S. House of Representatives, May 15, 2013.
37. "Pigford II Settlement," Government Accountability Office, GAO-13-69R, Dec. 7, 2012, pp. 2–3.
38. LaFraniere, "U.S. Opens Spigot After Farmers Claim Discrimination."
39. Rich Lowry, "The Obama/Clinton Reparations," National Review, April 13, 2013.

Chapter 6: The Holder Rule of Ignorance and Deceit

1. "DOJ's *Quid Pro Quo* with St. Paul: How Assistant Attorney General Thomas Perez Manipulated Justice and Ignored the Rule of Law," Joint Staff Report, House Committee on Oversight and Government Reform, April 15, 2013.
2. Hearing Before the Committee on the Judiciary, House of Representatives, Serial No. 113-43, May 15, 2013, p. 35.
3. Ibid., p. 36.
4. Ibid., p. 110.
5. Ibid., p. 111.
6. Matthew Boyle, "Emails Reveal Justice Dept. Regularly Enlists Media Matters to Spin Press," *Daily Caller*, Sept. 18, 2012.
7. Jeff Poor, "CBS Reporter: White House, DOJ Reps 'Yelled' and 'Screamed' at Her over 'Fast and Furious' Scandal," *Daily Caller*, Oct. 4, 2011.
8. Hearing Before the Committee on the Judiciary, House of Representatives, Serial No. 113-43, May 15, 2013, p. 107.
9. "Eric Holder's Long History of Lying to Congress," *Investor's Business Daily*, May 31, 2013.
10. Andrew McCarthy, "Eric Holder Misled Congress? Surely You Jest . . . ," *National Review*, May 29, 2013; see also "Justice Undone: Clemency Decisions in the Clinton White House," House Committee on Government Reform, Report No 107-454, May 14, 2002.
11. *U.S. v. Clarendon Ltd.*, 1:35CV00780
12. Andrew McCarthy, "Unpardonable: Holder's Marc Rich Shuffle," *National Review*, Jan. 21, 2009.

13. Ibid.
14. "Budget Hearing—Department of Justice—Attorney General," House Appropriations Subcommittee on Commerce, Justice, Science, and Related Agencies, March 1, 2011, p. 66 or hour 2:49.
15. *Judicial Watch, Inc. v. U.S.*, Civil Action No. 10-851 (D. D.C. July 23, 2012), p. 13.
16. H.Res. 711 (June 28, 2012).
17. Hearing Before the Committee on the Judiciary, House of Representatives, Serial No. 113-43, May 15, 2013, p. 39.
18. Letter from Deputy Attorney General James Cole to John Boehner, Speaker of the U.S. House of Representatives, June 28, 2012.
19. Letter of Sen. Charles E. Grassley to Ronald C. Machen, Jr., U.S. Attorney, District of Columbia, June 29, 2012.
20. Jennifer Rubin, "Holder Is At It Again: Do These Guys Ever Tell the Truth?" *Washington Post*, May 17, 2013.
21. Ibid.
22. "United States Department of Justice," Hearing Before the Committee on the Judiciary, House of Representatives, Serial No. 112-127, May 3, 2011, p. 45.
23. "Oversight of the U.S. Department of Justice," Hearing Before the Committee on Justice, U.S. Senate, Serial No. J-112-50, Nov. 8, 2011, p. 9.
24. "Fast and Furious: The Anatomy of a Failed Operation," Joint Staff Report, House Committee on Oversight and Government Reform, Part II of III, Oct. 29, 2012, p. 11.
25. Ibid., p. 103.
26. Ibid.
27. Ibid., p. 9.
28. "United States Department of Justice," Hearing Before the Committee on the Judiciary, House of Representatives, Serial No. 112-152, June 7, 2012, p. 423.
29. Ibid.
30. Interview with Andrew McCarthy, Dec. 19, 2013.

Chapter 7: Fast and Furious

1. "Primer on the Fast and Furious Scandal," CBS News, Feb. 12, 2013.
2. Press Conference of Attorney General Eric Holder, U.S. Department of Justice, Feb. 25, 2009.
3. Matthew Boyle, "Fast and Furious Product of Deliberate Strategy," *Daily Caller*, Oct. 29, 2012.

4. Mark Landler, "Clinton Says U.S. Feeds Mexico Drug Trade," *New York Times*, March 25, 2009.
5. Katie Pavlich, *Fast and Furious: Barack Obama's Bloodiest Scandal and Its Shameless Cover-Up* (New York: Regnery, 2012).
6. Ryan Mauro, "Where Drug Cartels Really Get Their Arms," *FrontPage-Mag*, April 12, 2011.
7. William La Jeunesse, "The Myth of 90 Percent: Only a Small Fraction of Guns in Mexico Come From U.S.," Fox News, April 2, 2009.
8. Speech by Attorney General Eric Holder at the Mexico/United States Arms Trafficking Conference, April 2, 2009.
9. Catharine Evans, "Fast and Furious Traced to White House," *American Thinker*, July 29, 2011.
10. Testimony of Secretary Janet Napolitano Before Senate Homeland Security and Governmental Affairs Committee, March 25, 2009.
11. Speech of Deputy Attorney General David W. Ogden at the ATF Firearms Trafficking Summit, Albuquerque, New Mexico, June 30, 2009.
12. "The Department of Justice's Operation Fast and Furious: Accounts of ATF Agents," Joint Staff Report for Rep. Darrell Issa and Sen. Chuck Grassley, June 14, 2011.
13. John Dodson, *The Unarmed Truth: My Fight to Blow the Whistle and Expose Fast and Furious* (New York: Threshold Editions, 2013).
14. Sari Horwitz and James V. Grimaldi, "U.S. Gun Dealers with the Most Firearms Traced over the Past 4 Years," *Washington Post*, Dec. 13, 2010.
15. Letter from Sen. Chuck Grassley to Kenneth E. Melson, Acting Director, Bureau of Alcohol, Tobacco, Firearms, and Explosives, Jan. 27, 2011.
16. Letter from Senator Chuck Grassley to Kenneth E. Melson, Acting Director, Bureau of Alcohol, Tobacco, Firearms, and Explosives, Jan. 31, 2011.
17. Letter from Office of Legislative Affairs, U.S. Department of Justice, to Sen. Chuck Grassley, Feb. 4, 2011.
18. "Agent: I Was Ordered to Let U.S. Guns Into Mexico," *CBS Evening News*, March 3, 2011.
19. Matthew Boyle, "Holder Less than Candid on Fast and Furious," *Daily Caller*, Oct. 4, 2011.
20. Matthew Boyle, "Holder Personally Named in New Fast and Furious Documents," *Daily Caller*, Oct. 3, 2011.
21. Ibid.
22. "Rep. Blake Farenthold on the Latest Fast and Furious News," NRA News, Oct. 5, 2011, https://www.youtube.com/watch?v=nccW4wKhfUk&feature=youtu.be.

23. "Rep. Raul Labrador Calls for Resignation of Attorney General Holder Over 'Fast and Furious' Testimony Discrepancies," Press Release, Oct. 6, 2011.
24. Matthew Boyle, "Congressman to Holder: 'We're Not Interested in Kumbayah, Drop Your Rhetoric and Resign Immediately,'" *Daily Caller*, Oct. 8, 2011
25. Matthew Boyle, "Congressman: Obama May be Accessory to Murder with Fast and Furious," *Daily Caller*, Oct. 5, 2011.
26. Boyle, "Holder Less Than Candid on Fast and Furious."
27. Matthew Boyle, "Holder Claims His Testimony Was Accurate, Pushes Back Against 'Inflammatory Rhetoric,'" *Daily Caller*, Oct. 7, 2011.
28. Matthew Boyle, "Rep. Joe Walsh to Eric Holder: Resign Immediately and Take Responsibility for Operation Fast and Furious," *Daily Caller*, Oct. 26, 2011.
29. Matthew Boyle, "Rep. Pete Olson: If Holder Refuses to Leave We'll Force Him to Resign Through Impeachment," *Breitbart News*, Nov. 13, 2011.
30. Tim Mak, "Issa Subpoenas Holder on Fast and Furious," *Politico*, Oct. 22, 2011.
31. Matthew Boyle, "During Senate Testimony Holder Changes Misleading Testimony from May Hearing," *Daily Caller*, Nov. 8, 2011.
32. "Justice Withdraws Inaccurate Fast and Furious Letter It Sent to Congress," NPR Blog The Two Way, Dec. 2, 2011.
33. Matthew Boyle, "Issa to Obama: Either You're Involved in Fast and Furious or Your Executive Privilege Claim is Unjustified," *Daily Caller*, June 26, 2012.
34. Alan Silvereib, "House Holds Holder in Contempt," CNN, June 29, 2012.
35. Matthew Boyle, "Grassley: Politics in US Attorney General Holder's Decision," *Daily Caller*, June 29, 2012.
36. Josh Gerstein, "Judge Won't Allow Holder Appeal Now in Contempt Case," *Politico*, Nov. 18, 2013.
37. *Committee on Oversight and Government Reform v. Holder*, Case No. 12-1332 (D. D.C. Nov. 18, 2013).
38. 498 F.2d 725 (D.C. Cir. 1974).
39. Hans von Spakovsky and Elizabeth Slattery, "Packing the D.C. Circuit," *Human Events*, Oct. 31, 2013.
40. Todd F. Gaziano, "Executive Privilege Can't Shield Wrongdoing," Heritage Foundation Backgrounder, June 22, 2012.
41. Matthew Boyle, "Grassley: Federal Judge Should Overturn Obama's Fast and Furious Executive Privilege Claim," *Daily Caller*, Aug. 29, 2012.

42. Matthew Boyle, "Darrell Issa Vows Fast & Furious Justice on Brian Terry Murder Anniversary," *Breitbart News*, Dec. 15, 2013.
43. Evan Perez, "Fast and Furious Gun Turns Up After Mexican Resort Shootout," CNN, Dec. 31, 2013.
44. Hunter Stuart, "Fast and Furious Gun Linked to Murder of Mexican Police Chief, Bodyguard," *Huffington Post*, July 6, 2013.
45. Gerardo Reyes and Santiago Wills, "Fast and Furious Scandal: New Details Emerge on How the U.S. Government Armed Mexican Drug Cartels," Fusion.net, Sept. 28, 2012.
46. Matthew Boyle, "Gowdy: Fast & Furious Deaths, Consequences Will 'Last for the Rest of Our Lives," *Breitbart News*, Dec. 19, 2012.
47. "Gun From Botched Fast and Furious Operation Turns Up After Mexican Resort Shootout," Fox News, Jan. 2, 2014.
48. Matthew Boyle, "Issa Says Holder Should Apologize to Mexico: Justice Has Blood on Their Hands," *Daily Caller*, Jan. 26, 2012.
49. Katie Pavlich, "Grassley and Issa Send Letter to ATF: We Are Appalled by Agents Lack of Judgment," Townhall, Jan. 10, 2014.
50. Boyle, "Darrell Issa Vows Fast & Furious Justice on Brian Terry Murder Anniversary."

Chapter 8: Protecting National Security

1. Huma Khan, "Shoe-Bomber Reid Was Read His Rights 'Within 5 Minutes of Being Removed from the Aircraft': Obama Administration Continues Pushback on National Security Criticism," ABC News, Feb. 3, 2010.
2. "Mukasey: 'Amateur Night' at Justice Department Over Terror Trial Confusion," Fox News, Feb. 2, 2010.
3. Diane Sawyer, "9/11 Mastermind to Be Tried at Gitmo," ABC News, April 4, 2011.
4. Josh Meyer and Tom Hamburger, "Eric Holder Pushed for Controversial Clemency," *Los Angeles Times*, Jan. 9, 2009.
5. Joseph F. Connor, "Terrorists Killed My Dad," *Los Angeles Times*, Jan. 16, 2009.
6. Ron Kolb, "Hillary, Terrorism and the FALN," *RealClearPolitics*, May 29, 2008.
7. Huma Khan, "More on Holder and FALN," ABC News, Jan. 16, 2009.
8. Joseph Connor, "Eric Holder: Incompetent or Malfeasant Ideologue?" *Breitbart*, Oct. 9, 2011.
9. Meyer and Hamburger, "Eric Holder Pushed for Controversial Clemency."

10. "Senate Condemns Clinton for FALN Clemency," CNN, Sept. 14, 1999.
11. Connor, "Terrorists Killed My Dad."
12. Kolb, "Hillary, Terrorism and the FALN."
13. Andrew C. McCarthy, "The Ruler of Law," *New Criterion*, Sept. 2011.
14. Raffaela Wakeman, "September 2013 Guantanamo Recidivism Report from DNI," Lawfareblog.com, Sept 6, 2013.
15. Meghan Clyne, "A Bleeding Heart to 'Fight' Terror," *New York Post*, July 17, 2009.
16. Andrew C. McCarthy, "'Representing' al-Qaeda," *National Review Online*, March 29, 2010.
17. Clyne, "A Bleeding Heart to 'Fight' Terror."
18. Andy McCarthy, "Who Are the Gitmo 9?," *National Review Online*, Feb. 24, 2010.
19. Mike Levine, "Exclusive: Unknown DOJ Lawyers Identified," Fox News, March 3, 2010.
20. Jennifer Rubin, "Gen. 'Stonewall' Holder," *Weekly Standard*, May 10, 2010.
21. Andrew C. McCarthy, "The Gitmo Volunteers," *National Review Online*, March 5, 2010.
22. Debra Burlingame and Thomas Joscelyn, "Gitmo's Indefensible Lawyers," *Wall Street Journal*, March 15, 2010.
23. McCarthy, "The Gitmo Volunteers."
24. These memoranda were principally written by John Yoo, now a law professor at the University of California, Berkeley, and Jay S. Bybee, a federal appeals court judge who headed the Office of Legal Counsel. These memoranda were released by Eric Holder and the Obama administration despite CIA Director Leon Panetta's argument that "full disclosure would damage the government's ability to recruit spies and harm national security." Daniel Klaidman, "Independent's Day," *Newsweek*, July 11, 2009.
25. The CIA contractor, David A. Passaro, was convicted of assault for hitting an Afghan captive with a flashlight. Carrie Johnson, Jerry Markon, and Julie Tate, "Inquiry Into CIA Practices Narrows," *Washington Post*, Sept. 19, 2009.
26. Siobhan Gorman, "Seven CIA Directors Ask Obama to Stop Criminal Probe," *Wall Street Journal*, Sept. 18, 2009.
27. "Obama White House v. CIA; Panetta Threatened to Quit," The Blotter, ABC News, Aug. 24, 2009.
28. Johnson, Markon, and Tate, "Inquiry Into CIA Practices Narrows."
29. *United States v. Richardson*, 418 U.S. 166 (1974).

30. "Statement of Attorney General Eric Holder on Closure of Investigation into the Interrogation of Certain Detainees," U.S. Department of Justice, Aug. 30, 2012.
31. Marc A. Thiessen, "The CIA's Exoneration and Holder's Reckoning," *Washington Post*, July 4, 2011.
32. "Statement of Attorney General Eric Holder on Closure of Investigation into the Interrogation of Certain Detainees," U.S. Department of Justice, Aug. 30, 2012.
33. Thiessen, "The CIA's Exoneration and Holder's Reckoning."
34. *U.S. v. Slough*, Criminal Action No. 08-0360 (D. D.C. Dec. 31, 2009).
35. *U.S. v. Slough*, Criminal Action No. 08-0360 (D. D.C. Dec. 31, 2009), Slip Op. at 22.
36. 385 U.S. 493 (1967).
37. *U.S. v. Slough*, Criminal Action No. 08-0360 (D. D.C. Dec. 31, 2009), Slip Op. at 3.
38. "The Real Blackwater Scandal," *Wall Street Journal*, Jan. 3, 2010.
39. James Risen, "Ex-Blackwater Guards Face Renewed Charges," *New York Times*, April 22, 2011.
40. "New Charges in Blackwater Shootings," Associated Press, Oct. 17, 2013.
41. Glenn Greenwald, "The Bin Laden Raid Exposes the Obama Administration's Selective Secrecy," *Guardian*, Aug. 23, 2012.
42. Ann E. Marimow, "A Rare Peek Into a Justice Department Leak Probe," *Washington Post*, May 19, 2013.
43. "Journalists or Criminals? Attorney General Eric Holder's Testimony before the Committee and the Justice Department's National Security Leak Investigative Techniques," House Committee on the Judiciary, Majority Staff Report to Chairman Bob Goodlatte, July 31, 2013, Executive Summary.
44. Leonard Downie, "The Obama Administration and the Press—Leak Investigations and Surveillance in Post–9/11 America," Committee to Protect Journalists, Oct. 10, 2013.
45. Ibid.
46. Patrick Howley, "Emails: White House, State Department Coordinated with Journalist on National Security Leaks," *Daily Caller*, Oct. 23, 2013.
47. "Journalists or Criminals? Attorney General Eric Holder's Testimony before the Committee and the Justice Department's National Security Leak Investigative Techniques," House Committee on the Judiciary, Majority Staff Report to Chairman Bob Goodlatte, July 31, 2013, p. 3.
48. David E. Sanger, "Obama Order Sped Up Wave of Cyberattacks Against Iran," *New York Times*, June 1, 2012.

49. Howley, "Emails: White House, State Department Coordinated With Journalist on National Security Leaks."
50. Ibid.
51. "Journalists or Criminals? Attorney General Eric Holder's Testimony before the Committee and the Justice Department's National Security Leak Investigative Techniques," House Committee on the Judiciary, Majority Staff Report to Chairman Bob Goodlatte, July 31, 2013, p. 4.
52. Howley, "Emails: White House, State Department Coordinated With Journalist on National Security Leaks."
53. "CIA Foiled al-Qaeda Bomb Plot Around Anniversary of Bin Laden Death," *Guardian*, May 7, 2012.
54. "Journalists or Criminals? Attorney General Eric Holder's Testimony before the Committee and the Justice Department's National Security Leak Investigative Techniques," House Committee on the Judiciary, Majority Staff Report to Chairman Bob Goodlatte, July 31, 2013, p. 1.
55. Mark Sherman, "Government Obtains Wide AP Phone Records in Probe," Associated Press, May 13, 2013.
56. Letter from Gary Pruitt to Eric Holder, May 13, 2013.
57. Mark Hosenball and Tabassum Zakaria, "AP Records Seizure Just Latest Step in Sweeping U.S. Leak Probe," Reuters, May 15, 2013.
58. Presidential Statement on Signing the Privacy Protection Act of 1980, Oct. 14, 1980.
59. Jennifer Rubin, "Five Questions About the AP Surveillance," *Washington Post*, May 17, 2013.
60. Steven Nelson, "AP Leak Investigation Isn't Quite Over, Despite Charges," *U.S. News & World Report*, Sept. 24, 2013.
61. Ibid.
62. Mark Hosenball, "Exclusive: Did White House 'Spin' Tip a Covert Op?," Reuters, May 18, 2012.
63. Ibid.
64. Ibid.
65. Nelson, "AP Leak Investigation Isn't Quite Over, Despite Charges."
66. James Rosen, "NK's Post UN Sanctions Plans, Revealed," Fox News, June 11, 2009.
67. "Journalists or Criminals? Attorney General Eric Holder's Testimony before the Committee and the Justice Department's National Security Leak Investigative Techniques," House Committee on the Judiciary, Majority Staff Report to Chairman Bob Goodlatte, July 31, 2013, p. 6,
68. Affidavit of Reginald B. Reyes, In the Matter of Search of E-Mail Account of James Rosen, Case No. 10-291-M-01 (D. D.C. May 28, 2010).
69. "Journalists or Criminals? Attorney General Eric Holder's Testimony

before the Committee and the Justice Department's National Security Leak Investigative Techniques," House Committee on the Judiciary, Majority Staff Report to Chairman Bob Goodlatte, July 31, 2013, p. 17.

70. Ibid., p. 16.
71. Ibid., pp. 15–16.
72. Michael Issikoff, "DOJ Confirms Holder OK'd Search Warrant for Fox News Reporter's Emails," NBC News, May 27, 2013.
73. "Journalists or Criminals? Attorney General Eric Holder's Testimony before the Committee and the Justice Department's National Security Leak Investigative Techniques," House Committee on the Judiciary, Majority Staff Report to Chairman Bob Goodlatte, July 31, 2013, p. 19.
74. Ibid., p. 30.
75. Brian Stelter and Michael D. Shear, "Justice Dept. Investigated Fox Reporter Over Leak," Fox News, May 20, 2013.
76. Marimow, "A Rare Peek Into a Justice Department Leak Probe."
77. Sari Horwitz, "Justice Dept. Tightens Rules on Subpoenaing Records of Journalists," *Washington Post*, July 12, 2013.
78. The prior guidelines were found at 28 C.F.R. § 50.10 and were incorporated into the Justice Department's U.S. Attorney's Manual at § 9-13.400.
79. Matt Vasilogambros, "Feinstein: White House Behind National Security Leaks," *National Journal*, July 24, 2012.
80. Toby Harnden, "Joe Biden Opens His Mouth About US Navy Seals," *Telegraph*, May 4, 2011.
81. Jeffrey T. Kuhner, "The Betrayal of the Navy's SEAL Team 6," *Washington Times*, June 7, 2013.
82. Ibid.
83. "Scooter Obama Outs Navy SEAL Team 6 Leader for Movie," *Investor's Business Daily*, May 24, 2012.
84. Rowan Scarborough, "Navy SEALS Cite Shabby Treatment as Team Obama Helps Hollywood Instead," *Washington Times*, Nov. 17, 2013.
85. Maureen Dowd, "Downgrade Blues," *New York Times*, Aug. 6, 2011.
86. Glenn Greenwald, "The bin Laden Raid Exposes the Obama Administration's Selective Secrecy," *Guardian*, Aug. 23, 2012.
87. Rowan Scarborough, "Details of bin Laden Raid Leaked First by Obama Aides," *Washington Times*, Sept. 16, 2012, "Judicial Watch . . . obtained via the Freedom of Information Act a series of internal emails that show close cooperation between the movie's director and screenwriter and Obama political appointees at the CIA, Pentagon and White House."
88. Daniel Halper, "Gates to National Security Team on Osama Raid: 'Shut the F– Up,'" *Weekly Standard*, June 6, 2012.

89. Jo Becker and Scott Shane, "Secret 'Kill List' Proves a Test of Obama's Principles and Will," *New York Times*, May 20, 2012.
90. Greenwald, "The bin Laden Raid Exposes the Obama Administration's Selective Secrecy."
91. Interview with Joe Connor, Dec. 3, 2013.

Chapter 9: Corruption Abroad

1. 15 U.S.C. § 77dd-1.
2. Ammon Simon, "Wal-Mart and the Foreign Corrupt Practices Act," *National Review Online*, Dec. 21, 2012.
3. Mike Koehler, "Lanny Breuer and Foreign Corrupt Practices Act Enforcement," White Collar Crime Report, Bloomberg BNA, March 22, 2013.
4. http://www.justice.gov/criminal/pr/speeches/2012/crmspeech-1211161.html, Nov. 12, 2012.
5. Matthew Rosenberg, "With Bags of Cash, C.I.A. Seeks Influence in Afghanistan," *New York Times*, April 28, 2013.
6. Koehler, "Lanny Breuer and Foreign Corrupt Practices Act Enforcement."
7. Ibid.
8. Assistant Attorney General Lanny A. Breuer Speaks at the New York City Bar Association, Sept. 13, 2012; http://www.justice.gov/criminal/pr/speeches/2012/crm-speech-1209131.html.
9. Koehler, "Lanny Breuer and Foreign Corrupt Practices Act Enforcement."
10. Mike Koehler, "An Examination of Foreign Corrupt Practices Act Issues," 12 *Richmond Journal of Global Law & Business* 317,332 (2013).
11. See Prepared Remarks by Former Attorney General Alberto R. Gonzales, May 2012, http://www.wallerlaw.com/portalresource/lookup/wosid/cp-base-4-13102/media.name-/TAP%20-%20Speech%20to%20LCJ%20by%20Judge%20Gonzales%202012%2005.pdf.
12. John L. Smith, "FBI Stung After Sting Involving Corrupt Foreign Practices," *Las Vegas Review-Journal*, Feb. 29, 2012.
13. Ibid.
14. Del Quentin Wilber, "Racy, Vulgar Texts Hurt Justice Department's Largest Sting Operation Targeting Foreign Bribery," *Washington Post*, Feb. 13, 2012.
15. Ibid.
16. Ibid.
17. Smith, "FBI Stung After Sting Involving Corrupt Foreign Practices."

18. Wilber, "Racy, Vulgar Texts Hurt Justice Department's Largest Sting Operation Targeting Foreign Bribery."
19. "A Guest Post from the Africa Sting Jury Foreman," FCPA Professor, Feb. 6, 2012, http://www.fcpaprofessor.com/a-guest-post-from-the-africa-sting-jury-foreman.
20. Transcript of Judge Leon's Remarks Dismissing the Indictments with Prejudice for Amaro Goncalves and 15 Co-Defendants," *U.S. v. Goncalves*, Case No. 09-CR-335 (D.D.C. Feb. 21, 2012).
21. "Africa Sting—A 'Long and Sad Chapter in the Annals of White Collar Criminal Enforcement," FCPAProfessor, Feb. 22, 2012, http://www.fcpaprofessor.com/2012/02/page/2.
22. Ibid.
23. Walter Pavlo, "Government Witness, Richard Bistrong, Gets Jail Time While Targets Walk," *Forbes*, Aug. 2, 2012.
24. *U.S. v. O'Shea*, Indictment H-09-629 (S.D. TX Nov. 16, 2009).
25. Richard L. Cassin, "Judge to DOJ: Your Principal Witness Knows Almost Nothing," FCPAProfessor, Jan. 19, 2012, http://www.fcpablog.com/2012/1/19/judge-to-doj-your-principal-witness-knows-almost-nothing.
26. Ibid.
27. Dane Schiller, "After Losing Everything, Mexico Bribery Suspect Acquitted," *Houston Chronicle*, Jan. 17, 2012.
28. Ibid.
29. Ibid.
30. "California Company, Its Two Executives and Intermediary Convicted by Federal Jury in Los Angeles on All Counts for Their Involvement in Scheme to Bribe Officials at State-Owned Utility in Mexico," Department of Justice, Office of Public Affairs, May 10, 2011, http://www.justice.gov/opa/pr/2011/May/11-crm-596.html.
31. Lisa Riordan Seville, "Battling Corporate Crime," *The Crime Report*, Jan. 8, 2012; thecrimereport.org/news/article/2012-01-battling-corporate-crime.
32. Order Granting Motion To Dismiss, *US v. Aguilar*, Case No. 10-01031 (C.D. Cal. Dec. 1, 2011), p. 1.
33. Ibid., p. 2.
34. Ibid., p. 20.
35. Ibid., pp. 14–15.
36. Ibid., p. 32.
37. Ibid., p. 38–39.
38. Ibid., p. 40.
39. Samuel Rubenfeld, "U.S. Drops Appeal in Lindsey Manufacturing FCPA Case," *Wall Street Journal*, May 29, 2012.

40. "Writer's Cramp at the DOJ?," FCPAProfessor, Feb. 3, 2012, http://www.fcpaprofessor.com/writers-cramp-at-the-doj.

Chapter 10: What Is to Be Done?

1. Andrew McCarthy, "The Rule of Law," *New Criterion*, Sept. 2011.
2. "Investigation into the Office of Legal Counsel's Memorandum Concerning Issues Relating to the Central Intelligence Agency's Use of 'Enhanced Interrogation Techniques' on Suspected Terrorists," Office of Professional Responsibility, U.S. Department of Justice, July 29, 2009, p. 11.
3. "Memorandum for the Attorney General," Associate Deputy Attorney General David Margolis, Jan. 5, 2010.
4. Letter of Jan. 9, 2009, to H. Marshall Jarrett, Office of Professional Responsibility, U.S. Department of Justice.
5. "Vindicating John Yoo," *Wall Street Journal*, Feb. 22, 2010.
6. See Hans A. von Spakovsky, "Revenge of the Liberal Bureaucrats," *Weekly Standard*, Jan. 23, 2009.
7. "Vindicating John Yoo," *Wall Street Journal*, Feb. 22, 2010.
8. Charlie Savage, "For Holder, New Congress Means New Headaches," *New York Times*, Dec. 30, 2010.
9. At the Justice Department, a "detail" is when a lawyer is temporarily assigned to a different office inside Justice, another federal agency, or even to Congress. The lawyer remains a DOJ employee and all benefits and salary continued to be paid by DOJ.
10. J. Christian Adams, *Injustice: Exposing the Racial Agenda of the Obama Justice Department* (New York: Regnery, 2011), p. 163.
11. Ibid., p. 162.
12. Ibid., p. 163.
13. "Top Management and Performance Challenges Facing the Department of Justice—2013," Memorandum for the Attorney General, the Deputy Attorney General, from Michael E. Horowitz, Inspector General, Dec. 11, 2013, reissued Dec. 23, 2013.
14. "Annual Report—2012," Office of Professional Responsibility, U.S. Department of Justice, p. 16, fn. 10.
15. Fine issued a four-hundred-page report on the faux scandal of the firing of nine U.S. attorneys by the Justice Department during the Bush administration that claimed the process used to remove them "was seriously flawed." He made a federal case out of a molehill, basically ignoring the fact that U.S. attorneys are political appointees who serve at the pleasure of the president and can be terminated at

any time for any reason or no reason. There was nothing to investigate in the president's termination of nine political appointees. But refusing to investigate this supposed scandal that had been whipped up by political opponents of the administration would not have served Fine's political allies. It was his decision to investigate this matter that was "seriously flawed." See "An Investigation into the Removal of Nine U.S. Attorneys in 2006," Office of the Inspector General and Office of Professional Responsibility, U.S. Department of Justice, Sept. 2008.

16. "A Review of the Operations of the Voting Section of the Civil Rights Division," Office of the Inspector General, U.S. Department of Justice, March 2013, p. 188.
17. Andrew M. Grossman, "Use and Abuse of Consent Decrees in Federal Rulemaking," Testimony Before Subcommittee on the Courts, Commercial and Administrative Law, Committee on the Judiciary, U.S. House of Representatives, Feb. 3, 2012.
18. Ibid.
19. "Department Policy Regarding Consent Decrees and Settlement Agreements," Memorandum from Edwin Meese III to All Assistant Attorneys General and United States Attorneys, U.S. Department of Justice, March 13, 1986.
20. "Sunshine for Regulatory Decrees and Settlements Act of 2013," Committee on the Judiciary, House Report 113-230, Sept. 26, 2013.
21. "Authority of the United States to Enter Settlements Limiting the Future Exercise of Executive Branch Discretion," Memorandum from Randolph D. Moss, Acting Assistant Attorney General for Office of Legal Policy, to Associate Attorney General Raymond Fisher, U.S. Department of Justice, June 15, 1999.
22. See H.R. 1493 and S. 714.
23. Grossman, "Use and Abuse of Consent Decrees in Federal Rulemaking."
24. See H.R. 317.
25. Interview by Hans von Spakovsky with Edwin Meese III, Jan. 12, 2014.
26. Hans von Spakovsky, "Porteous Impeached: The Vote Breakdown," *National Review Online*, Dec. 8, 2010.
27. Interview by Hans von Spakovsky with Edwin Meese III, Jan. 12, 2014.
28. Isaac Chotiner, "Eric Holder, Cave Man—Why the Attorney General Always Disappoints Himself," *New Republic*, June 20, 2013.
29. Ibid.
30. McCarthy, "The Rule of Law."
31. *Worcester v. Georgia*, 31 U.S. (6 Pet.) 515 (1832).

32. This quote by Jackson is probably apocryphal and derived from a letter in which he said that the Supreme Court's decision was "still born" and that the court could not "coerce Georgia to yield to its mandate." Paul F. Boller and John H. George, *They Never Said It: A Book of False Quotes, Misquotes & False Attributions* (New York: Oxford University Press, 1989), p. 53.
33. McCarthy, "The Rule of Law."

INDEX

ABOUT THE AUTHOR

JOHN FUND is a nationally recognized columnist and author whose work has appeared in the *Wall Street Journal*, *National Review*, *Esquire*, and the *New Republic*. He has written several books that touch on Justice Department issues, including *Stealing Elections* and *Cleaning House*. He has also collaborated with bestselling authors such as Rush Limbaugh on their books.

HANS VON SPAKOVSKY, now a senior fellow at the Heritage Foundation, is a former presidential appointee to the Federal Election Commission, serving there from 2006 to 2007. He is also a former counsel to the assistant attorney general for civil rights in the Justice Department. He is the coauthor (with John Fund) of *Who's Counting: How Fraudsters and Bureaucrats Put Your Vote at Risk*.